MUCKRAKING SOCIOLOGY
Research as Social Criticism

*trans*action/**Society** Book Series

TA/S-1   *Campus Power Struggle* / Howard S. Becker
TA/S-2   *Cuban Communism* / Irving Louis Horowitz
TA/S-3   *The Changing South* / Raymond W. Mack
TA/S-4   *Where Medicine Fails* / Anselm L. Strauss
TA/S-5   *The Sexual Scene* / John H. Gagnon and William Simon
TA/S-6   *Black Experience: Soul* / Lee Rainwater
TA/S-7   *Black Experience: The Transformation of
          Activism* / August Meier
TA/S-8   *Law and Order: Modern Criminals* / James F. Short, Jr.
TA/S-9   *Law and Order: The Scales of Justice* / Abraham S. Blumberg
TA/S-10   *Social Science and National Policy* / Fred R. Harris
TA/S-11   *Peace and the War Industry* / Kenneth E. Boulding
TA/S-12   *America and the Asian Revolutions* / Robert Jay Lifton
TA/S-13   *Law and Order: Police Encounters* / Michael Lipsky
TA/S-14   *American Bureaucracy* / Warren G. Bennis
TA/S-15   *The Values of Social Science* / Norman K. Denzin
TA/S-16   *Ghetto Revolts* / Peter H. Rossi
TA/S-17   *The Future Society* / Donald N. Michael
TA/S-18   *Awakening Minorities: American Indians, Mexican Americans,
          Puerto Ricans* / John R. Howard
TA/S-19   *The American Military* / Martin Oppenheimer
TA/S-20   *Total Institutions* / Samuel E. Wallace
TA/S-21   *The Anti-American Generation* / Edgar Z. Friedenberg
TA/S-22   *Religion in Radical Transition* / Jeffrey K. Hadden
TA/S-23   *Culture and Civility in San Francisco* / Howard S. Becker
TA/S-24   *Poor Americans: How the White Poor Live* / Marc
          Pilisuk and Phyllis Pilisuk
TA/S-25   *Games, Sport and Power* / Gregory P. Stone
TA/S-26   *Beyond Conflict and Containment: Critical Studies of
          Military and Foreign Policy* / Milton J. Rosenberg
TA/S-27   *Muckraking Sociology: Research as Social
          Criticism* / Gary T. Marx
TA/S-28   *Children and Their Caretakers* / Norman K. Denzin
TA/S-29   *Poverty in America: The Dynamics of Change* / Marc Pilisuk and
          Phyllis Pilisuk
TA/S-30   *Human Intelligence* / J. McVicker Hunt

MUCKRAKING
SOCIOLOGY

Research as
Social Criticism

Edited by

GARY T. MARX

Transaction Books
New Brunswick, New Jersey
Distributed by E.P. Dutton & Co., Inc.

Unless otherwise indicated, the essays in this book originally appeared in *trans*action/**Society** magazine.

Copyright © 1972
Transaction, Inc.

Transaction Books
Rutgers University
New Brunswick, New Jersey 08903

Library of Congress Catalog Card Number: 71-186711
ISBN: 0-87855-036-4 (cloth); 0-87855-532-3 (paper)

Printed in the United States of America

Contents

Preface   vii

Gary T. Marx   1
   Introduction

I. JUSTICE

Alan J. Davis   31
   Sexual Assaults in the Philadelphia
   Prison System

Stuart Nagel and Lenore J. Weitzman   50
   Sexism in the Courts

Gary T. Marx   75
   Civil Disorder and the Agents of
   Social Control

II. DECISION MAKERS

Harold M. Baron   99
with Harriet Stulman, Richard Rothstein and Rennard Davis
   Black Powerlessness in Chicago

25672

Kenneth M. Dolbeare and James W. Davis, Jr.   118
    Little Groups of Neighbors—American Draft Boards

Theodore J. Lowi   132
    Apartheid U.S.A.

Gordon Fellman, Barbara Brandt and Roger Rosenblatt   154
    Dagger in the Heart of Town:
    Mass. Planners and Cambridge Workers

James M. Graham   177
    Amphetamine Politics on Capitol Hill

III. SOCIAL CLASS

Robert Coles   207
    Life in Appalachia—The Case of Hugh McCaslin

Dorothy Nelkin   233
    Invisible Migrant Workers

Thomas M. Martinez   249
    Why Employment-Agency Counselors Lower Their
    Clients' Self-Esteem

IV. EDUCATION

David Wellman   265
    The Wrong Way to Find Jobs for Negroes

Rosalie H. Wax   289
    The Warrior Dropouts

Walter E. Schafer, Carol Olexa and Kenneth Polk   306
    Programmed for Social Class: Tracking in High School

V. HEALTH

Anselm L. Strauss   333
    Medical Ghettos

Richard Titmuss   352
    The Gift of Blood

About the Authors   382

Preface

For the past decade, *trans*action, and now **Society**, has dedicated itself to the task of reporting the strains and conflicts within the American system. But the magazine has done more than this. It has pioneered in social programs for changing the social order, offered the kind of analysis that has permanently restructured the terms of the "dialogue" between peoples and publics, and offered the sort of prognosis that makes for real aterations in economic and political policies directly affecting our lives.

The work done in the magazine has crossed disciplinary boundaries. This represents much more than simple cross-disciplinary "team efforts." It embodies rather a recognition that the social world cannot be easily carved into neat academic disciplines; that, indeed, the study of the experience of blacks in American ghettos, or the manifold uses and abuses of agencies of law enforcement, or the sorts of overseas policies that lead to the celebration of some dictatorships and the condemnation of others, can best be examined from many viewpoints and from the vantage points of many disciplines.

The editors of **Society** magazine are now making available in permanent form the most important work done in the magazine, supplemented in some cases by additional materials edited to reflect the tone and style developed over the years by *trans-action*. Like the magazine, this series of books demonstrates the superiority of starting with real world problems and searching out practical solutions, over the zealous guardianship of professional boundaries. Indeed, it is precisely this approach that has elicited enthusiastic support from leading American social scientists, many of whom are represented among the editors of these volumes.

The subject matter of these books concerns social changes and social policies that have aroused the long-standing needs and present-day anxieties of us all. These changes are in organizational lifestyles, concepts of human ability and intelligence, changing patterns of norms and morals, the relationship of social conditions to physical and biological environments, and in the status of social science with respect to national policy making. The editors feel that many of these articles have withstood the test of time, and match in durable interest the best of available social science literature. This collection of essays, then, attempts to address itself to immediate issues without violating the basic insights derived from the classical literature in the various fields of social science.

As the political crises of the sixties have given way to the economic crunch of the seventies, the social scientists involved as editors and authors of this series have gone beyond observation of critical areas, and have entered into the vital and difficult tasks of explanation and interpretation. They have defined issues in a way that makes solutions possible. They have provided answers as well as asked the right questions. These books, based as they are upon the best materials from *trans*action/**Society** magazine, are dedicated to highlighting social problems, and beyond that, to establishing guidelines for social solutions based on the social sciences.

The remarkable success of the book series to date is indicative of the need for such "fastbacks" in college course work and, no less, in the everyday needs of busy people who have not surrendered the need to know, nor the lively sense required to satisfy such knowledge needs. It is also plain that what superficially appeared as a random selection of articles on the basis of subject alone, in fact, represented a careful concern for materials that are addressed to issues at the shank and marrow of society. It is the distillation of the best of these, systematically arranged, that appears in these volumes.

THE EDITORS
*trans*action/**Society**

Introduction

GARY T. MARX

It is clear that the social sciences and especially sociology are undergoing important changes. In the present decade of ferment and realignment, traditional perspectives, methodologies, styles, assumptions and masters are being questioned. An early sign of this was the establishment of *trans*action in 1963*; the first issue stated, "The social scientist studying contemporary problems and the complex relationships among modern men knows that he can no longer discharge his social responsibilities by retreating from the world until more is known." A sociology at once more critical, and concerned with studying immediate human problems, reaching a wide audience and granting legitimacy to a wider range of methods, has come to partly displace the

---

trans*action magazine was renamed **Society magazine effective February 1972.

concern with technique and broad theory which has characterized American sociology in recent decades.

Unlike other volumes in the *trans*action/**Society** series focusing on particular substantive areas, this volume is intended to illustrate a particular *style* of social science research. While the articles differ in terms of method and subject matter, they are sufficiently similar to illustrate an important type of contemporary social research, which *I* have identified as "muckraking" research. Such research at its best documents conditions that clash with basic values, fixes responsibility for them and is capable of generating moral outrage. Use of the term "muckraking" implies nothing invidious; it originated from "muckrake," an instrument used for gathering dung into a heap. Following the turn-of-the-century activities of inspired journalists such as Lincoln Steffens and Upton Sinclair, muckraking came to be defined as "the searching out and public exposure of misconduct on the part of prominent individuals and the discovery of scandal and incriminating evidence." The type of social research represented by the articles included in this book is terribly incriminating and certainly deals with scandalous states of affairs. One of its main purposes is to document and publicize. In pointing out the gap between values and actual practices and in questioning established orthodoxies it serves as a vehicle for social criticism and, hopefully, social change. This is social criticism of a very focused nature; it can be differentiated from the broad essay with an explicit theoretical orientation which uses social science data to critique the entire social order and its major assumptions and values. Muckraking thus seems to be an appropriate description of the consequences, if not always the intent, of this new style of critical research.

Such research uses the tools of social science to document unintended (or officially unacknowledged) consequences of social action, inequality, poverty, racism, exploitation, opportunism, neglect, denial of dignity, hypocrisy, inconsistency, manipulation, wasted resources and the displacement of an organization's stated goals in favor of self-perpetuation. It may show how, and the extent to which, a dominant or more powerful class, race, group or stratum takes advantage of, misuses, mistreats or ignores a subordinate group, often in the face of an ideology that claims it does exactly the opposite. In pointing out a state of affairs that strikingly clashes with cherished values, muckraking research may have an exposé, sacred cow-smashing, anti-establishment, counter-intuitive, even subversive quality, for it grows out of and helps sustain social upheaval and questioning. Although sociology like any other intellectual undertaking always has this potential, it is not often realized.

Ironically, such research also can have a conservative aspect: it shows how far the society may be from fulfilling its own traditional values. As Gunnar Myrdal observes in *An American Dilemma*, "America is . . . conservative in fundamental principles. . . . But the principles conserved are liberal and some, indeed, are radical." As with Myrdal such research is characteristically American in its optimistic belief that something can be done. The frequent discrepancy between a society's abstract values and its actual practices, when documented with ability, tact and luck by the social researcher, makes possible the legitimization of such research in the eyes of many not normally given to a critical perspective of their own society.

*trans*action has been an important impetus to such

focused work, both as a means of dissemination and as role model for other journals and research. The magazine does not restrict itself only to this type of research, nor does all research on social problems fall within the framework considered here. Present-day sociology is far from being generally defined in such terms, whatever the media may report about its annual professional meetings.

Perhaps as a consequence of their insecurity or perceived powerlessness, or the nature of their profession, with its self and socially sensitizing concepts, and its lack of a widely agreed upon paradigm for ordering social facts and directing the discipline, many contemporary social analysts have spent a great amount of time analyzing their role. Much of their concern focuses on the responsibilities of the researcher, on the uses and misuses of research and even on how potentially helpful research can be (no matter to whom).

What roles *are* open to the social researcher and in what ways can and should his work be relevant to social change? Should sociology be a disinterested calling pursued for purely intellectual and esthetic reasons, or should it be committed to, and involved in, solving current problems? To what extent do our social problems stem from a lack of obtainable technical knowledge rather than simply from the way political power is used and resources allocated? To what extent is a science of man analogous to the physical sciences possible and desirable? Even if useful knowledge can be obtained, won't it always be of most use to those already in power, given their greater resources?

Without entering fully into the issues of how social science can and cannot make a difference, I wish to argue that an important and little acknowledged potential for change lies in the educative role it can play in raising public issues. Such data and analysis can give us a clearer picture of our world, stripped of protective verbiage and without the usual selective perceptions (and misperceptions). If this picture involves a striking contrast between values and practices, it can be politically useful to those seeking change. It can expose the fallacies in certain common-sense beliefs about social problems and can show how certain ideas rationalize an unsatisfactory status quo. Careful social science documentation of a problem may convey a certain legitimacy over and above the testimony of an anguished group. As Herbert Gans and Howard Becker have noted, social science can help articulate the value claims and suffering of ignored and powerless groups. There is an important role for some social researchers to play here—perhaps one far easier to carry out than discovering cause and effect knowledge that can be directly applied. As Robert Merton has written, "The function of social research, then is not simply to supply information useful in remedying problems already known, it serves to make the problems known." The social researcher can of course also be instrumental to change by studying sources of resistance and how advocates of change can be mobilized, by designing and helping implement new programs and conceptions of society and by evaluating the consequences of innovations. He can also help by analyzing "deviant cases" where desirable but uncommon social outcomes occur, and through conventional and unconventional political action.

The Selections

Turn-of-the-century muckrakers tended to hold particular individuals (usually big businessmen) responsible for the social conditions which disturbed them and to ignore the role of social structure. Theological underpinnings or the rugged individualism of the era often led them to adopt the "evil man" theory of injustice. The role of government tended to be seen as indirect, a consequence of default and failure to regulate.

In contrast, muckraking social science researchers, aware of the increased centralization and government responsibility in so many areas of life, have focused primarily on institutional responsibility. The particular institutions looked at are often agencies of government, or at least theoretically subject to appreciable government regulation and control: schools, courts, welfare, police, prisons, hospitals, urban renewal and labor. For example, this volume includes articles on sexual assaults in prison vans and jails, the ways in which schools fail to meet the needs of Indian youth and how the tracking system in high schools may further the achievement gap between whites and blacks rich and poor, how employment agencies may lower their clients self-esteem, the unanticipated consequences of an OEO job-training program, unemployment in Appalachia, and the invisibility and exploitation of migrant farm laborers. Other articles include ways in which police occasionally cause riots rather than control them, how the courts treat women unequally, the federal role in creating segregation, the social costs of building a highway through a low-income community, the extent to which blacks are excluded from positions of power in government and industry, the gap between the official ideology of Selective Service boards and actual practices, the power of the amphetamine drug lobby to affect legislation, the hidden cost of commercial blood banks, and the ways in which medicine fails the poor. The criticism does not concern the idea of government involvement as such but rather the form of its involvement or the negative consequences of its noninvolvement. It is interesting that relatively less attention has been paid to the private sector. Much research attempts to link the actions of those at the top with the life conditions of those at the bottom, rather than simply studying one or the other.

To be credible, muckraking research must respect the traditional canons of science and be judged by them, although it may not be inspired by the esthetic contemplation of ideas for their own sake or the desire to advance an abstract body of knowledge. An additional criterion might be the extent to which such research creates shock and indignation and the belief that the situation must be changed. The articles included here strikingly satisfy these criteria, at least for those sharing humanistic values.

Unfortunately, space limitations precluded articles on abortion, maternal mistreatment of children, the evasion of fair-housing laws, problems of American foreign policy, consumer exploitation, problems faced by homosexuals and alcoholics as a result of society's response to them, and a wide range of other topics that can be seen to fall within the range of a critical and muckraking social science. Yet the book is representative of research being done within this framework.

No single method characterizes muckraking research, though observation and focused case studies seem to lend themselves better to instilling attitudes conducive to social change, at least among laymen, than do elaborate statistical analyses or abstract theoretical treatments. The audience to which such research is directed introduces constraints on how the data can be presented. Here we have aimed for diversity in method and subject matter. This book contains studies which employ a number of methodological approaches: participant observation, quantitative data, ethnographic accounts, a case study of one individual, and institutional analysis. The subject matter is, unfortunately, less diverse: most of the articles touch upon problems of race or class in one form or another. Along with sex, age (both the young and the very old) and region these are the major bases of inequality in American life and consequently they have attracted the most research attention.

To be sure, action with unintended or unacknowledged consequences which clash with basic societal values and rationalizing myths is not the special property of the rich and the powerful—populist glorifications and the romanticization of suffering aside. Almost any aspect of social life might be covered here, though not in the same degree or with the same consequences. One might hazard the proposition that wherever there are social structure, norms and legitimation, an underside of life can be observed. Hypothetically, one might well investigate blue-collar theft and sabotage on the job, prejudice among minorities, the damage that students do to teachers, the relatively high suicide and illness rates among police, and the occasional failure of some members of excluded groups to take full advantage of the limited opportunities that may be available. Another topic might be authoritarian and manipulative behavior and oversimplified explanations on the part of protestors who espouse an ideology of democracy and participation and claim that their analysis is scientific.*

---

*For many social scientists this has become increasingly important in their teaching if not necessarily in their research. Many educators facing the

Yet the social consequences of "underdog" groups' activities are considered appreciably less serious by most social scientists than the consequences of action by those in high status positions. Given the equalitarian and democratic values of many researchers, it may not be surprising that they generally focus on the consequences of the behavior (or neglect) of the powerful. There are doubtless other reasons why social scientists avoid certain kinds of critical research—such as that directed at major foundations and government agencies which offer them research support or the college administrators and trustees who hire them. Whose ox the researcher is to gore is clearly a political question, even if the goring partakes of the neutrality of science.

Such social research poses a number of important questions about social change, the sociology of sociology, methodology and the careers and identity of social scientists. In what time periods does a muckraking orientation appear? How is it linked to the history of American sociology? What kinds of people do such research and what difficulties do they face? What special methodological or ethical problems may be involved? What are the implications of strongly held value positions for one's research results? What implications does such research have for the development of social

---

more silent generation of the 1950s felt compelled to shake up the conventional world view of their students, and in Peter Berger's words to convey the fact "that the wisdom of sociology is this—things are not what what they seem." Now, faced with a new generation indignant over the right issues, but sometimes for the wrong reasons, occasionally given to rhetoric and oversimplification, romantically valuing emotions over thought and action over analysis, sometimes uninformed and uninterested in history, international comparisons and complex data from their own society (and the techniques needed to understand and make use of these), the educator may feel compelled to spend time analyzing critical perspectives as well as the conventional wisdom.

science? How significant is such research for social change?

Origins and Parallels

The present period of critically oriented research has important parallels and ties to earlier periods of American social science. The twentieth century has witnessed cycles of social science involvement with what have traditionally been defined as social problems (or what, from some current perspectives are seen as social symptoms—those with power being seen as the social problem) followed by the less dirty work of studying noncontroversial areas or developing techniques and general theories. Controversial work has been most frequent during the first two decades of this century and since the 1960s. Any intellectual pursuit is of course affected by the internal development of a body of thought, by conflicts between systems of thought, and by the diffusion of intellectually fashionable ideas. Yet critical research seems especially conditioned by external social events.

Karl Mannheim has written that systematic sociology develops only as a nation begins to be unsure of itself. As many observers have noted, to a great degree modern sociology developed out of the deep changes affecting nineteenth-century Europe. In the American context, social science became even more explicitly a means of reform. From its inception through the first decades of this century, American sociology took a critical stance and sought reform, albeit rather conservative reform by today's standards. The orientation of men such as Ward, Ross, Small, Park and Ogburn and their students was greatly influenced by social, political and economic changes. Industrialization, immigration, ethnic and racial violence, war, depression and the social move-ments these spawned, led them to ask hard questions about their society and to be skeptical of its convention-al wisdom. The agrarian background of these earlier researchers made them especially sensitive to the prob-lems of cities undergoing rapid urbanization. Their religious concerns, noblesse oblige and social position contributed to a vicarious interest in experiencing and documenting the problems of those considered less fortunate; the rich ethnographic accounts they pro-duced attest to their success.

While these researchers were initially outsiders to the problems they studied (unlike many contemporary social researchers), they were insiders with respect to the traditional prestige criteria of American society and held dominant positions within their profession. In-fluenced by empiricism and pragmatism, they used observation and limited interpretive frameworks to acquire useable knowledge. Their work generally did not identify much with the broad belief systems and sweeping moral imperatives that characterized latter nineteenth-century European social thought. While moral issues certainly concerned them, they saw the world as too complex to fit into any single explanatory framework. The problems they selected for study thus tended to be microscopic rather than macroscopic, and as a consequence the approach was less radical. Their belief in the promise of American equality, liberty and democracy (whose failure inspired their critical re-search) prevented these researchers from searching for wholly new social systems and interpretive frameworks.

The optimism and apparent prosperity of the 1920s somewhat muted the critical orientation of many social analysts, though for some the shock of the depression years helped revive it. But sociology reflected the relative quietism in American society during the 1940s and 1950s and the unhospitable political climate by also turning inward; this was further strengthened by the great interest in psychoanalysis among many researchers during this time period. Problems for study were defined by business and government to an important extent. Concern with pressing social issues was thought unscientific. Yet this irrelevant, and to some, irreverent concern with method and concept eventually permitted more insightful treatment of social issues. As the pendulum swung back toward concern with socially meaningful problems, sociology found it had gained new techniques, greater sophistication and resources, and increased respectability.

The critical work of men such as David Riesman, William H. Whyte and C. Wright Mills, which was affected by the spread of large-scale bureaucracies and the more visible presence of many aspects of a mass society also helped spread criticism to other areas.

The present period of unfortunate involvement in Southeast Asia and the emergence of qualitatively new problems on a previously unimagined scale has led to a mood of doubt and self-questioning. The powerful role of the United States in world affairs and the diverse potentials of its technology are also relevant to the reemergence of critical research. As T.B. Bottomore has observed, "In a society of such wealth and power, capable of doing such immense good or harm to the whole world, the social critic can scarcely fail to acquire a sense of the seriousness and urgency of his task. . . . The actions and responsibilities of a great world power provoke a major undertaking of self-criticism."

The present decade illustrates the reciprocal relationship between critical social science and social movements. The civil rights, student power and antiwar movements were important to the reorientation of contemporary social research, just as the feminist and ecology movements are beginning to inspire research in the 1970s.

The present-day researcher may feel that his work is worthwhile to the extent that he contributes to existing protest movements and avoids writing only in the abstract. A group making demands may sensitize the sociologist to studying its problems, and his data and theories may offer reciprocal insight to the group and help it to further press its claims and mobilize potential members.

Unlike many of the earlier muckrakers who seemed to become radicalized in the process of doing their work, current researchers may come to social research after a period of not completely successful political activism. In entering graduate school many seek to deepen their understanding in order to more effectively work for change. They bring a critical and questioning perspective with them which may be accentuated by the skepticism produced by graduate training. As they grow older, fatigue, new family and career responsibilities, or cooptation, may lead muckraking social researchers to find they lack the energy for the sustained political involvement which may have initially spurred their research interests. Unlike Lenin they may come to find writing about revolution more to their taste than participating in it. In one of those divine coincidences which make it possible to rationalize preference as necessity, the kind of research represented by these articles can become an alternative to the political activism of one's youth, while incidentally building a career and helping maintain one's feelings of relevance. It may be argued that a division of labor is needed between activism and research. Some may be better suited and able to make a greater contribution through research. One argument stresses the prior need to understand how society works ("the pragmatic social engineering argument") before it can be changed, another the need to carefully document problems in order to mobilize public opinion ("the truth will make men mad enough to change society,") and still another urges research if for no other reason than to counter the research of those whose politics and methods are disagreed with ("ascientific Machiavellism").

In addition to taking cues from social movements, muckraking research has been anticipated and inspired by the writing of informed activists and journalists outside the university community such as Michael Harrington, Jessica Mitford, Charles Silberman and Ralph Nader. This also seems to be true of early twentieth-century researchers—Ward wrote a book surveying and going beyond the work of the muckrakers and Robert Park came to sociology from journalism and saw as one of sociology's principal tasks "getting the big story." This effort to get at the facts and the real nitty-gritty of urban social life owes much to journalists and activists who, more directly involved with everyday life, are quicker to sense problems and trends and are less locked into a given theoretical framework.

Currently muckraking research is disproportionately carried out by younger people, often those who are racial or ethnic outsiders, and less likely to be in positions of prestige and power. Because they are less committed to vested interests and traditional outlooks within the profession, they may be freer to innovate and offend. The earlier struggle for the respectability and scientific status of sociology is not a factor inhibiting them the way it may have inhibited some of their elders. Meanwhile, the number of sociologists and centers for graduate training has greatly increased, and the ability of a few powerful men and schools to shape entire disciplines has declined. Greater literacy, affluence and ease of media exposure have increased the audience for critical research, just as earlier muckrakers were aided by the emergence of inexpensive mass circulation magazines.

Maturing in a highly politicized age, coming from urban areas, personally touched by issues of the draft or racial and ethnic prejudice, and likely to have been harrassed at some point as a result of their life style and politics, these younger social researchers are more likely than earlier researchers to root their questioning in their own experiences.

Some Potential Problems

If in broad outline the increased prominence of muckraking social research is a positive development and a necessary condition for social change, it also has limitations and presents difficulties. Both methodological and ethical problems may occur in the attempt to conduct such research. Precisely because the research deals with matters of some delicacy, obtaining entry to the data required may be difficult, particularly when this involves studying the actions and machinations of those in positions of power and those whose business it is to administer the lives of others. The more a group has to hide, the more protective it is likely to be. The price of entry may be providing those studied with the data, the right to prior censorship or guarantees to maintain the participants' anonymity. Such requirements are unlikely to be satisfactory if an important aim of the study is to publicize unsatisfactory conditions. One must either violate a trust in the interest of a personally defined broader social good, or pursue the research in a less convincing manner through second-hand sources or not at all. If the first option is taken it may become difficult for other social researchers to gain access. Persons in positions of public accountability may sometimes cooperate fully and openly with the researcher, accepting responsibility for their actions; or in some cases they may want a situation beyond their control documented and publicized; or they may not realize they are vulnerable and have something that should be protected. Though here the researcher may feel uneasy about publicly criticizing an organization which has extended friendship and trust and been generous with its time and information. It may also be possible to keep the analyzed unit anonymous while arguing that it is representative of similar institutions. While access to those lower in status and power may be technically easier, there are important questions regarding rights to privacy.

Then there are issues personally troublesome to some researchers. Particularly when it involves directly studying a deprived group, the researcher may worry that he is, in a sense, profiting from other people's misery. Clearly, if it were not for contemporary problems such as poverty and race relations, many social scientists would be out of work, or at least working elsewhere. As Robert Blauner has noted in writing about the problem of academic colonialism, minority communities increasingly resent outside researchers, who are seen to use people as subjects but to offer them little in direct return. The benign motives which inspire research may be seen as paternalistic interferences. The tendency to obtain research support from those at the top to study those at the bottom or outside, and a tendency to oversell the potential of social science (while enhancing egos and budgets) makes the researcher vulnerable to charges of perpetuating the status quo by feeding research upward into the hands of the powerful.

The researcher may experience a tension between his personal values of egalitarianism, participation and anti-elitism and the "fact" of his technical superiority in many aspects of the research process. He may feel equally guilty or uncomfortable when he tries to reconcile his expressed belief in cultural relativism and tolerance of other people with his secret belief that he is really better than the people he is studying.

The researcher may also face overt attacks from aggrieved communities, which may argue that as an outsider he or she is unable to understand or adequately present the problems of the group. The possibility that social research may debunk some of the claims of an oppressed group, as well as of more powerful groups, may also be seen as threatening.

The muckraking researcher might argue that almost everyone else in American society has some kind of a hustle and that the consequences of his, on balance, may be better than most. More detached and specially trained outside observers are often in a position to gain unique insights. The scientist's freedom of inquiry (which unfortunately sometimes results in intellectual anarchy and moral indifference) may also be used as a justification. It could also be argued that research on these problems is a better use of resources than marketing research or military research. If those holding egalitarian and democratic values and committed to as rational an analysis as possible do not study such problems they may not be studied at all, or treated in ways pleasing neither to one's science nor one's politics. While such rationalizations are readily available, the researcher involved in such work and presumably already sensitized to issues of injustice and exploitation may find them inadequate in the face of the personal attacks he may receive from representatives (if not always those representative) of an aggrieved community.

If viewed from the perspective of some interest group, almost any social research may be critical. However, as suggested, many current researchers, like earlier muckrakers, self-consciously seek topics likely to yield critical conclusions. But muckraking social science research tends to be more systematic, controlled and generalizable in its documentation, since it is bound by the traditional canons of scientific inquiry. Journalistic license is not so acceptable, which usually makes for less dramatic, if more credible presentations.

The strain toward objectivity may not always be present, however, and when it is, it may create inner conflict in the researcher who holds strong value positions. Whether an area chosen for research because it is thought likely to yield material for social criticism in general will be as accurately presented as one chosen out of intellectual curiosity is still a difficult question. Will the intensity of one's political commitment result in haste, in failure to master the more difficult social science techniques? More seriously, will it inhibit respect for the standards of scholarship that grant social science whatever legitimacy it has in the outside world? Is social rhetoric presented as social research? As the world of social science becomes divided into the good guys and the bad guys, does civility decline and self-righteousness run rampant among those who should ideally be bound to each other by their respect for the truth, wherever they may be pursuing it? There are, of course, no sure answers to the above questions, but they do suggest some potential pitfalls of committed research.

The needs of social science and of opinion mobilization may conflict. In a politically charged research milieu there may be undue pressures to forego work on nonsubstantive questions of technique and theory or nonrelevant substantive topics.

Without arguing that the needs of science should always have priority, the importance of a variety of approaches to the study of society should be acknowledged. Advances in sociological understanding of relevant questions may come from giving free play to the imagination and working on questions far removed from whatever issues have received public attention. It is possible that in some cases intense public pressures (and extensive resources) for quick data and solutions may interfere with understanding. The quality of descriptive documentation which characterizes much muckraking research may not contribute much to cumulative scientific knowledge (though for many of those involved in such research, the need for social change takes priority over building social science.) It might also be argued that less sophisticated methodology or theory may have a greater impact on public opinion. Nuance and subtlety may not be conducive to indignation over social policies, particularly on the part of laymen.

Of course it could also be argued that sophisticated techniques or theory will turn up better results and offer more convincing interpretations; though the increased understanding which may come from more specialized language and technique may make it difficult to communicate in plain English. While it is incumbent upon social analysts not to confuse profundity with incomprehensibility and to write as clearly as they can, there is also an important role here to be played by journalists trained in social science interpretation and translation.

The radical potential of social research lies in its cynical (if not always compassionate) stance toward men's rationalizations and ideologies. As outside observers social scientists may consider aspects of reality that men as actors are unaware of and would deny. However, social science may also have a conservatizing effect on its practitioners (beyond the rewards that can serve to seduce and coopt the appropriately pedigreed and licensed). It may make them overly aware of the complexity of the social world, of the many levels at which cause may be sought, and of the interdependence and tendency of many social phenomena to persist in time, in spite of well intentioned efforts to eliminate them. (However, a radicalizing influence may result as one comes to reject limited changes in focused institutions in favor of transforming the entire social order). It may also be easier to document some of the brutal facts of poverty, inferior education and inadequate housing, than to assess clear responsibility for them. Sometimes it may even turn out that victims cooperate in their victimization and that there are secondary gains to those mistreated.

From the perspective inspired by Max Weber and George Herbert Mead social science understanding may require that one imaginatively try to project oneself into the position of another person or group. Certainly each social group has the right to be taken seriously by the researcher (though certainly not to be liked or admired) no matter how abhorrent they may seem to him. Yet to realize with Harry Stack Sullivan that "we are all more human than otherwise" can greatly dampen the moral fervor a researcher begins with. Empathizing with the group seen as responsible for a problem may cause the researcher to develop an appreciation of the group's problems and fears and even on occasion to accept its point of view. This can greatly dampen the moral fervor with which he or she may have started. There are more than a few cases of social researchers becoming somewhat sympathetic to the point of view of the police, the far right, hard hats and ghetto merchants as a result of studying them; just as there are cases of researchers who come to assume more than the observer's role they began with in criminal, drug and homosexual milieus.

Even with respect to documentation, careful research sometimes may reveal the situation to be far less grave than one initially imagined. Or research may reveal how little we actually know about many problems, our smattering of social science facts and ideological hunches and sympathies to the contrary.

Does one report such gaps in knowledge, or report data in a highly selective or distorted fashion, or ignore the data and go on and do new research on a topic or in a manner which will hopefully reveal less ambiguous and more striking results? Whatever one decides in such situations a price must be paid, either to one's honesty as a scientist or by failure to help the political cause in question.

In graduate training and in the professional face presented to the public the norms of scientific honesty are stressed. Yet a serious sociological study of sociologists, rather than of others, would no doubt reveal the usual gap between principles and practices. This is not always as bad for mankind or public policy as for the advancement of science.

Assuming, however, that the above difficulties have been avoided and the data has turned out the way one had hoped, it is nevertheless easy to overemphasize the significance of such research. George Bernard Shaw reportedly once remarked, "I have solved practically all the pressing questions of our time, but . . . they go on being propounded as insoluble just as if I had never existed." The social researcher may experience similar feelings though he is more likely to have identified a problem than to have solved it. Many facts well capable of creating indignation have been carefully documented for generations without change occurring, such as the concentration of economic power, racism and the implications of social class for life chances.

Once the world stands naked, its ugliness exposed, what then? Are the facts which the researcher may find upsetting self-evident, and will they generate reform attitudes in others? What obligation does the researcher have to see that his findings are widely propagated and correctly interpreted and to make concrete policy suggestions and then to work toward their implementation?

The analyst may not be sure what to do with his incriminating data once he has it, particularly since social criticism research of the kind represented by these articles is often undertaken by the scholar acting as a free agent. While he is free from the constraints of sponsored research, he may also find that he has a revealing picture but lacks the resources to see anything come of it. Much has been written about the difficulties of getting social research used, even if it has been commissioned by an organization that would profit from its implementation. How much more difficult then to apply findings of research carried out with neither the support of a large organization nor a specific mandate other than the good of the society at large as defined by the researcher. Journals such as *trans*action play an important role in diffusing such information, even if many of those reached may already be convinced of the need for reform. Yet a broker is still needed to more closely link research with relevant political constituencies.

Research is perhaps best when the analyst can go beyond specifying an undesirable end result (showing how it conflicts with official ideology and commonsense assumptions, how it developed, what its main dimensions are, where it is located, and what its human costs are) to clearly indicate the basic causes, responsible agent(s) and the mechanisms by which this situation may be changed. Some analysts go even further and seek the power to bring about envisioned changes and perhaps even to participate in their implementation. As we move from documentation, to causal analysis, to policy suggestions, to actual policy implementation of a given piece of research there is probably a decline in the proportion of social scientists involved at each successive step. It is easier to document and describe than to explain, and to criticize existing institutions and policy failings than to suggest new ones. The greater difficulty of explanation stems from the crudity of our measures and the very complexity of behavior, affected as it is by culture and history and human consciousness. This should create some humility and help establish indignation over a given problem in ratio to one's ability (or that of others) to propose ways in which it might be improved. That criticism and debunking are rather inexpensive and emotionally pleasing should not lead to overindulgence in them without the possibility of concrete suggestions for reform. Without at least some effort in this direction muckraking research may run the danger of being little more than shocking exposés sometimes bordering on sensationalism, bathed in the self-congratulatory smugness of the analyst free from the manifest sins of those lesser mortals submitted to his analysis.

Until recently sociologists have been hesitant to involve themselves in questions of policy. Partly this stems from a mistaken belief about scientific purity, from hesitancy to say anything concrete in the face of data whose implications are usually at least somewhat equivocal, and from the difficulties of translating research into action. But social scientists are also generally trained and rewarded for taking the world as it is: little attention is given to the free play of the imagination and thinking about alternative social forms.

Some analysts may also recoil at policy-making's implicit manipulation of behavior and choosing for others. Particularly with respect to deviant and non-middle class groups, the researcher may be torn between recommending that the group be left alone so as to avoid the persecutions, stigmas and prejudices which so increase its problems, and recommending policies which will change the social conditions responsible for the group's distinctiveness. Unfortunately, the resolution is too often withdrawal, no recommendations and simple contentment with having documented a problem. A division of labor here may be practical. Many social analysts lack the temperament and skills for community political struggles and policy implementation. To the extent that the average person tries to play all roles in the social change process, his contribution in any one phase must necessarily be diluted.

Aside from the question of whether he can be a multifaceted super-change agent, the social researcher, too often encapsulated in a ghetto of like-minded people and perhaps overemphasizing the importance of his calling, may forget that facts which he found so compelling may not necessarily seem this way to others—even assuming that he can gain access to the media.

The consequences of such research are affected by factors such as the way it is presented and the audience reached, the degree of indignation and political aware- ness among the unprivileged, the relative power and extent of gains and losses of groups affected by proposed changes, and the general political atmosphere at the time of publication. The message men take from communication depends very much on what they bring to it and the context in which they receive it, beyond the attributes of the message. A wide array of psycho- logical defenses and institutional rationales, not to mention different value preferences, will often prevent others from coming to terms with information that may seem apparent and poignant to the social analyst in a liberal milieu. One man's indignation may be another's pleasure or boredom. In this volume the article by Lowi on the Federal role in creating segregation is not likely to create indignation on the part of many racists (who are unlikely to read it in any event). The article by Martinez showing how employment agencies lower their clients' self-image may be seen as a smart business practice by those thoroughly imbued with the profit- making ethos.

The article by Barron on the powerlessness of blacks

in Chicago may be seen by some as proof of lack of ambition and ability. Much research in this tradition is concerned with conveying the life conditions and human misery of excluded, stigmatized and ignored lower status groups. This is needed and important. Yet, if not presented with an analysis of the institutions most directly responsible for producing such behavior (and even then) some readers will take the description offered as further proof of how inferior and alien the excluded group is and will interpret their condition in terms of personal pathology and failing of the individual or his community. A careful description and analysis may also be taken as proof that the situation could not be otherwise. Research which documents violations of the most widely held consensual standards—such as Davis' article on sexual assaults in Philadelphia prisons or research on extreme parental mistreatment of children—is more likely to create reform sentiment. Research which exposes a condition directly touching the receiver of the message (particularly if he or she is of high status) rather than that which calls for sympathy and compassion for the revealed plight of others is even more likely to create such an end.

As for the implicated institution or group, if they do not ignore a study altogether, shift responsibility to some other group or report that the problem is "being studied," they may label the research "unscientific," "biased" and the view of an uninformed outside ax-wielder who does not appreciate their problems, dangers and responsibilities. They may attempt to discredit data as a result of its sponsor or the past political activities of the researcher. They may try to cut off research funds, restrict further research access or limit publication channels. If rich and sophisticated enough (and they are usually far richer if not always more sophisticated than their critics) they may produce their own experts and counter-science (e.g., cigarette company research casting doubt on the link between smoking and cancer, the "counter-riot commissions" that emerged in some cities to dispute the reports of liberal commissions, southern foundations encouraging research on "white superiority," and the use of social scientists to testify in favor of urban renewal or school segregation). Such defense may take the form of offering methodological critiques, presenting data from another source, drawing on the same body of data but selectively emphasizing a different aspect of it, or even offering a different explanation for the same body of facts. Even where there is agreement on facts and explanation, there may be disagreement on significance. Does one say that *fully* 5 percent of police contact with low-income whites results in excessive police violence, or *only* 5 percent, that a majority of blacks live in conditions of poverty or that only one in three of the American poor are black?

Institutions under fire may sidestep critical studies by insinuating they are utopian and romantic. They may insist that a "hard realistic look" at the data will show how much progress has been made and how much better things are for the group in question than for comparable groups elsewhere in the world, or in other states or cities. By introducing an historical or comparative perspective, the evaluational frame of reference is made relative rather than absolute and some of the sting may be taken from the critique. Even where the research has more benign effects, it is still well to keep in mind the exceptional flexibility and adaptability of American society and its remarkable capacity for cooptation.

Muckraking research may show various institutions where their failings are most visible and lead to window dressing (such as the symbolic black in the front office) without basic alterations in patterns. Praising the results of a study or initiating a commission of inquiry may simply be an inexpensive way of giving the impression that something is being done. The researcher may sometimes come to feel that the main consequence of his work is to clarify for himself and his professional colleagues what is happening in a world beyond his reach and control.

Although their efforts were significant, early journalistic muckrakers became disillusioned rather quickly and were active for only a short period of time. Cynics have noted that after they left the scene the nation settled back into business as usual. Though there were certainly some improvements and some blatantly devious practices disappeared, others came to be more carefully hidden and in time, the new regulatory agencies were captured by those they were set up to control. The research themes and political concerns of sociologists radicalized during the depression years have also become more moderate over time.

Perhaps the current trend toward muckraking research will also be reversed. Certainly cooptation, fatigue, cynicism and frustration may discourage socially relevant research. Intense political pressure from the right (repression, denial of resources) and the left (harassment, difficulties of research access), the increased ability of established interests to defuse threatening social science data, and intellectual cycles of involvement and retreat from social issues may also have an impact.

Social change is usually subtle, uneven and multifaceted. Analyzing the precise contribution of social scientists who wish to contribute to it is difficult and can be self-indulgent. Compared to other decades in American sociology and most other countries the amount of research informed by reform instincts is significant. Even if it is far from making a major dent, change has been achieved on some fronts and on others perhaps things have been kept from greater deterioration. In spite of much recent social science attention, many of our problems are still with us—some worse than ever. However, research such as that represented by this collection has contributed to greater public awareness and more sophisticated and humane theories about domestic social issues. Considering that until recently this was a rather smug, optimistic and in some ways self-deluded society, blind to many of its problems, this is not an insignificant factor.

FURTHER READING

Critics of Society by T.B. Bottomore (New York: Pantheon Books, 1968).

Crusaders for American Liberalism by Louis Filler (Yellow Springs, Ohio: Antioch Press, 1961).

A Sociology of Sociology by Robert W. Friedrichs (New York: Free Press, 1970).

The Coming Crisis in Western Sociology by Alvin W. Gouldner (New York: Basic Books, 1970).

The Uses of Sociology by Paul Felix Lazarsfeld, William H. Sewell and Harold L. Welensky (New York: Basic Books 1967).

The Sociological Imagination (2nd ed.) by Charles Wright Mills (New York: Oxford University Press, 1967).

Radical Sociology by J. David Colfax and Jack L. Roach (New York: Basic Books, 1971).

"Ethical Dilemmas and Political Considerations in Social Research" by M. Useem and G. Marx in *Social Science Methods*, edited by R. Smith.

Sexual Assaults in the Philadelphia Prison System

ALAN J. DAVIS

A Note on This Report

This chapter is based on the results of a three-month investigation conducted jointly by the Philadelphia District Attorney's office and the Police Department, under the supervision of the author. It culminated in a 103-page report submitted to Judge Alexander F. Barbieri and the public on Sept. 11, 1968. More than half of the report contains detailed recommendations for controlling sexual assaults and for the general reform of the Philadelphia prison system. Many of these recommendations are now being implemented by the city administration. This chapter relates only to those portions of the report analyzing sexual assaults and comparing the physical and psychological characteristics of the victims and aggressors.

In the summer of 1968, Joseph F. Mitchell, a slightly-built 19-year-old, was brought to trial before Alexander F. Barbieri, judge of the Court of Common Pleas No. 8 in Philadelphia County. Mitchell's lawyer, Joseph E.

Alessandroni, told Judge Barbieri that his client, while being transported in a sheriff's van, had been repeatedly raped by a gang of criminals. A few weeks later, Alessandroni informed the judge that George DiAngelo, a slender 21-year-old whom Barbieri had committed to the Philadelphia Detention Center merely for pre-sentence evaluation, had been sexually assaulted within minutes of his admission.

Judge Barbieri thereupon appointed me, then Chief Assistant District Attorney of Philadelphia, to investigate these allegations. Police Commissioner Frank L. Rizzo started a parallel investigation; then these two investigations were merged.

In the Philadelphia prison system there are three facilities: the Detention Center, Holmesburg Prison, and the House of Correction. The period we chose to study was from June 1966 to July 31, 1968—a little over two years. Out of the 60,000 inmates who passed through the prison system in those 26 months, we interviewed 3,304—virtually all of them inmates during the period of our investigation. We also interviewed 561 out of the 570 custodial employees. We took 130 written statements from those who had given us important information, and gave polygraph ("lie-detector") examinations to 45 of them. We asked 26 employees to take polygraph tests: 25 refused, and the one employee who took the test "passed." We asked 48 inmates: seven refused, and of the 41 remaining, 10 failed the test and 31 passed. (We ignored the statements of those prisoners and employees who either would not take the test or who failed it.) In addition, we interviewed several people whom we believed had special information, and we reviewed all of the reports dealing with homosexuality issued by the prison system since June 1966. Finally, we made a number of detailed personal inspections of the prison facilities and of the sheriff's vans.

In brief, we found that sexual assaults in the Philadelphia prison system are epidemic. As Superintendent Hendrick and three of the wardens admitted, virtually every slightly-built young man committed by the courts is sexually approached within a day or two after his admission to prison. Many of these young men are repeatedly raped by gangs of inmates. Others, because of the threat of gang rape, seek protection by entering into a homosexual relationship with an individual tormentor. Only the tougher and more hardened young men, and those few so obviously frail that they are immediately locked up for their own protection, escape homosexual rape.

After a young man has been raped, he is marked as a sexual victim for the duration of his confinement. This mark follows him from institution to institution. Many of these young men return to their communities ashamed and full of hatred.

This, then, is the sexual system that exists in the Philadelphia prisons. It is a system that imposes a punishment that is not, and could not be, included in the sentence of the court. Indeed, it is a system under which the least hardened criminals, and many men later found to be innocent, suffer the most.

A few typical examples of such sexual assaults may convey the enormity of the problem. In an early draft of our report, an attempt was made to couch this illustrative material in sociological, medical and legal terminology less offensive than the raw, ugly language used by the witnesses and victims. This approach was abandoned. The incidents are raw and ugly. Any attempt to prettify them would be hypocrisy.

A witness describes the ordeal of *William McNichol*, 24 years old and mentally disturbed:

"That was June 11th, I was assigned to E Dorm. Right after the light went out I saw this colored male, Cheyenne—I think his last name is Boone. He went over and was talking to this kid and slapped him in the face with a belt. He was saying come on back with us and the kid kept saying I don't want to. After being slapped with the belt he walked back with Cheyenne and another colored fellow named Horse. They were walking him back into E Dorm. They were telling him to put his hand down and stop crying so the guard will not know what is going on. I looked up a couple of times. They had the kid on the floor. About 12 fellows took turns with him. This went on for about two hours.

"After this he came back to his bed and he was crying and he stated that 'They all took turns on me.' He laid there for about 20 minutes and Cheyenne came over to the kid's bed and pulled his pants down and got on top of him and raped him again. When he got done Horse did it again and then about four or five others got on him. While one of the guys was on him raping him, Horse came over and said, 'Open your mouth and suck on this and don't bite it.' He then put his penis in his mouth and made him suck on it. The kid was hollering that he was gagging and Horse stated, 'you better not bite it or I will kick your teeth out.'

"While they had this kid they also had a kid named William in another section in E Dorm. He had his pants off and he was bent over and they were taking turns on him. This was Horse, Cheyenne, and about seven other colored fellows. Two of the seven were brothers.

"Horse came back and stated, 'Boy, I got two virgins in one night. Maybe I should make it three.' At this time

he was standing over me. I stated, 'What are you looking at?' and he said 'We'll save him for tomorrow night.' "
Julius Brown, 18 years old:

"Brown stated that he has been in Holmesburg since March 29, 1968, and that about a week and a half ago, on Thursday, he was in I block; his cell was number 926. On this date, in the morning after breakfast, James Williams called him into his cell; he went into Williams' cell. Donald Reese was in there also. Further that he had owed Williams four cartons of cigarettes. Williams said to him that he would have to give the cigarettes back right now or he would have to give them something else. He [Brown] then started to walk out of the cell and Williams pushed him down. Williams picked up the window pole, Reese picked up a bench and stood blocking the door. Reese told him that if he goes to the guard they are going to get him anyway; there were other men outside the cell.

"Further that he walked out of the cell, they were all around him and walked to cell 971, and they pushed him inside. He went over and sat on the toilet seat. Twin [Roger Jones] came into the cell, they made him lay down on the floor, and Twin pulled his [Brown's] pants down and made him lay face down. Twin pushed his [Brown's] legs apart and Twin put his penis into his [Brown's] rectum. He was on him until he discharged. When he got through, Brown saw that he was bleeding from the rectum. Then Twin, Williams, Reese, and McDuffy told him that if he went to the guard their boys would get him to D block, and he was scared then to tell the guard. Further that he did cry out when Twin did this to him, but the guard wouldn't be able to hear him because the block is long.

"Brown went on to say that the next day after chow

[breakfast] James Williams, McDuffy, Ike (Isaiah Franklin), and Leftenant got him in cell 972 [Roger Jones's cell]. They told him that everything is cool now as long as he doesn't tell. Further that he had never been in jail before and he was too scared to tell anybody. Then four of them did it to him—they put their penises into his rectum, James first, Ike second, Leftenant third, Mc-Duffy fourth. Twin did not bother him that time. That after they did this he was bleeding and got sick.

"That night, Roach [Thomas Roach] came into his cell and changed with his partner. Roach told him that he would have to do it. When the guard came to check the cells, Roach turned over so he wouldn't be recognized. After the guard counted and left, Roach got on top of him, put his penis into his [Brown's] rectum, and discharged."

Charles Williams, 19 years old:

"On Tuesday morning, the first week of June at about 9:30 AM, I was in my cell 412 on D block and I had started to clean up. A tall, heavy-set fella came into the cell and asked for a mirror and shaving brush and a comb, and that my cell partner said he could borrow.

"He then said that he heard something about me concerning homosexual acts. I told him what he had heard was not true. He then started to threaten me and if I didn't submit to him. Then I hit him with my fist in his face before he could hit me. Then about three more men came into the cell, and they started to beat me up, too. I fought back the best I could and then I fell on the floor and I got kicked in the ribs. Three guys were holding me while the other one tore my pants off; I continued to fight until one of the guys knocked me out. One of the guys was holding me on the floor and had my arm pinned to the floor. And about seven or eight guys came into the cell and they took turns sticking their penis up my ass. When they finished they left my cell, and I was still laying on the floor."

Clarence Garlick, 26 years old:

"Back in April this year, about 10:30 AM I was in my cell 455 on block D when Joe Lovett came into my cell. I was laying on my bed. When he came in I jumped up. He told me to get greased up. I told him I wasn't going to do nothing. He told me, 'You're going to do something.' He started punching me. I had backed up into a corner of the cell. He seen some mineral-oil grease I had on the table and he reached over and handed it to me saying, 'Put this on.' I put some on and layed down on the bed. He took out his penis and got on top of me. After he did what he wanted to do he got up and got some toilet paper and wiped himself off and went out of the cell."

"This is the second incident. He came to me on July 18, 1968, in the morning about 10 o'clock. I was standing up in the doorway of my cell, 455. He told me to 'get it fixed.' I told him I wasn't going to do nothing, that today was my birthday. He walked on away."

"The next day, on the 19th, he came to me again. I was in my cell, this was about the same time. He stated, 'Today isn't your birthday, you're going to do something.' I told him I wasn't going to do anything. He started punching me again. I told him I was going to call the guard. He stated, 'Go ahead and call, you'll only call him one time and I'll knock you out.' He got the grease from off the table and handed it to me, told me to put some on, which I did. I laid down on the bed, he took out his penis and got on top. A friend he walks with, Kincaid, was standing out by the door, he was laughing. Joe got up after he got through, got toilet paper and wiped himself off. He then walked out of the cell."

During the 26-month period, we found, there had been 156 sexual assaults that could be documented and substantiated—through institutional records, polygraph examinations or other corroboration. Seven of the assaults took place in the sheriff's vans, 149 in the prisons. Of the sexual assaults, 82 consisted of buggery; 19 of fellatio; and 55 of attempts and coercive solicitations to commit sexual acts. There were assaults on at least 97 different victims by at least 176 different aggressors. With unidentified victims and aggressors, there were 109 different victims and 276 different aggressors.

For various reasons, these figures represent only the top of the iceberg.

1) Our investigators, as mentioned, interviewed only a twentieth of the inmates who passed through the prison system. We discovered 94 assaults—excluding those reported in institutional records. This suggests that if all 60,000 inmates had been interviewed, 20 times 94—or 1,880—additional assaults would have come to light.

2) Almost all of the victims still in prison were so terrified of retaliation by other prisoners that they were very reluctant to cooperate with us.

3) Many guards discouraged complaints by indicating that they did not want to be bothered. One victim screamed for over an hour while he was being gang-raped in his cell; the block guard ignored the screams and laughed at the victim when the rape was over. The inmates who reported this passed a polygraph examination. The guard who had been named refused to take the test.

Then too, some guards put pressure on victims not to complain—such complaints, after all, would indicate that the guards were failing in their duty. We found many cases where victims, after filing complaints, had "voluntarily" refused to prosecute, and a number of them told us that guards urged them to rely on prison discipline rather than to bring the facts out into the open. Very often, these guards asked the victim if he wanted his parents and friends to find out about his humiliation.

4) Without prompting from the prison guards, many victims and their families wanted to avoid the shame and dishonor they believed would follow such a complaint.

5) Inmates have little faith in the ability of a guard to protect them from retaliation should they complain. Their fears are justified by the lack of supervision by guards and the inadequate facilities to provide security for complainants.

6) Inmates who complain are themselves punished by the prison system. It is usual procedure to place a victim of a sexual assault on "lock-in feed-in," obstensibly for his own protection. This means that after a complaint is made, and especially if it is pressed, the complainant is locked in his cell all day, fed in his cell, and not permitted recreation, television or exercise until it is determined that he is safe from retaliation. Many victims consider this "solitary confinement" worse than a homosexual relationship with one aggressor.

7) Sometimes very little comes of a complaint. Some complaints are just not acted upon; action, when taken, usually consists of putting the aggressor in the "hole" for 30 days or less. Meanwhile, the victim also is usually locked in, and looks forward—when released—to terror from the aggressor's friends, and from the aggressor himself when he is let out of the "hole." Finally,

8) Many of the victims themselves distrust and are hostile to constituted authority, and could not bring themselves to cooperate by filing a complaint.

Taking all of these facts into consideration, we conservatively estimate that the true number of assaults in the 26-month period was about 2,000. Indeed, one guard put the number at 250 a year in the Detention Center alone.

Of the estimated 2,000 assaults that occurred, 156 of which were documented, the inmates reported only 96 to prison authorities. Of this 96, only 64 were mentioned in the prison records. Of these 64, only 40 resulted in internal discipline against the aggressors, and only 26 incidents were reported to the police for prosecution.

Now, in our study of sexual assaults we excluded any that were cases of truly "consensual" homosexuality. Nonetheless, it was hard to separate consensual homosexuality from rape, since many continuing and isolated homosexual liaisons originated from a gang rape, or from the ever-present threat of gang rape. Similarly, many individual homosexual acts were possible only because of the fear-charged atmosphere. Thus, a threat of rape, expressed or implied, would prompt an already fearful young man to submit. Prison officials are too quick to label such activities "consensual."

At the opposite end of the spectrum from innocent victims of homosexual rape are the male prostitutes. These homosexuals—known as "sissys," "freaks" or "girls"—were supposed to be segregated from the general prison population, yet they were readily available. We learned of repeated instances where homosexual "security" cells were left unguarded by a staff that was too small or too indifferent, or who turned their backs so that certain favored inmates could have sexual relations.

Many of these male prostitutes were created not only by force and the threat of force, but by bribery. The fact is that a person with economic advantage in prison often uses it to gain sexual advantage. Typically, an experienced inmate will give cigarettes, candy, sedatives, stainless-steel blades or extra food pilfered from the kitchen to an inexperienced inmate, and after a few days the veteran will demand sexual repayment. It is also typical for a veteran to entice a young man into gambling, have him roll up large debts, and then tell the youth to "pay or fuck." An initial sexual act stamps the victim as a "punk boy," and he is pressed into prostitution for the remainder of his imprisonment.

Despite the important role that economic advantage plays in the creation of homosexuality, it is virtually impossible to obliterate economic distinctions among inmates. Even a small accumulation of money or luxuries gives an inmate substantial economic advantage: In the prison economy, a shopworker earns 15 to 25 cents a day; half of the inmates have no prison jobs at all, and most inmates get little or no material help from friends or relatives outside the prison.

It is the duty of prison officials to reduce the economic power that any inmate might exercise over another inmate. Yet we discovered one area in which Philadelphia prison officials, either through neglect or indifference, disregarded this duty. As a result, at least one inmate became so powerful economically that he was able to choose, as cellmates, a series of young men he found attractive, and then use bribery to sexually subvert each one.

The University of Pennsylvania and a private concern operate a large laboratory on H block of Holmesburg

Prison, where they test inmates' reactions to new medicines and to experimental commercial products like soaps, shaving creams, suntan lotions and toilet tissue. The prisoners are excellent "human guinea pigs" 1) because they live under controlled conditions, and 2) because they will submit to tests for a fraction of the fee that a free individual would demand. Prison officials—because there is very little other activity for the prisoners, and because the laboratory pays 20 percent of the inmates' wages to the prison system— have allowed the project to expand to the extent that it constitutes a separate government within the prison system.

All the inmates at Holmesburg wanted to "get on the tests" because, by prison standards, they can earn a fortune. Just by wearing a chemical patch on his back, for example, a prisoner can earn $10 to $15 a week. By participating in some tests that last longer, a prisoner— for doing almost nothing—will receive over $100. Altogether, the Holmesburg inmates earn more than $250,000 a year from the project. A few prisoners end up with bodies crazyquilted with motley scars and skin patches, but to these men, in the context of a prison economy, it seems well worth it.

To save money another way, the operators of the project also use inmates as laboratory assistants. An experienced assistant, working an eight-hour day, will get $100 a month—in the prison economy, the equivalent of a millionaire's income. Even a few prison guards are employed in the project, after their regular hours, and they work side by side with the prisoners.

Generally, the U. of P. project has had a disastrous effect upon the operations of Holmesburg Prison; it is one of the reasons why morale of the employees is at the lowest in that institution. The disproportionate wealth and power in the hands of a few inmates leads to favoritism, bribery and jealousy among the guards, resulting in disrespect for supervisory authority and prison regulations. What is more, the project contributed to homosexuality in the prison.

Stanley Randall, a 38-year-old con man serving a four- to 11-year sentence, was employed in laboratory cell 806, H block, as an assistant. Although prison and laboratory officials at first denied it, Randall had the power to decide which inmates would serve as subjects on various tests. Since the 806 cell disbursed $10,000 to $20,000 a year, Randall's power was considerable.

Randall's special taste was newly admitted young inmates. Through his influence with the guard staff he had his pick of these young men assigned to him as cellmates—and for as long as he wished. When his victims moved in, Randall solicited them to engage in sexual acts in return for his giving them a steady stream of luxuries and for "getting them on the tests." At least half a dozen of these inmates submitted, and went on to profit handsomely from the University of Pennsylvania project.

Although top prison officials assured us that no inmate was permitted to earn more than $1200 a year, and that $400 was unusually high, in six months Randall's present cellmate had earned over $800. The record was held by a prior cellmate of Randall's, who had earned $1740 in just 11 months. When we asked university project managers about these high incomes, they told us they had never heard of any $1200-a-year limit. The prison's accounting office had apparently never heard of this $1200-a-year limit either, because that office had credited these high amounts to the accounts of Randall's cellmates.

How had Randall managed to get his choice of cellmates? One guard told us that H-block guards had been instructed by "higher-ups" not to interfere in the affairs of inmates working for the U. of P. Another guard reported he had received such instructions, and said they had come from the guard lieutenant. The lieutenant denied this, and agreed to take a lie-detector test. Later he reversed his position and refused. Randall admitted he had often given cigars to this lieutenant.

Other inmates besides Randall exploited their powerful positions. One inmate worker, for example, forged test results and fee vouchers, and got fees for inmates who had not actually been test subjects. It also seems that at least a few guards were also corrupted.

As a result of our investigation, prison officials have relieved the powerful inmate workers of their positions with the U. of P. project. They are also considering phasing out the project entirely.

How did sexual aggressors in the prisons differ from their victims? On the average, aggressors tended to be older, heavier, taller, and more serious offenders. Data on hundreds of victims and aggressors yielded the following comparisons:

Table 1

	Victims	Aggressors
Average Age	20.75	23.67
Average Height	5'8¼"	5'9"
Average Weight	140.9	157.2

Both victims and aggressors tended to be younger than the average inmate, as comparison with the following table shows:

Table 2
Average Age of Prisoners (July 31, 1968)

Detention Center	27.9
Holmesburg	29.3
House of Correction	28.9
All Prisons	28.8

Yet although aggressors on the average are older and larger than victims, these differences are rather slight. In many cases, there may be no differences, and in others they are reversed. Still, after having observed hundreds of victims and aggressors we believe that there are other, more subjective, physical criteria which can be used to differentiate between aggressors and victims:

1) Victims tend to look young for their age.

2) Victims tend to look less athletic and less physically coordinated.

3) Victims tend to be better looking.

A comparison of 164 aggressors and 103 victims showed that 68 percent of the former and only 38 percent of the latter had been charged with serious felonies. Among aggressors, violent assaultive felonies were particularly common. Thus, 14 aggressors had been charged with rape, but only three victims; six aggressors had been charged with weapons offenses, and no victims; 34 aggressors with robbery and aggravated robbery, but only eight victims; and seven aggressors with assault with intent to kill, but only one victim. As many victims as aggressors, however, had been charged with homicide. On the other hand, many more victims than aggressors were charged with relatively less serious offenses, such as the larceny of a car, going AWOL from the armed forces, violating parole and delinquency.

We also made a study of the 129 documented assaults in which the races of both aggressors and victims had been ascertained, and found that a disproportionate number involved Negro aggressors and white victims:

Table 3

Type of Incident	Number of Incidents	Percentage
White Aggressors & White Victims	20	15
Negro Aggressors & Negro Victims	37	29
White Aggressors & Negro Victims	0	0
Negro Aggressors & White Victims	72	56
Total	129	100

These statistics in part reflect the fact that 80 percent of the inmates are Negro—it is safer for a member of a majority group to single out for attack a member of a minority group. Then too, Negro victims seemed more reluctant than white victims to disclose assaults by Negro aggressors. But it also seems true that current racial tensions and hostilities in the outside community are aggravated in a criminal population.

Now, we are not professionally qualified to offer a scientific theory to explain the sexual aggression in the Philadelphia prison system. We have, however, reached certain conclusions that should be recorded for possible use by psychiatrists, psychologists and social scientists. The conclusions and the analysis set forth are based upon our observations, upon pertinent literature, and upon discussions with a psychiatrist and a psychologist who are experts in forensic psychology.

1) We were struck by the fact that the typical sexual aggressor does not consider himself to be a homosexual, or even to have engaged in homosexual acts. This seems

to be based upon his startlingly primitive view of sexual relationships, one that defines as male whichever partner is aggressive and as homosexual whichever partner is passive.

2) It appears that need for sexual release is not the primary motive of a sexual aggressor. After all, in a sexually segregated population, autoeroticism would seem a much easier and more "normal" method of release than homosexual rape. As recent studies have shown (Masters and Johnson, *Human Sexual Response*, 1966), autoerotic stimulation yields a measure of physical release and pleasure similar to that yielded by sexual intercourse.

3) A primary goal of the sexual aggressor, it is clear, is the conquest and degradation of his victim. We repeatedly found that aggressors used such language as "Fight or fuck," "We're going to take your manhood," "You'll have to give up some face," and "We're gonna make a girl out of you." Some of the assaults were reminiscent of the custom in some ancient societies of castrating or buggering a defeated enemy.

4) Another primary goal of many of the aggressors, it appears, is to retain membership in the groups led by militant sexual aggressors. This is particularly true of some of the participants in gang rapes. Lacking identification with such groups, as many of the aggressors know, they themselves would become victims. And finally,

5) Most of the aggressors seem to be members of a subculture that has found most nonsexual avenues of asserting their masculinity closed to them. To them, job success, raising a family, and achieving the respect of other men socially have been largely beyond reach. Only sexual and physical prowess stands between them and a

feeling of emasculation. When the fact of imprisonment, and the emptiness of prison life knock from under them whatever props to their masculinity they may have had, they became almost totally dependent for self-esteem upon an assertion of their sexual and physical potency.

In sum, sexual assaults, as opposed to consensual homosexuality, are not primarily caused by sexual deprivation. They are expressions of anger and aggression prompted by the same basic frustrations that exist in the community, and which very probably were significant factors in producing the rapes, robberies, and other violent offenses for which the bulk of the aggressors were convicted. These frustrations can be summarized as an inability to achieve masculine identification and pride through avenues other than sex. When these frustrations are intensified by imprisonment, and superimposed upon hostility between the races and a simplistic view of all sex as an act of aggression and subjugation, then the result is assaults on members of the same sex.

Assuming that this analysis is valid, then the principal psychological causes of sexual assaults in the Philadelphia prison system are deeply rooted in the community—in that millions of American men, throughout their lives, are deprived of any effective way of achieving masculine self-identification through avenues other than physical aggression and sex. They belong to a class of men who rarely have meaningful work, successful families, or opportunities for constructive emotional expressional and individual creativity. Therefore, although sexual assaults within a prison system may be controlled by intensive supervision and effective programing, the pathology at the root of sexual assaults will not be eliminated until fundamental changes are made in the outside community.

December 1968

Postscript: November 1971

During the first year following my report, the City committed an additional $1,000,000 to improvement of the county prisons and the initiation of new programs for the prisoners. The next year, however, the city cut back the prison budget to the point where it had been prior to my report. On July 4, 1970, a riot errupted at Holmesburg Prison, which resulted in serious injuries to dozens of prisoners, and destruction of portions of the facility. No reforms resulted from the riot, and the county prison system remains in the same state as in 1968.

Sexism in the Courts

STUART NAGEL *and* LENORE J. WEITZMAN

Are women treated equally in American courts? Or does sexism tip the scales of American justice against women when they are defendants and litigants before the bar? In the literature dealing with women's rights, researchers have found that "in several states, higher penalties are imposed on a woman who commits the same crime." However, this conclusion is based on those few state statutes and appellate test cases which describe the law on the books rather than law in action. Our research will focus instead on the law in action. We will ask if, in practice, women are sentenced to more time in prison than men for the same crimes. Are women favored or disfavored in criminal, personal injury and divorce proceedings? How does the presence of women jurors and judges affect the relative treatment of male and female litigants?

Analogies are frequently drawn between the treatment of women and blacks in many areas (e.g., employment) of American society. Is this similarity applicable to the courtroom? A comparison of black-white and male-female sentencing practices is examined for comparative insights.

Women as Criminal Defendants

In 1962, Lee Silverstein of the American Bar Foundation (ABF) compiled data on 11,258 criminal cases, using 194 counties located in all 50 states as his sample. While the main focus of his study was on procedures for providing attorneys to indigent defendants, Silverstein also gathered information on the race, sex and age of the defendants and the treatment they received at all stages of the criminal justice process—from preliminary hearing through sentencing.

Two basic patterns of discrimination emerge. The first—the disadvantaged pattern—involves unfavorable treatment of defendants who are poor, black or have only elementary education. These defendants in socially inferior positions receive unfavorable treatment at virtually all stages of the criminal justice process, including 1) receiving a preliminary hearing, 2) being released on bail, 3) having a hired attorney rather than assigned counsel or no attorney, 4) being subjected to relatively shorter pretrial detainment while in jail if not released on bail, 5) receiving a jury trial, 6) being dismissed or being acquitted 7) receiving probation or a suspended sentence if convicted and 8) receiving a relatively short sentence if jailed.

The second discriminatory syndrome—the paternalistic pattern—particularly applies to juvenile offenders and involves unfavorable treatment only in the area of safeguards for the innocent, such as having an attorney or a jury trial. It involves favorable treatment, however, in being kept out of jail pending trial, in not being convicted and in not being sentenced to jail if convicted.

Both the disadvantaged and paternalistic patterns of discrimination against women are apparent to some degree in the ABF findings. However, when female criminal defendants are compared with their male counterparts, the resulting treatment pattern most readily fits the paternalistic mold. Paternalistic discrimination against and for women, as in the case of juveniles, is found in both grand larceny cases and in felonious assault cases, although women are somewhat more likely to be jailed when they commit assault. Due perhaps to the fact that assault is considered a more masculine type of crime than larceny, women's and men's jail sentences correspond more closely in these cases.

To the extent that male and female larceny and assault cases are comparable, the data suggest that the difference in treatment may be explained by a judicial attitude which assumes women (and juveniles) to be weaker, and therefore more likely to be harmed by pretrial and postconviction jailing.

Although blacks and indigents are particularly discriminated against when it comes to being released on bail, in the larceny and assault cases studied, the opposite holds true for women (Table 1). Of the 63 female larceny defendants, 76 percent were released on bail, while of the 771 male larceny defendants, only 50 percent were released on bail—a 26 percent difference. This practice works to avoid keeping juveniles and women in jail pending trial or after conviction. The same pretrial jail-avoidance phenomenon is evident in

Table 1 — HOW THE TREATMENT OF FEMALES DIFFERS
FROM MALES AS DEFENDANTS IN CRIMINAL CASES

	NUMBER OF DEFENDANTS Percentage Receiving Treatment			
	Females	%	Males	%
GRAND LARCENY CASES				
A. BEING JAILED				
1. Released on bail	63	76	771	50
2. Had less than 2 months delay of those awaiting trial in jail	10	60	231	67
3. Case dismissed or acquitted	71	24	841	13
4. Received suspended sentence or probation of those convicted	47	64	656	43
5. Received less than one year imprisonment of those imprisoned	9	33	241	45
B. FORMAL SAFEGUARDS				
6. Received preliminary hearing	42	57	606	55
7. Had or given a lawyer	61	90	781	87
8. Received a jury trial of those tried	18	47	283	31
FELONIOUS ASSAULT CASES				
A. BEING JAILED				
1. Released on bail	43	77	615	58
2. Had less than 2 months delay of those awaiting trial in jail	6	17	152	49
3. Case dismissed or acquitted	45	36	638	23
4. Received suspended sentence or probation of those convicted	25	44	415	36
5. Received less than one year imprisonment of those imprisoned	9	89	172	57
B. FORMAL SAFEGUARDS				
6. Received preliminary hearing	31	74	451	73
7. Had or given a lawyer	42	88	620	89
8. Received a jury trial of those tried	24	19	262	45

the assault cases, where there is a 19 percent difference.

Likewise, the data show that women receive more lenient treatment if they are convicted in grand larceny cases; 64 percent of the women received a suspended sentence or probation, as compared to only 43 percent of the men. A related although weaker difference is also apparent in the felonious assault cases studied.

Of those defendants who actually received jail sentences, there are too few (20 or less) women in the sample who were jailed pending trial or imprisoned after conviction to make a meaningful comparison possible on length of imprisonment. Possibly as a means of avoiding imprisonment and the stigma of a criminal record, fewer women are convicted than their male counterparts. The study shows that 24 percent of the women were acquitted or had their larceny cases dismissed, as compared to only 13 percent of the men. A similar difference is present in the assault cases cited.

Convicted defendants given indeterminate sentences were not included when computing the number imprisoned because these sentences lack the necessary precision for comparison. Of the 363 women sentenced in the total sample, 27 percent received indeterminate sentences, while 35 percent of the 5,898 men's sentences were indeterminate. Although these sentences are usually associated with such crimes as murder and arson (which men are more likely to commit), men usually receive a slightly higher percentage of indeterminate sentences than do women for the same type of crime. Such sentences generally have higher maximums than fixed terms and may result in longer prison stays.

When it comes to formal safeguards for the innocent, judicial treatment is mixed. When women defendants are compared with men defendants in either larceny cases or assault cases with respect to having a lawyer, no discriminatory pattern emerges. Likewise, no discrimination is evident with regard to receiving a preliminary hearing, although this is probably not as important a safeguard for the innocent as are having counsel or receiving a jury trial. (Of these three safeguards, only preliminary hearings have not been made a due process right for adults by the Supreme Court.)

However, women—in conformity with the paternalism hypothesis—are more likely to receive informal treatment with regard to not receiving a jury trial, at least in the assault cases, where the percentage difference between men and women is 26. This disparity is contrary to the best interests of women, because juries are generally less likely to convict than are judges. To be convicted by a jury normally requires the unanimous agreement of 12 persons, a task harder for the prosecutor to achieve than that of convincing a single judge. The University of Chicago Jury Project research indicates that while both juries and judges tend to favor women in their criminal verdicts, juries do so to a greater extent.

Although the numbers are small, a comparison of women by race indicates that white women are less likely to be jailed before or after conviction than are black women, and they are also less likely to have a lawyer to represent them. This is because they are less apt than blacks to be so poor that they are appointed counsel by the court. And while black women (unlike black men) receive more favorable treatment than do white men with regard to being jailed before or after conviction—in this case, sexual paternalism and racial discrimination are mixed—there is no consistent pattern whereby black women receive or do not receive a jury trial. Therefore, while women seem to fit the paternalistic mold more neatly.

The ABF data, then, indicate that women are substantially less likely to be held in jail before or after trial, but are more likely to lack a jury trial. While all the differences discussed were sufficiently significant that they could not readily be attributed to chance, some of them might be attributable to the fact that women commit grand larcenies and felonious assaults on a less grand scale than men do, and that therefore they have less at stake to merit a jury trial and less guilt to merit a severe sentence.

It is interesting to note that male juveniles and female adults are treated about equally. Although the male juveniles are less likely to have an attorney, a jury trial or a preliminary hearing, the female adults are more likely to be kept out of jail before and after conviction.

In addition to assuming that women are weaker and more open to harm from jailing, judges may also give shorter sentences to women than to men convicted of similar crimes because they think this weaker nature also makes women less dangerous to society, more easily deterred from repeating their crime and more speedily rehabilitated. Custodial care, deterrence from further crime and rehabilitation being the official goals of imprisonment in any case, women are thus already assumed to be in a position of conforming to them. Women and especially juveniles are also less likely to be hardened criminals—in the sense that they are somewhat less likely to have prior criminal records.

Likewise, judges might feel that both juveniles and women should be treated in a more fatherly, less legalistic way, and that jury trials and defense counsel interfere with this paternalistic informality.

The few statutes which provide different sentences for women and men for the same type of crime generally provide more indeterminate sentences for women, just as juvenile statutes provide more indeterminate sentences for juveniles. The legislators who pass these laws probably believe that women and juveniles are more accessible to rehabilitation than are adult males, and that indeterminate sentences contingent on progress made in prison will facilitate rehabilitation. (However, we know that indeterminate sentences usually result in a longer period of incarceration.) Testing this explanation would require determining the legislators' attitudes, although the judges who apply criminal statutes allowing for discretion are probably more instrumental to the increase or decrease of sexual discrimination than are the legislators who write them into law.

Women as Personal Injury Plaintiffs

In personal injury cases, where the defendant is usually an insurance company rather than an individual man or woman, the difference in the sex of the plaintiffs who have suffered personal injuries may be an important variable. How do sex differences affect treatment received?

There are separate stages at which discrimination can occur in personal injury cases—the first being whether or not the injured party files a complaint.

In Alfred Conard's 1964 study of the economics of personal injury cases in the state of Michigan, he compiled data on the background characteristics of automobile accident victims who subsequently became personal injury claimants. His key sex data (Table 2) show that of the seriously injured male accident victims, 38 percent filed suit, whereas of the seriously injured female accident victims, only 30 percent filed suit. This difference might be due to a higher rate of precomplaint settlements for women or to less severe injuries sus-

Table 2 — HOW THE TREATMENT OF FEMALES DIFFERS
FROM MALES AS VICTIMS AND PLAINTIFFS IN
PERSONAL INJURY CASES

	Female Plaintiffs	Male Plaintiffs
I. SUIT FILED		
1. Suit filed by seriously injured victim	30%	38%
II. LIABILITY ESTABLISHED		
2. Claim was paid in bodily injury cases	80%	77%
3. Victory in jury trial cases (to plaintiffs of all ages)	61%	62%
4. Victory in jury trial cases (to adult plaintiffs)	69%	76%
III. AVERAGE AMOUNT AWARDED		
5. Award in jury trial cases (to plaintiffs of all ages)	-2% below average	+1% above average
6. Award in jury trial cases (to adult plaintiffs)	-2% below average	+6% above average
7. Award for loss of victim's services (to spouse plaintiffs)	$5,585	$6,524
8. Award for victim's death (to spouse plaintiffs where victim employed age 21-29)	$67,524	$39,820
9. Award for urinogenital injuries	$11,835	$31,966

tained by them. An even more telling explanation might be that women are encouraged to be less aggressive in asserting their legal rights in personal injury cases.

Once the suit is filed, the next stage is establishing the defendant's liability to pay something to the injured plaintiff. The 1970 Department of Transportation study of personal injury claims (which used nationwide data) shows that there is virtually no difference between men and women in the likelihood of their winning claims (see Table 2). It is interesting to note that there is a lower victory rate in cases which go to a jury decision as compared to cases heard by a judge or settled without coming to trial—possibly because the nontrial cases more clearly favor the plaintiff—but there is no differentiation related to whether the plaintiffs are men or women.

A discriminatory pattern begins to appear if one leaves out minors and compares only adult male plaintiffs with adult female plaintiffs, since adult males win 76 percent of their jury trials and adult females only 69 percent of theirs. Sexual discrimination seems less prevalent in the comparison between boy and girl minors (especially preteenage minors) because the tendency is to class them simply as "children." The data reveal, however, that adults, whether male or female, have a better chance of winning their cases than children of either sex, probably because children frequently contribute through negligence to their own injuries, and juries tend to identify more closely with adult defendants than with child plaintiffs.

Once liability has been established, the next stage involves determining the amount of money to be awarded. Again there is little difference in the average amount awarded to male and female plaintiffs when adults and minors are grouped together, although a small percentage difference may involve a substantial number of dollars. However, the pattern of amounts awarded is again more favorable to men when only adults are compared: men received 6 percent above the average personal injury award for similar cases of injury with similar compensation for medical expenses and lost wages, while women averaged 2 percent below this figure.

The more interesting male-female comparisons relate to specific kinds of personal injuries. For instance, when husbands sue for loss of consortium (affection and sex) caused by their wives' injuries they collect more than when wives sue for loss of consortium caused by their husbands' injuries. This is so even though when women sue for their own injuries, they tend to collect less than men do. Our data also show that there are more than 11 times as many suits by husbands for the loss of their wives' services as by wives for the loss of their husbands' services—another odd phenomenon. Does this represent the fact that more wives than husbands suffer personal injuries, or is it rather a reflection of outmoded legal tradition? It would seem to be the latter, for in fact, these 28 suits in which the wife is plaintiff represent a sizeable increase over the three such cases shown in the 1964 Jury Verdict Research Report, and in some states the law still permits only husbands—and not wives—to sue for loss of a spouse's services—a holdover from the time when wives were considered part of their husbands' property—and one's property cannot sue for damages to the owner of the property. It may also have been felt unseemly for a woman to sue for the loss of the sexual services of her husband.

The generally larger amounts awarded to male plaintiffs for their personal injuries may be in part explained by the greater earning power of males, which may be temporarily or permanently reduced by the injury. This greater earning power may reflect employment and educational discrimination against women over which personal injury juries have no control. In cases where the injury results in death, male victims are clearly valued more highly than women in terms of monetary awards; because of this, women seem to be favored as plaintiffs. However, it must be remembered that where a wife-plaintiff is seeking to collect for a killed husband rather than a husband-plaintiff for a killed wife, one is mixing favoritism as to the victim's sex with discrimination as to the plaintiff's sex.

Differences in the amounts awarded to male and female plaintiffs for injuries not generally related to an individual's work capacity cannot be readily explained in terms of differential earning power. Urinogenital injuries fall into this category, and the inequality pattern here is greater than with any other type of bodily injury. In the sample studied, the average male plaintiff who wins a urinogenital injury case collects $31,966, while the average female plaintiff collects only $11,385. This represents an absolute difference of $20,131 or 170 percent. Monetary awards for injury to male genitalia run almost three times as high as those for injury to female genitalia—a direct indication of an apparently sexist value system in American courts.

Some of the difference may be accounted for by the fact that urinogenital damage was usually more severe and more likely to be permanent among the male plaintiffs. Because the child-bearing capacity of women is especially valued in American society, a more useful comparison would be between women who lose their capacity to bear children with men who lose their potency.

An overall view of the findings seems to reveal a pattern in which adult women are less likely than men to file suit, to establish liability and to receive a relatively high award, especially for certain types of injury. In this regard, the pattern of discrimination against women resembles that of black plaintiffs rather than juveniles. The victory rate for black plaintiffs was 57 percent as compared to a general rate of 61 percent and a rate of 46 percent for children under 12. Damage awards to black plaintiffs averaged 15 percent lower than the general level of awards. If children collect anything in court, they tend to get either very small or very large awards. This uneven distribution gives them an average award close to that of the general population. In personal injury cases, children, blacks and women, in that order, do worse on liability than adults, whites and men. Given this order of discrimination on a victory-rate continuum, women plaintiffs are thus closer to blacks than to children in the treatment they receive. On a damages-awarded continuum, however, women are closer to children than to blacks, with blacks farthest behind.

The basic issue in personal injury cases is whether the plaintiff succeeds in collecting money for damages. Since women are usually less favored in economic matters in our society, a similar pattern of negative discrimination should be evident in personal injury cases. This has, on examination, turned out to be correct. The paternalism hypothesis, which made some sense in relation to the treatment of women as criminal defendants, cannot be applied in the same terms to personal injury plaintiffs, because they are not in jeopardy of being placed in jail or stigmatized with criminal records. It could, however, be defined here as favoritism toward the weak in imposing negative sanctions, but disfavoritism in awarding or enforcing monetary awards. If it is so defined, we can legitimately say that the discrimination women experience fits both the disadvantaged and the paternalistic patterns. Its causes are probably: the traditional subordination of women in the family, employment and educational discrimination, the rationing of scarce monetary resources, even, in some cases, a Freudian castration fear and other sexual anxieties, as indicated by the huge discrepancy in awards for loss of urinogenital functions. As contemporary pressures for societal and legal change steadily erode these causal factors, differential victory rates and damages awarded should become more nearly equal.

Women as Divorce Litigants

The predominant impression among the general public is that divorce cases are a manifestation of female domination or even exploitation of men, because normally only women litigants seek and obtain alimony or child support. Despite this prevailing opinion, the facts about women as divorce litigants could well be said to show actual male domination and even exploitation.

In a sample of divorce cases in 22 states taken in 1963, wives were plaintiffs in 72 percent of the cases. Yet, even where women are the formal plaintiffs, existing data indicate this is often really a nominal status, and in reality it is the husband who has taken the de facto rather than the de jure initiative in dissolving the marriage. William Goode, on the basis of extensive interviews with a sample of 425 divorced women in 1956, concluded that "the husband more frequently than the wife is the first to desire a divorce, and it is the husband more often than the wife who adopts (whether consciously or not) a line of behavior which forces the other spouse to suggest a divorce as the appropriate solution."

Among the poor, desertion by the husband is a frequent substitute for divorce and is a major cause of eligibility for welfare aid. In the year 1967, 76 percent of the 1.3 million Aid to Dependent Children families in the United States had fathers absent from the home. Once again the man appears to be the active partner in the dissolution of the family.

The fact that wives seem to have better formal grounds for divorce and thus become the plaintiff-complainants may possibly show greater provocation on the part of husbands. An alternative explanation is that both husband and wife recognize that the wife has a better chance of winning the case. In divorce cases where decrees were granted, the wife as plaintiff lost only about 2 percent of the time, whereas the husband as plaintiff lost about 10 percent of the time. Although women have become more independent as a result of increased employment opportunities, they are still more economically dependent upon their husbands than their husbands are on them and would therefore tend to resist divorce were it not for their husbands' provocation, which may take the form of cruelty, nonsupport, desertion or some other ground.

In descriptions of the divorce trial process, there are many references to the often degrading paternalistic procedures to which women litigants are subjected. Begging for alimony may be particularly degrading, even if alimony is considered 1) income accrued as a result of inadequately compensated wifehood and motherhood and 2) payment for obtaining educational rehabilitation and training. Seeking child support may also be a frustrating ordeal, even if the judge recognizes the concept as covering both some of the considerable work the mother must do in caring for her children and some of the many out-of-pocket expenses involved in raising the children which the husband has fathered. Although it might at first glance appear to be a victory when the wife obtains custody of and responsibility for the children, which she does in about 95 percent of cases, husbands in fact admitted that about 85 percent of the time they agreed with the custody decrees.

A double standard of morality may also prevail in custody disputes, condemning extramarital activities by wives but tolerating them on the part of husbands. In some states, the double standard actually allows husbands to obtain a divorce on sexual grounds which are not allowed to wives—as, for example, a common provision that allows husbands to divorce wives who were pregnant at the time of the marriage, whereas there is no comparable legislation allowing wives to divorce husbands who have made other women pregnant at the time of the marriage.

The real test of possible discrimination in the judicial process comes not at the stage of initiation or filing suit, nor even at the stage of judgment, but rather at the stage of that judgment's enforcement. To a lesser extent, this reasoning also applies to criminal and personal injury cases, but a far higher percentage of the results of such cases are determined at the prejudgment stage. In addition, there seems to be no data available on the collection of personal injury damages by sex—as distinct from the awarding of damages—nor on the paroling of convicts by sex. We do however have some data on the monetary judgments awarded to women divorce litigants.

Table 3 illustrates the probability of a divorced woman being able to collect any child-support money. It is based on data gathered by Kenneth Eckhardt from a sample of fathers who were ordered to pay child support in divorce decrees in a metropolitan county in Wisconsin in 1955. Within one year after the divorce decree, only 38 percent of the fathers were fully complying with the support order. Twenty percent had only partially complied, and in some cases partial compliance constituted only one payment. Forty-two

Table 3 — THE POSSIBILITY OF A DIVORCED
WOMAN COLLECTING ANY CHILD SUPPORT MONEY

Years since court order	Number of open cases	Compliance Full	Partial	No	Nonpaying Fathers*
One	163	38%	20%	42%	19%
Two	163	28	20	52	32
Three	161	26	14	60	21
Four	161	22	11	67	18
Five	160	19	14	67	9
Six	158	17	12	71	6
Seven	157	17	12	71	4
Eight	155	17	8	75	2
Nine	155	17	8	75	0
Ten	149	13	8	79	1

*Nonpaying fathers against whom legal action was taken.

Based on data from Kenneth Eckhardt, "Deviance, Visibility, and Legal Action: The Duty to Support," 15 *Social Problems* 470, 473-74 (1968).

percent of the fathers had made no payment at all. By the tenth year, the number of open cases had dropped from 163 to 149 because of the death of the father, termination of his parental rights or the maturity of the children. By that year, only 13 percent of the fathers were fully complying and 79 percent were in total noncompliance.

If noncompliance with child-support orders is so great, we can reasonably expect it to be even greater with alimony orders, although alimony orders are in fact relatively infrequent. In a 1956 analysis of 12,000 Chicago divorce cases, the wife requested post-divorce alimony in only 7 percent of the cases. In 1922, the last year the United States Census Bureau kept alimony data, their figures showed alimony decreed in only 15 percent of a nationwide sample, although women were considerably less independent at that time.

Of 172,000 minor children involved in divorces in

Chicago in the period 1949-50, one third were awarded no child support at all. It should also be noted that the original child-support orders given by a court probably do not meet the full support needs of the children. Some of the orders may also be further judicially reduced when the husband remarries or when his financial status otherwise worsens. Thus, if only a minority of husbands are paying anything at all, and those husbands are paying only a substantially less than full support order, this means in practice that most of the actual child support is being carried by the mother or by the state.

In spite of potential sanctions such as contempt of court, civil action and criminal prosecution and despite the considerable incentive to the state to avoid unnecessary welfare payments, legal action is seldom initiated against the nonpaying father. This is especially the case as the children grow older and probably require even more support money. Yet Table 3 shows that only 19 percent of the 101 nonpaying fathers at the end of the first year had legal action taken against them, and in the tenth year only 1 percent of the 128 nonpaying fathers were faced with legal action. Indeed, monetary divorce awards may well be the least complied with and the least enforced of criminal or civil court orders.

The explanation for the lack of enforcement is not that the fathers are unable to comply. Support orders take into account the father's ability to pay. In fact, working-class fathers, though less financially well off, are more likely to be prosecuted than are middle-class fathers, because their ex-wives are more likely to be on welfare, and they themselves are more likely to have criminal records. The explanation for general nonenforcement of support orders probably lies in the pro-male bias of the prosecutors, judges and legislators who could more effectively enforce the law if they cared to. Some of the nonenforcement may also be due to the greater complexity of nonsupport cases (especially where there is a question of interstate enforcement) and to the less current nature of nonsupport decrees, as compared to the crush of other cases.

A realistic remedy for the nonenforcement of child-support orders may lie not in the more vigorous prosecution of errant males—although in some flagrant cases this might be merited—but in the imposition of some system of social insurance to cover the situation and preserve the dignity of those concerned. The concept of survivorship under Social Security could be expanded to include children of a deserting or divorced father, as well as of a deceased father. Other social alternatives include child allowances, the negative income tax or an expanded Family Assistance Plan. A national program of wholesome, well-run daycare centers and a government stimulation of possible employment opportunities would also enable those women who wish to work to support themselves and their children to do so, rather than have to ask for child support or welfare.

The amount and direction of inequality between treatment of male and female litigants may be affected by whether the judge is a man or a woman and the predominance of male or female jurors. While there is a significant lack of female judges and a corresponding lack of data comparing them with male judges in their treatment of male and female litigants, it may be possible to extrapolate some findings about male and female jurors to male and female judges. (The concern here is with the effect of the sex ratio of judicial decision-makers on discrimination against women as litigants. Studies that deal with the effect on sentences or awards in general are not directly relevant. However, such studies do show that housewives are less punitive in burglary and possibly in other theft cases too, but more punitive in father-daughter incest and possibly other male-female sex crimes.)

There are five meaningful hypotheses which one can formulate about the effect of the jurors' own sex on their treatment of male and female defendants in criminal and personal injury cases. (Since jury trials are a rare occurrence in divorce cases, they will not be considered here.) One hypothesis might be called the attraction-of-opposites hypothesis, predicting that men will favor women and women men. "If you are representing a personable young man," advises John Appleman in his *Successful Jury Trials* (1952), "try to seat kindly old ladies in the jury box. If you are presenting an attractive young woman, have as many male jurors, old or young, as possible."

Second is the chivalry hypothesis, which predicts that men will favor women and women will also favor women, because women need special treatment. A third, the brainwashing hypothesis, says men and women both favor men because they have both been indoctrinated to believe men are more valuable. Fourth is the equality hypothesis, which says men favor neither sex and women favor neither sex. This is the implicit or explicit hypothesis in those court cases which have held that it is not a denial of equal protection for a state to systematically decrease the chances of women serving on juries. Fifth is the likes-attract-likes hypothesis, which says men favor men and women favor women.

With regard to criminal cases, the most relevant data

appear in a study by Arnold Rose and Arthur Prell. In 1953, they asked a sample of students taking courses in introductory sociology and social psychology at the University of Minnesota what sentences they would hand down if they were serving as judges or jurors in a variety of hypothetical fact situations. One situation involved a male convicted of a certain crime. Another, placed elsewhere on the list of situations, involved a female convicted of the same crime. The male respondents tended to give the male defendant a lower sentence than the female defendant, whereas the female respondents tended to give the female defendant a lower sentence than the male defendant. In other words, men tended to favor males and women tended to favor females. To the extent that this finding can be extrapolated to real juries or real judges, it confirms the likes-attract-likes hypothesis.

There is data available from the Jury Verdict Research Corporation on the way actual juries have treated females as distinct from males in personal injury cases, taking into consideration the sex of the jury. The study answers two questions: "If I know the sex of the plaintiff, what can I predict with regard to victory and damages before male-dominated and female-dominated juries?" and, "If I know the dominant sex of the jury, what can I predict with regard to victory and damages for male and female plaintiffs?"

Both parts of the study show that controlling for the sex of the jury makes no significant differences with regard to establishing liability. Both parts, however, show that controlling for the sex of the jury does make a substantial difference with regard to the average amount awarded. For instance, male-dominated juries gave awards to male plaintiffs that were 12 percent above the average to be expected for the type of injury, medical expenses and lost wages, whereas male-dominated juries gave female plaintiffs awards 17 percent below the average expected. Female-dominated juries reversed the direction of favoritism between female and male plaintiffs, further reinforcing the data that the likes-attract-likes hypothesis is the valid one, at least for average amounts awarded.

Discrimination, or at least inequality, between men and women seems to be greater in the amount of damages awarded than in the establishment of liability. This may be attributed to the fact that extremely large awards, those over $100,000 for instance, tend to be rendered for work accidents that result in crippling injuries—and relatively few women are injured in such circumstances. But some of the liability-damages difference may be because the differential earning power rationale only applies to assessing damages, not to establishing liability, and male jurors may place more emphasis on that rationale.

Much of the difference may also be attributed to the greater subjectivity involved in determining the extent of damages, which allows prejudice to enter more readily than in the more legalistic decision involved in establishing liability. Likewise the greater inequality present at the bail and sentencing stages in criminal cases, as compared to the pretrial procedural safeguards, may also be partly attributable to the relatively greater subjectivity and lesser legalistic restraint involved in the setting of bail and sentencing.

Because the disparities in the treatment of male and female litigants can be affected by the sex of the decision-makers, this should be further reason for society to seek out more women judges and jurors, in addition to the reasoning that emphasizes more democratic representation. To obtain more women judges, we must encourage more women to become law students and lawyers who will in due course be eligible to become judges. As for jurors, a majority of states by law still allow women to be more easily excused or exempted from jury service than men, and women are therefore probably underrepresented on the juries of those states.

Although women are more easily exempted from jury service in most states, local administrators and judges play a crucial role in applying jury selection laws. A Pennsylvania study showed an imbalance toward male jurors in Lancaster County, an imbalance toward female jurors in Philadelphia County and approximate equality in Allegheny County—all under the same state law.

From this general review, we can conclude that women as litigants do not receive the same treatment as men. In criminal cases women are much less likely to be jailed before or after conviction and are more likely to lack a jury trial than are men charged with the same crime. In personal injury cases, adult women are less likely to win than are adult men, and they collect awards that are substantially smaller, especially for certain types of injuries and especially before male-dominated juries. In divorce cases, where there is always a woman on one side and a man on the other, the woman seems to win on the basis of a simple analysis of divorce decrees; but these decrees become meaningless when we look at the collection records.

These findings seem consistent with how women are treated in American society in general. There is a kind of paternalistic protectiveness, at least toward white women, which assumes that they need sheltering from such manly experiences as being jailed or being treated in an overly formal fashion in family law or criminal cases. At the same time, when it comes to allocating scarce valuable resources, such as personal injury monetary awards or money for child support, women are more likely to be slighted.

More equal treatment might be achieved by increasing the public awareness of the disparities in the treatment of male and female litigants and by increasing the representation of women as jury and judicial decision-makers. Needed, however, are more specifically focused changes within the legal system, which will in turn improve the legal process for men and women alike.

For example, the remedy for the disparities in the jailing of women lies not in lessening the frequency of their release on bond, or increasing their postconviction term of imprisonment, but in providing pretrial release for all persons—regardless of sex—mainly on the basis of the likelihood that they will in fact appear for trial. Likewise, society needs to provide postconviction sentencing for everyone, regardless of sex, again, mainly on the basis of whether that person is likely to be rehabilitated or deterred from future crime by a period of imprisonment.

Along related lines, the remedy for disparities in personal injury awards and child-support collections probably does not lie in lowering the damages awarded to males or in prosecuting wayward nonpaying fathers more vigorously. Instead, society should perhaps seek collective action, such as no-fault insurance and an expanded Social Security program.

Neither these measures nor any others, however, will be sufficient in themselves. Nothing will succesfully eliminate the discrimination that exists against women litigants—save the complete eradication of discrimination against all women in our society.

March 1972

FURTHER READING

"Women as Litigants" by Stuart S. Nagel and Lenore J. Weitzman in the *Hastings Law Journal*, (Winter 1971).

Women and the Law: The Unfinished Revolution by Leo Kanowitz (Albuquerque, N.M.: University of New Mexico Press, 1967).

Radical Lawyers: Their Role in the Movement and in the Courts edited by Jonathan Black (New York: Avon Books, 1971).

"Women's Servitude under Law" by Ann Garfinkle, Carol Lefcourt and Diane Schulder in *Law Against People: Essays to Demystify Law, Order, and the Courts* edited by Robert Lefcourt (New York: Vintage Books, 1971).

Civil Disorder and the
Agents of
Social Control

GARY T. MARX

The number of popular and scholarly perspectives that can be brought to bear on the interpretation of civil disorder in the United States seems limited only by the breadth of one's imagination and reading. Some of the more prominent would undoubtedly include those that emphasize the increased radicalism of social movements as they evolve; the relevance of world revolutionary struggle; the importance of external warfare; limited political access of certain groups; various types of social and political frustration; conspiracy and agitation; the mass media; relative deprivation and heightened aspirations; our frontier tradition and history of racial and labor violence; lower class and criminal subcultures; and youthful, Hobbesian, biological or territorial man.

All of these perspectives focus on factors in the predisorder situation conducive to violence. Each also tends to correspond either to a particular left- or right-wing ideology. Thus conservatives tend to see disturbances as meaningless, irrational events caused by agitators who prey upon the degenerate character of the lower classes, while liberals are more likely to see them as spontaneous patterned protests caused by the deprivation of these same classes. One perspective, however, finds support among both the extreme left and right, and seeks the cause in the disturbance situation itself. This is the view which suggests that the police cause riots (though, to be sure, the Right blames the police for being too soft, while the Left blames them for being too harsh).

Unintended Consequences of Social Action

One justification for social research is that it goes beyond our common-sense views of the world. Robert Merton has suggested that an important task of social research is to point out the latent or unintended consequences of human action. For example, however, corrupt early twentieth-century political machines were, they also helped the Irish and other immigrants to assimilate. Prostitution, whatever its moral implications, sometimes makes an important contribution to family stability. There are other cases with unintended consequences: propaganda designed to reduce prejudice may actually reenforce it; youth institutions may create juvenile delinquents who are later made into knowledgeable and embittered criminals by the prison system; mental hospitals may reinforce mental illness; welfare institutions may create dependency; and doctors sometimes injure or even kill patients.

In the same fashion a review of police behavior in civil disorders through the summer of 1967 suggests a number of instances in which the behavior of some agents of social control seemed to create as much disorder as it curbed. Some of the ways in which the behavior of various agents of control has had these unintended consequences are examined in this chapter.

As Park and Blumer and other researchers have noted, collective behavior has an emergent character. It involves elements that can't very well be predicted by a static consideration of conditions preceding the disturbance. Civil disorder involves a social process of action and counteraction. It is here that a consideration of police behavior is relevant.

I have found it useful to organize police behavior that was ineffective or seemed to create rather than control the disorders into the following three categories: inappropriate control strategies, lack of co-ordination among and within various control units, and the breakdown of police organization. I will be concerned primarily with police behavior up to the end of the summer of 1967.

Inappropriate Control Strategies

Crowd Dispersal. In the spirit of Gustav Le Bon, it is sometimes assumed that crowds are uniformly like-minded, anarchic, irrational and hell-bent on destruction. From this it may follow that all people on the street are actual or potential rioters, that crowds must always be broken up, that a riot will not terminate unless it is put down, and that only a technical approach involving the use of massive force is adequate.

In all too many cases police are still following nineteenth-century methods; a riot manual of the period stated that "crushing power, exercised relentlessly and without hesitation is really the merciful, as it is necessary, course to be pursued." Police are often responsible for the initial crowd, which gathers when they respond to fairly routine incidents with a large number of squad cars with loud sirens and flashing lights. In some cities I studied the traditional strategy of dispersing the crowd had unanticipated consequences and served to escalate and spread disorder. The problem then shifted from controlling a crowd to coping with guerrilla-like hit-and-run activities.

While the initial formation of a crowd seemed to be an important factor in most disturbances I studied, it does not follow that crowds should always be dispersed, nor that when they are dispersed, force is the only means that should be used. While a crowd may encourage its members to lose some of their inhibitions, their anger may be heightened and released by precipitous police action.

In New Haven in 1967, for example, the crowd's mood was still tentative in spite of some initial minor violence. A small crowd walked down the street toward police lines. As the perimeter of the lines was reached, police fired three canisters of tear gas. The crowd then ran back, breaking windows and began seriously rioting.

According to a report on the 1964 Harlem riot, New York City's Tactical Patrol Force attempted to clear an intersection by swinging their clubs and yelling "Charge!" As they plowed into the crowd and broke it into smaller segments, "Hell broke loose in Harlem." The angry but until then peaceful crowd began pulling fire alarms, starting fires and beating up whites.

In Englewood, New Jersey, police efforts to force black bystanders into houses, whether or not they belonged to them, angered and sparked violence on the part of young men. In Rockford, Illinois, instances of rock and bottle throwing were inspired by police efforts to move a late-night bar crowd off the streets.

A peaceful rally protesting school practices in

Philadelphia was violently broken up by the Civil Disobedience Squad using "riot plan number three." This elicited a violent response from the black youth. The Superintendent and President of the School Board subsequently blamed the police for starting the riot.

Contrary to official riot control manuals (and usually the wishes of higher authorities) as police encounter a crowd they may break ranks, raise their night sticks above their shoulders and hit people on the head rather than the body.

Beyond the issue of police provoking a hostile but as yet nondestructive crowd to retaliatory violence or committing a symbolic act that serves as a catalyst for the expression of the crowd's anger, the members of the crowd, once dispersed, may do more damage than the crowd itself. Here an analogy might be what happens when one beats a burning log to put out a fire, only to see the sparks and embers scatter widely. Both the Milwaukee and New Haven disorders were spread in this fashion. Scattered bands of rioters may have presented police with a more difficult control situation than the original crowd.

Failure to Negotiate. The treatment of disorder as a technical problem of law and order to be solved only by force has meant that negotiations and the use of counterrioters were often ruled out. Such ironclad rules popular in many police circles has completely obscured the variation in types of disorder. When the disturbance seems apolitical, unfocused and primarily expressive, and is not related to current issues or demands, and when there is no minimal organization among rioters and no one willing to take counterriot roles, authorities may have no alternative—from their viewpoint—but the graduated use of force. However, when the disturbance develops out of specific issues (the demand for receiving promised jobs, a particular instance of police brutality, discrimination by a business firm, disagreement over school policies and so forth), when grievances and demands are clearly articulated, when there seems to be some organization among rioters and actual or would-be spokesmen and potential counterrioters come forth, the disturbance may be stopped or dampened by entering into a dialogue, considering the grievances, and using counterrioters. To resort to force is more likely to inflame the situation and increase the likelihood of future disorders.

The refusal to negotiate and use strategies other than a show of white force may have had disastrous consequences in Watts. The director of the Los Angeles Human Relations Commission had worked out a plan to send in black plainclothes officers and antipoverty workers to make inconspicuous arrests and spread positive rumors ("the riot is over") and to withdraw white officers to the perimeter. Young gang leaders promised to use their influence to stop the riot and were led to believe that the above conditions would be met.

The Deputy Chief of Police rejected this proposal stating among other things that he was not going to be told how to deploy his troops and that, "Negro police officers are not as competent as Caucasian officers and the only reason for sending them in would be because they have black skins and are invisible at night." To the Director of the Human Relations Commission he said, "I don't want to hear anything you have got to say, you're part of the problem. *We know how to run a riot* and we are going to handle it our way." In response to the promises of gang leaders to stop the riot, he stated, "We are not going to have hoodlums telling us how to run the police department." And, "We are in the business of trying to quell a riot and we haven't got time to engage in any sociological experiments." Following his refusal a full-scale riot ensued.

All Blacks are Rioters. Just as it is sometimes erroneously assumed that all men at a gay bar are gay or all women standing on certain street corners at a particular time are prostitutes, so to the police any black person out on the street during a period of civil disorder may be suspect. In some cities, orders to clear an area and the panicky use of force (along with beliefs about the efficacy of getting tough) have resulted in indiscriminate abuse of anyone with a black face, including innocent bystanders, government officials, policemen in civilian clothes, ministers and Negro youth trying to stop the disorder.

Previous role relationships have an important effect on behavior in disaster situations. While collective behavior is essentially defined by the emergence of new, spontaneous norms, it nevertheless occurs within a context of ongoing familial, religious, economic, political and social relationships. In many cities the resources of the black community were effectively used in counterriot activities—quelling rumors, urging people to go home, and trying to channel indignation into less destructive protest.

During the summer of 1967, in some cities such as Tampa, Florida, and Elizabeth, New Brunswick and Plainfield, New Jersey, police were even ordered out of the disturbance area and local residents successfully patrolled the streets. The issue of whether or not police should be withdrawn is a complex one that far transcends the simplistic rhetoric of its opponents and supporters. While it was successful in the above cities, in several other cities it had the opposite effect. Counter-riot sentiment was generally not counterprotest and in many cases represented considerations of strategy rather than principle. However, the *existence* of a sizeable reservoir of counterriot sentiment that can be activated in the place of, or alongside, other control activities is not really at issue. And motivation aside, failure to effectively use counterrioters may have prolonged a number of disturbances.

In Cincinnati, despite an agreement between the Mayor and black leaders that the latter would be given badges and allowed to go into the riot area to help calm things, police refused to recognize the badges and arrested some of their wearers on charges of loitering. A somewhat similar situation resulted in Milwaukee. In Newark the Mayor and Governor gave permission to Negro volunteers to go among the people to calm the situation. Their activities were inhibited by enforcement personnel. According to the Governor, they ". . . were chased around so much by people who suspected them as participating in the riot that they had to abandon their efforts."

Beyond the general confusion in the disorders and a racially inspired (if not racist) inability to differentiate among Negroes, police harassment was related to their view of the disorders as a technical problem to be met only by a show of force and their feeling that police competence and jurisdiction were being infringed upon. Because counterrioters were often black activists, and in some cases youthful gangs, their feelings may have been accentuated.

Official Anticipation: Thus far, I have considered disturbances that had a pattern of riotous or at least disorderly Negro behavior followed and sometimes encouraged by the official response. However, in other instances the dynamics of the disturbance worked in the opposite direction. Here authorities (with poor intelligence reports) precipitated confrontation by anticipating violence where none was imminent and by overreacting to minor incidents that happened to occur when a major riot was going on elsewhere.

While adequate planning and preparation are vital to effective control, they may help create a state-of-siege mentality, increase susceptibility to rumors, and exert a self-fulfilling pressure. This is particularly true when they are accompanied by a get-tough, act-quickly philosophy. Following the Newark riot, disorders broke out in 14 cities in the surrounding area, and after Detroit, eight additional Michigan cities reported disorders. An important factor in the spread of violence from major urban centers to outlying communities was the expectation of a riot and subsequent overreaction on the part of white authorities.

In New Jersey, a month and a half before Newark erupted, there were reports of planned violence, and counterplans were designed. On June 5, 1967, the police chiefs of more than 75 New Jersey communities met in Jersey City to discuss the supposed plans of militant blacks to foment violence. Jersey City, Newark and Elizabeth were reportedly given "triple A" ratings for violence over the summer. The authorities drew up plans to coordinate control efforts and rehearsed procedures for calling in the National Guard and state police. Riot control training was held in a number of communities.

When Newark finally erupted many officials found their expectations confirmed and they acted on their fears of anticipated local violence. In one New Jersey city officials reacted to the rumor that Stokely Carmichael was bringing carloads of black militants into the community, although Carmichael was in London at the time. In Jersey City 400 armed police occupied the black area several days before any disorders occurred. In Englewood, where police outnumbered participants three to one, black residents had earlier been angered by riot control exercises in which the wind blew tear gas into surrounding Negro homes. In Elizabeth, police greatly increased patrols in the black area and residents expressed opinions such as, "The community felt it was in a concentration camp." The appearance of armed police patrols increased the likelihood of confrontation and greatly strained relations with local Negroes. Whatever an individual's feeling about civil rights, having his neighborhood saturated with armed men in uniform in the face of minimal, sporadic or sometimes no disorders often created indignation. A frequent demand was for police withdrawal or a less visible show of arms. In six of seven New Jersey cities that had disorders at the time of Newark, removal of police from the ghetto signalled an end to violence.

Sniping. While much sniping was attributed to police and other control agents firing at each other, fire-crackers and the snapping of broken power lines, response to the sniping that actually did occur was inadequate. Mass firing at buildings by men on the ground, who often used their private weapons, occurred, and an inadequate system of accounting for ammunition and lack of supervision by a superior officer all created havoc. Many innocent people were killed and wounded which helped to escalate the violence. Such firing in some cases created the very sniper fire it was supposedly trying to stop, as angry Negroes retaliated. In Detroit the fact that a policy of not shooting rioters was reversed without public announcement may have increased the death toll.

Lack of Coordination Among Control Units

In the face of major, unanticipated disorders involving a wide area and large numbers of people engaged in hit-and-run guerrilla-like tactics, decentralized, autonomous local police, organized primarily to fight crime, control traffic and keep the peace, were usually ineffective. The control of such disturbances requires training and actions that are almost opposite to those used in normal police operation. As a result, other control units differing in training, organizational structure, ethos and familiarity with the local area were often called in. Not surprisingly difficulties resulted.

The inability to admit failure, bureaucratic entanglements, petty rivalries and political considerations usually delayed the calling out of higher levels of force, and lack of prior planning and an unclear chain of command all meant further delays once other control agents finally did arrive on the scene.

Local, state and National Guard units did not merge easily. Guard units, accustomed to acting in patrols, were fragmented and guardsmen were isolated from commanding officers, while police used to working as one or two-man autonomous patrol units had to become disciplined members of military units relying on commands from superiors instead of their own discretion. While officers from different units were together, they often responded to separate orders. In Newark the three enforcement agencies were issued separate orders on weapons use.

Technical as well as social communication problems contributed to ineffective coordination of control activities and clearly furthered the disorders. Regular radio frequencies were heavily overtaxed, and local police, state police and the National Guard operated on different frequencies. Though this had been a problem two years earlier in Watts, little had changed by the time of Detroit and Newark. In the beginning stages of the latter riot, state police were unable to get a clear definition of riot perimeters or where activity was heaviest. They could not obtain information about the movement of local police patrols and were obliged to follow local police and fire trucks responding to citizens' calls. Inability to communicate was a factor in police and guardsmen firing at each other and in the belief in widespread sniping.

Poor communication within departments also had serious consequences. One reason the Los Angeles Police Department failed to employ sufficient manpower was the reluctance of subordinate commanders to expose themselves to ridicule and downgrading by possible overreaction. While the Los Angeles police possess some of the most skilled investigators in the world, trained to deal with master criminals, they could not get a true picture of what was happening in the early stages of Watts. Early on the third day of the riot, field forces knew the situation was out of control but the downtown command post was still optimistic. This is the classic problem of information flow in a bureaucracy. A highly professional department was unable to admit that a handful of what it considered hoodlums could create a major disturbance that it couldn't control.

In Plainfield, contrary actions by county and city police greatly inflamed the disorders. Plainfield was primarily a political disturbance, with meetings and negotiations between blacks and city authorities alternating with violence. At one such meeting, held under the auspices of community-relations personnel and with the understanding of city police, several hundred young men gathered in a county park to discuss their grievances and to choose leaders to represent them. During the meeting the violence greatly subsided. Peace was shortlived, however, as the assembly was abruptly broken up by county police who said they could not meet in the park without a permit. This incensed the young men. Within an hour violence flared and that night a patrolman was killed and the destruction reached its highest point.

Further conflict among different levels of authority emerged in Plainfield between the police and local and state officials. Police felt "left out," "tired" and "poorly treated" and threatened to resign *en masse* (and to some observers almost mutinied) after they were excluded from negotiations that led to the release of arrested rioters, the institution of a policy of containment following the killing of a fellow officer, and the termination (by a State official) of a house-to-house search for stolen carbines. The New Jersey riot inquiry felt that the circumscription of local police activities was such "as virtually to destroy the department's morale. . . (and) to limit seriously the effectiveness of the force."

In still other cases, as in Los Angeles, Boston and New York, agreements reached by the mayor's special representatives, human relations officials and police-community relations officers who had rapport with rioters were not honored by other policemen, creating great indignation and a sense of betrayal.

In Los Angeles, the police community relations inspector was reportedly not called into the inner circle of police advisors. The Chief of Police was unaware that his department had been represented at an important community meeting held during the riot.

A potentially ugly incident might have emerged in Detroit (May 21, 1968) when mounted police outside a building tried to drive supporters of the Poor People's March back into a building, while police on the inside were trying to drive them out.

In Rockford, Illinois, in 1967, as people poured out of bars that were closing, police tried to drive them off the street that other police had already barricaded.

In Birmingham in 1963 police circled several thousand blacks, on one side swinging their clubs and from the other side turning water hoses on them catching bystanders as well as protesters. This was no doubt all too well coordinated.

Breakdown of Police Organization: One Riot or Two?

An additional source of police ineffectiveness and abuse stems from the breakdown of organization within enforcement agencies.

In most discussions of riots undue emphasis has been given to the behavior of rioters. The normal concepts used to analyse collective behavior have been applied to them—emotional contagion, the spread of rumors, panic and the expression of frustration, the lessening of inhibitions, innovative behavior. Yet in several major disturbances, these concepts might equally be applied to the police. Police, lacking training and experience and often uncertain of what they were to do, sometimes became fatigued (frequently working 12-hour or more shifts with insufficient rest and little food). They were likely to be thrown off balance by the size of the disturbance and by being drawn frantically from one area to another, in some cases because of false alarms seemingly coordinated with attacks and looting. As large numbers of people taunt, defy, insult and attack them and they see their fellows injured and in some cases killed, patience thins and anger rises. Rumors about atrocities committed against them may spread.

Police may take violent black rhetoric and threats (which are partly related to expressive oral traditions, ritual posturing and political infighting) too literally; for few police are killed by snipers and there are reports that some snipers misfire on purpose. The lack of attacks on known racists certainly indicates this.

The belief may spread that they are in a war and all black people are their enemy. Traditional misconceptions about riotous crowds may contribute to an exaggeration of the dangers confronting them. And as police control of the "turf" is effectively challenged and rioters gain control of the streets by default, the word may spread (as in Watts, Newark, and Detroit) that rioters have "beat the police." Losing face, humiliated by their temporary defeat and with their professional pride undermined, police may have a strong desire for revenge and to recoup their "honor."

In a context such as the above, superior officers may lose the power to control their men. The chain of command and communication between and within enforcement agencies, often unclear to begin with, may completely break down. The most dangerous part of the disturbance is now at hand as the environment changes from a riot to a war. Some police behavior seems as much, or more, inspired by the desire for vengeance, retaliation and "to teach the bastards a lesson" as by the desire to restore law and order.

The words of Lee and Humphrey, written shortly after the 1943 Detroit riot, are clearly relevant 26 years later. "War is to the army much what civilian outbreaks are to the police. Both offer socially acceptable outlets for the residuum of aggressiveness characteristic of each."

On the third day of the Detroit riot, an officer was overheard telling a young black on a newly stolen bicycle, "The worm is turning." And turn it did as the police took off their badges, taped over squad car numbers (this, of course, greatly reduced the number of complaints filed), and began indiscriminantly and excessively using force against rioters, bystanders and in some cases each other. The death and injury toll climbed rapidly. Some of the firing stopped only when control officials ran out of ammunition. At this time the Algiers Motel killings or "game" (from the perspective of involved police) occurred. According to an account by John Hersey, one of the police officers involved in this incident stated " . . . there was a lot of rough-housing, you know, everything just went loose, [following the killing of a police officer on the third day of the riot]. The police officers weren't taking anything from anyone." This would seem to be something of an understatement.

According to one high police official in secret testimony, by the fourth day of the riot "the police were out of control." There are some reports of police keeping looted goods taken from prisoners and robbing them, and of doing damage to "soul brother" stores spared by the rioters. Claims of brutality filed included charges of the mistreatment of women and the carving of initials on prisoners.

The chairman of the Newark Human Rights Commission reported that " . . . men were being brought in, many of them handcuffed behind their backs, being carried like a sack of meal, and the fifth policeman would be hammering their face and body with a billy stick. This went on time after time. Many times you would see a man being brought into the police station without a mark on his face and when he was taken out, he was brutally beaten." It has been said in jest, although there is an element of truth in it, that Newark was a classical race riot except the Italians wore blue uniforms.

Police behavior often seems to become progressively worse as the disorders wear on. In Watts, Newark and Detroit this was partly related to the entrance of higher level control units into the disturbance. The assignment of Guardsmen to accompany policemen may be seen by the latter as offering a chance to reverse earlier humiliation and gain revenge for injury and death suffered by the police. At the same time, inexperienced Guardsmen, isolated from the authority of their commanding officers, may become subject to the same collective behavior phenomena as police and blacks, further adding to the disorder. Police may come to see rioters and suspected rioters, like those convicted of crimes, as having forfeited their civil rights.

The head of the Detroit police, a former reporter, was hesitant to call out the Guard. According to a report by Gary Wills, he said "I've been on too many stories where the guard was called up. They're always shooting their own people. . . . These poor kids were scared pissless; and they scared me."

What is especially tragic is that the symbols of police legitimacy become the cloak under which indiscriminate force is exercised upon the Negro community. It is a mistake to attribute such behavior only to the desire for revenge or a hatred of Negroes. Part of it would seem to be equivalent to the behavior of front line soldiers who kill many of their own men in their first combat experience. That the breakdown of police organization transcends racism may also be seen in their response to student protests such as at Columbia University and various antiwar demonstrations.

It is important to recognize that not only was police behavior in the latter stages of several major riots excessively brutal and probably ineffective, but that such acts were not idiosyncratic or random but were woven into a social fabric of rumor, panic, frustration, fatigue, fear, racism, lack of training and inexperience and the breakdown of police organization. While such a situation creates widespread fear in the Negro community and may inhibit some rioters, it can lead to (and partly results from) escalation in the level of black violence as the same social processes go on.

There is an interaction process and gradual reciprocal increases in the severity of action taken on both sides. The fact that police abuses were most pronounced in Newark and Detroit, where disturbances were the most serious, does not necessarily lend itself to a one-sided causal interpretation. Here we see the emergent character of the disorders. Just as the belief that blacks want to kill them spreads among police so it may spread among black people.

An additional element in the misuse of official force is the view held by some policemen that they can (and indeed must) "hold court in the street," given the presumed leniency and complexity of the legal system. Gathering evidence that will hold in court during mass disorders and demonstrations is difficult; those arrested can often be charged with nothing more than a misdemeanor; sentencing for riot offenses tends to be lighter than for similar offenses committed in nonriot situations. The use of violence in such situations may also be related to the policemen's effort to save face and their belief that respect for their authority must be reestablished.

Yet police in Japan and Britain have learned to cope with similar provocations. Even in the United States police overreaction is the exception rather than the rule. We simply don't hear about the large number of instances when police show professional behavior and restraint because they are not newsworthy. Unlike the more enduring problems of reducing the crime rate and eliminating corruption, this is one area where real change is possible if the police are given appropriate leadership, training and strategy.

The breakdown of police organization and the misuse of force has not happened to anywhere near the same extent in all cities that have had demonstrations and riots. An important question for analysis is why did this breakdown occur in the ghetto riots of Watts, Newark and Detroit—but not in Cincinnati or Boston? Why at the Chicago Democratic Convention but not at the counter-inaugural in Washington, D.C. where many of the same groups were involved? Why at Columbia and Harvard but not at M.I.T. or Dartmouth? Why at the People's Park in Berkeley but not at Woodstock? Given the immense number of factors involved and the variability of confrontations, the conditions under which such police behavior appears can never be exactly predicted. Yet it would seem to be related to some things which cannot readily be changed, such as the extent to which police disagree with, or are threatened by, the issues raised by protestors, whether police expect disturbance participants to be sufficiently punished by the legal system, the extent of injuries and provocation faced by police and the size and length of the disorders. Yet factors that *are* amenable to change may be even more important. Among them are training, the extent to which a flexible approach to crowds is used, that doesn't rely only on force and stresses communication between authorities and protestors and the right of peaceful assembly, the extent to which police share social characteristics with protestors, the clarity of orders stressing restraint, the general climate created by officials and the tightness of the police command structure. Other factors are whether civilian monitors and high-level government and police officials are on the scene, and whether it is made clear to police that they will be punished for misbehavior. Filming the scene and having names or numbers on helmets and sewn on uniforms might also increase accountability.

Quis Custodiet Ipsos Custodes?

A crucial question raised by some of this material is "Who controls the agents of social control?" One of the central intellectual problems for social analysts is the basis of social order. If one resolves the question of social order by relying on shared values and the internalization of standards then there may not be much of an issue. Yet even those who answer the question of social order by stressing the importance of external force usually ignore the problem of controlling the agents of control. In several major disturbances the tragic answer to the question of "who guards the guards" seemed to be "no one."

One of the manifestly unfair aspects of social organization is that those with official power are usually those (or are intimately tied to those) who possess the power to legitimately sanction the misuse of this power.

One means by which the police have traditionally been controlled is by the exclusionary rule of the courts, whereby illegal means used in acquiring evidence or making arrests are grounds for the dismissal of a case. However, this rule only has an effect when convictions are sought (a factor often beyond the control of the police). In addition many police abuses do not involve the gathering of evidence. The closeness of the police to the courts and their interdependence may inhibit the regulatory role of the latter, particularly at lower levels.

Individuals can also bring costly and time-consuming civil damage suits against the police, although those most likely to need redress may be least likely to have the resources necessary for a long court struggle—and establishing proof is difficult. The anonymity and confusion of a crowd situation and the tendency to remove badges makes identification of offending officials unlikely. In the rare cases where police are criminally prosecuted for riot offenses, juries tend to find in their favor. In most states National Guardsmen are granted immunity from criminal and/or civil liability.

Police have also been controlled through direct political means. The rise of "good government"-inspired civil service reforms and the decline of the urban political machine makes this less likely today. Most of the now defunct Civilian Review Boards met with great police resistance, had no formal enforcement power and could not initiate inquiries.

The means of control favored by the police is self-regulation, in a fashion analogous to specialized professions such as medicine or law. It is argued that police work is highly technical and only those who practice it are competent to judge it. Internal review mechanisms have been inadequate to say the least; there is evidence to suggest that, like the rest of us, the police can resist anything but temptation. Knowledge that they are unlikely to be subjected to post-riot santioning may have lessened restraints on their use of violence. In many departments there is a strong norm of secrecy surrounding police misbehavior; even when known, infractions often go unpunished.

The consequences, costs and benefits of various means of regulating the police have not been carefully studied. It is clear from some of the data considered in this chapter and from more recent events such as the Chicago Democratic Convention, the People's Park episode in Berkeley and attacks on groups such as the Black Panthers that the control of the police is sometimes not much affected by the courts, various other checks and balances, internalized norms of fair play, nor internal police organization. The question of control and responsiveness of the police is certainly among the most pressing of domestic issues.

It has been often suggested that the most hideous crimes have been committed in the name of obedience rather than rebellion. In the Gordon Riots of 1780, demonstrators destroyed property and freed prisoners but evidently did not kill anyone, while authorities killed several hundred rioters and hanged an additional 25. In the Reveillon Riots of the French Revolution, several hundred rioters were killed, but rioters killed no one. Up to the end of the summer of 1967, this pattern was being repeated; police, not rioters, are responsible for most of the more than 100 riot deaths that have occurred. To aan important extent this pattern stems not from differences in will, but from the greater destructive resources of those in power, from their holding power to begin with, and from their ability to sanction. In a related context, the more than 100 civil rights murders of recent years have been matched by almost no murders of racist whites. (Since 1968, this pattern may be changing.)

As long as racism and poverty exist American society needs relentless protest. It also needs police. It is increasingly clear that police are unduly scapegoated, stereotyped and maligned; they are, as well, often underpaid, undertrained, given contradictory tasks, and made to face directly the ugly consequences of the larger society's failure to change. It is equally clear that solutions to America's racial problems lie much more in the direction of redistributing power and income, eliminating discrimination and exploitation than in changing the police. Nevertheless, one important change called for in the Kerner Commission's plea to "end the destruction and violence, not only in the streets of the ghetto but in the lives of the people" is surely more enlightened police behavior.

Black Powerlessness
In Chicago

HAROLD M. BARON
with Harriet Stulman, Richard Rothstein *and* Rennard Davis

A Note on Methodology

In studying the exclusion of Negroes from the decision-making structure in Chicago, our working assumption was that the men who hold power are those who have been elevated to policy-making positions in powerful institutions, like banks, law firms and unions. This approach differed from the more popular methodologies of studying community power—thus, we did not try to identify the top decision-makers, and we did not assume that a power elite was at work.

To identify policy-making posts, we relied on these assumptions:

1) In each major area of metropolitan life, certain enterprises have a disproportionate amount of power—because of their control over human and material resources, or because of their responsibility for making public policy.

2) Individuals who occupy policy-making posts in these key enterprises have a disproportionate amount of power *within* these institutions.

3) Policy decisions are made at every level of a bureaucracy. But certain posts within a bureaucracy will structure the range of

99

decision-making for all other posts. Posts that have this responsibility we call "policy-making," and these are the posts we studied.

Under stable conditions, policy-making is the most important way in which power is exercised. In any firm or government department, policy-makers are relatively few. They are the ones who set the major goals and orientation, while the more numerous *management* is responsible for their implementation.

Just as our definition of "policy-making position" was restrictive, so was our definition of "power." In our study, power means the ability to make and enforce decisions for an institution, for a community, or for society at large—and the ability to determine in whose interest these decisions are made.

Our study began with a census of those Negroes occupying public or private policy-making positions. First we identified Cook County's major institutional areas—that is, related types of formally organized activities, such as local government, religious organizations, and business firms. In those areas where we could *not* be exhaustive in our research, we selected one or more representative groups. Corporate law firms, for example, were chosen to represent business-oriented professions and services.

Within each institutional area, we developed criteria to determine how large an individual enterprise or organization had to be before it has significant potential influence and power over other organizations. Next, we determined which positions within these powerful enterprises or organizations had policy-making authority. Finally, we conducted interviews with knowledgeable informants to learn which of the policy-making positions were held by Negroes.

In our study, the chairman of the board of the largest industrial firm was given the same statistical weight as the vice-president of the smallest bank included in the survey. While differentiating between them would have been useful for a study of the total process of decision-making in the Chicago area, our aim was to document only the inclusion or exclusion of Negroes. If there is any methodological bias in our study, then, it operates in favor of employing less strict criteria in determining important positions in order to include at least a few Negroes.

Our census was based on information for the year 1965. Since then, although there have been some shifts in the number and percentage of Negroes in particular organizations, the pattern of power traced remains fundamentally the same.

Until recently, the three principal targets of the civil-rights movement in the North were discrimination and inferior conditions in 1) housing for Negroes, 2) jobs for Negroes, and 3) the education of Negroes. But after failing to bring about major changes, many Negroes realized that one reason the status quo in housing, jobs and education continues is that the black community lacks control over decision-making. Negroes remain second-class citizens partly because of the discrimination of individual whites, but mainly because of the way whites control the major institutions of our society. And therefore the fourth major goal of Negro organizations and the civil-rights movement has become the acquisition of power.

It was because of this concern with power for black people that, more than two years ago, the Chicago Urban League—a social-welfare organization dedicated to changing institutions so as to achieve full racial equality—started to study the decision-making apparatus in Cook County, Illinois, and particularly how it affects or ignores Negro citizens. (Cook County takes in the city of Chicago, and two-thirds of the population of the surrounding suburban ring included in the Chicago Standard Metropolitan Statistical Area.) Among the questions we posed were:

1) What is the extent of Negro exclusion from policy-making positions in Chicago?

2) Where Negroes *are* in policy-making positions, what type of positions are these, and where are Negroes in greatest number and authority?

3) Do Negroes in policy-making positions represent the interests of the Negro community? and

4) How might an increase in the percentage of Negro policy-makers affect socioeconomic conditions for Negroes in general?

What we found was that in 1965 some 20 percent of the people in Cook County were Negro, and 28 percent of the people in Chicago were Negro. Yet the representation of Negroes in policy-making positions was minimal. Of the top 10,997 policy-making positions in the major Cook County institutions included in our study, Negroes occupied only 285—or 2.6 percent.

In government (see Table 1), out of a total of 1,088 policy-making positions Negroes held just 58. This 5 percent is about one-fourth of the percentage of Negroes in the total county population. Of the 364 elective posts in the survey, however, Negroes occupied 29, or 8 percent, indicating that the franchise has helped give Negroes representation. Yet Negroes had the most positions, percentagewise, on appointed supervisory boards, such as the Board of Education and the Chicago Housing Authority. There they occupied 10 of the 77 policy-making positions, or about 13 percent.

Negroes were better represented on appointed supervisory boards and in elected (nonjudicial) offices than they were in local administrative positions, or in important federal jobs based in Chicago. Thus, Negroes held 12 percent of the nonjudicial elected posts in Chicago's government, but only a little over 1 percent of the appointive policy-making positions in the city administration. The same anomaly appears at the federal level. There is one Negro out of the 13 U.S. Congressmen from Cook County (8 percent), but Negroes held only one out of 31 Presidential appointments (3 percent), and eight of the 368 top federal civil-service posts (2 percent).

Nonetheless, Negroes have—proportionately—two-and-a-half times as many important posts in the public sector as they have in the private sector. As Table 2 indicates, Negroes are virtually barred from policy-making positions in the large organizations that dominate the private institutions in the Chicago area. Out of a total of 9,909 positions, Negroes fill a mere 227. This 2 percent representation is only one-tenth of the proportionate Negro population.

The whitest form of policy-making in Chicago is in the control of economic enterprises. Out of 6,838 positions identified in business corporations, Negroes held only 42 (six-tenths of 1 percent). Thirty-five of these were in insurance, where Negroes occupy 6 percent of the 533 posts. But all 35 were in two all-Negro insurance firms. The other seven positions were in four smaller banks. In banks in general, Negroes occupied three-tenths of 1 percent of the policy posts. There were no Negro policy-makers at all in manu-facturing, communications, transportation, utilities and trade corporations.

Out of the 372 companies we studied, the Negro-owned insurance companies were the only ones dominated by blacks (see Table 3). And if we had used the same stringent criteria for banks and insurance companies that we used for nonfinancial institutions, there would have been no black policy-makers in the business sector at all.

Now, amazingly enough, Chicago has proportionately more Negro-controlled businesses larger than neighbor-hood operations than any other major city in the North. Therefore, similar surveys in other Northern metropolitan areas would turn up an even smaller percentage of Negro policy-makers in the business world.

Table 1—THE EXCLUSION OF NEGROES
FROM GOVERNMENT
Policy-Making Positions in the
Cook County Public Sector (1965)

	Policy-Making Positions	Positions Held by Negroes	Percent
1. Elected Officials			
U.S. House of Representatives	13	1	8
State Legislature	120	10	8
Cook County—nonjudicial	34	3	9
Chicago—nonjudicial	59	7	12
Cook County—judicial	138	8	6
Total:	364	29	8
2. Appointive Supervisory Boards			
Total:	77	10	13
3. Local Administrative Positions			
City of Chicago	156	2	1
Chicago Board of Education	72	7	9
Metropolitan Sanitary District	7	0	0
Cook County Government	13	1	8
Total:	248	10	4
4. Federal Government			
Civil Service	368	8	2
Presidential Appointments	31	1	3
Total:	399	9	2
Grand Total:	1,088	58	5

The legal profession, represented by corporate law firms, had no Negroes at high policy levels. We are convinced that the same situation would be found in other professions, such as advertising and engineering.

The very prestigious universities—the University of Chicago, Northwestern University, Loyola University, DePaul University, Roosevelt University, the Illinois Institute of Technology, and the University of Illinois (the only public university of the seven)—had a negligible 1 percent Negro representation. Most of these universities had few Negro students, faculty members or administrators. Five of the seven had no Negro policy-makers. The University of Illinois had one. Roosevelt University, the sole institution that had a number of Negroes at the top, was the newest, and the one with the least public support. When this university was founded, its leaders had made a forthright stand on racial questions and a firm commitment to liberal principles.

We included these major universities in our survey because other institutions—public and private—have been placing increasingly greater value on them. Every year hundreds of millions of dollars in endowment and operating funds are given to the Chicago-area schools. After all, their research activities, and their training of skilled personnel, are considered a key to the region's economic growth. One indication of the tremendous influence these universities have is that they have determined the nature of urban renewal more than any other institutional group in Chicago (aside from the city government). Without a doubt, the universities have real—not nominal—power. And perhaps it is a reflection of this real power that only five out of 380 policy-making positions in these universities are held by

Table 2—THE EXCLUSION OF NEGROES
FROM PRIVATE INSTITUTIONS
Policy-Making Positions in the
Cook County Private Sector (1965)

	Policy-Making Positions	Positions Held by Negroes	Percent
1. Business Corporations			
Banks	2,258	7	*
Insurance	533	35	6
Nonfinancial Corporations	4,047	0	0
Total:	6,838	42	*
2. Legal Profession			
Total:	757	0	0
3. Universities**			
Total:	380	5	1
4. Voluntary Organizations			
Business & Professional	324	3	1
Welfare & Religious	791	69	9
Total:	1,115	72	6
5. Labor Unions			
Internationals	94	15	16
District Councils	211	20	9
Locals	514	73	14
Total:	819	108	13
Grand Total:	9,909	227	2
Grand Total for Public & Private Sectors:	10,997	285	2

*Below 1 percent.
**Includes the University of Illinois, which is a public body.

Negroes.

The exclusion of Negroes from the private sector carries over to its voluntary organizations: Negroes are found in only 1 percent of the posts there. It is in the voluntary associations that it is easiest to make symbolic concessions to the black community by giving token representation, yet even here Negroes were underrepresented—which highlights the fundamental norms of the entire sector.

The sectors and individual groups in the Chicago area with the highest Negro representation were those with a Negro constituency—elective offices, supervisory boards, labor unions, and religious and welfare organizations. These four groups accounted for 216 of the posts held by Negroes, or 75 percent, although these four groups have only 19 percent of all the policy-making positions we studied. Labor unions had a larger percentage—13 percent—than any other institution in the private sector. In welfare and religious organizations, whose constituents were often largely Negro, Negroes occupied 8 percent of the positions, the same percentage of the elected public offices they held.

Now, either the black constituency elected the Negroes directly (in the case of elective offices and trade unions); or the Negroes were appointed to posts in an operation whose clients were largely Negro (principal of a Negro school, for example); or Negroes were given token representation on bodies that had a broad public purpose (like religious organizations). By "token representation," we mean—following James Q. Wilson—that "he is a man chosen because a Negro is 'needed' in order to legitimate [but not direct] whatever decisions are made by the agency."

Of the three ways a black constituency had of getting

Table 3—THE EXCLUSION OF NEGROES
FROM PRIVATE ESTABLISHMENTS
Percentage of Negro Policy-Makers in the
Cook County Private Sector by Establishment (1965)

	Total Establishments	Percentage of Negro Policy-Makers			
		none	1-5%	6-15%	16-50%	51%+
1. Business Corporations						
Banks	102	98	0	4	0	0
Insurance	30	28	0	0	0	2
Nonfinancial Corporations	240	240	0	0	0	0
2. Legal Profession	54	54	0	0	0	0
3. Universities*	7	5	0	2	0	0
4. Voluntary Organizations						
Business & Professional	5	3	2	0	0	0
Welfare & Religious	14	2	4	7	1	0
5. Labor Unions						
Internationals	4	0	1	1	2	0
District Councils	23	13	0	5	5	0
Locals	33	14	2	8	7	2
Total:	512	457	9	27	15	4

*Includes the University of Illinois, which is a public body.

itself represented, the most important was the first. The statistics clearly show the importance of the Negro vote. The elected political offices and the elected trade-union offices account for only 11 percent of all the policy-making positions in Cook County. Yet almost half of all the Negro policy-makers were found in these two areas—137 out of 285.

Nonetheless, even in the major areas where Negro representation was the greatest—labor unions, elective offices, supervisory boards, and religious and welfare organizations—many institutions still excluded Negroes from positions of authority.

There are, of course, few Negroes in the building-trade unions, most of which bar Negroes from membership. Only two out of the 12 building-trade-union organizations we studied had even one Negro in a decisive slot. These two Negroes made up a mere 1.5 percent of the policy-making positions in the building-trade unions.

The greatest degree of black representation was found in the former Congress of Industrial Organizations (CIO) industrial unions. Only one-fourth of these units in the survey totally excluded Negroes from leadership. In almost half, the percentage of Negro policy-makers was over 15 percent—which is above token levels.

The former American Federation of Labor (AFL) unions (not including those in the building trades) had a higher rate of exclusion than those of the CIO. Two-fifths of these AFL unions had no Negroes at all in policy-making posts. But one-third of this group had leaderships that were 15 percent or more Negro. And the only two black-controlled locals large enough to be included in this study were in AFL unions.

In elective offices, the Negro vote certainly does give Negroes some representation—though far below their proportionate number. In public administration, however, where advancement to policy-making offices comes through appointment and influence, Negroes are all but excluded from decisive posts, at both the federal and local levels. Although a very high percentage of all Negro professionals are in public service, they do not reach the top.

The only major governmental operation that had a goodly number of Negroes at the upper level of the bureaucratic hierarchy was the public-school system. Nine percent of the top positions were occupied by Negroes. This unique situation is the result of some fairly recent appointments, made as concessions after an intense civil-rights campaign directed at the Chicago Board of Education. In this instance, one can consider these civil-rights actions as a proxy for Negro votes. Still, this high-level representation in the Chicago school hierarchy did not seem to reflect any uniform policy of including Negroes in management. At the level of principalship that was not included as a policy-making position in this study, only 3 percent of the positions were occupied by blacks.

The voluntary welfare and religious associations that were sufficiently important to be included in the study usually had at least a few Negro policy-makers. Only two out of 14 bodies had no Negroes in policy positions (see Table 3), while four organizations had token representation—below 5 percent. None had a Negro majority in the key posts. Only the Chicago Urban League (with 43 percent) had Negroes in more than 15 percent of its policy slots. If individual religious denominations had been among the organizations counted in the survey, there would have been some black-dominated groups. As it was, Negro representation in the United Protestant Federation, which *was* included, came largely from the traditionally Negro denominations. It is of interest to note that, in recent years, Protestant groups have provided some of the few instances in which Negroes have been elected to important offices by a constituency that was overwhelmingly white.

Not only were Negroes grossly underrepresented in Chicago's policy-making posts, but even where represented they had less power than white policy-makers. The fact is that the number of posts held by Negroes tended to be inversely related to the power vested in these positions—the more powerful the post, the fewer the black policy-makers.

As we have seen, Negroes were virtually excluded from policy-making in the single most powerful institutional sector—the business world. In *all* sectors, they were generally placed in positions in which the authority was delegated from a higher administrator, or divided among a board. Rarely were Negroes in positions of ultimate authority, either as chief executive or as top board officer.

When Negroes ran for a board or for a judicial office on a slate, their number had been limited by the political parties apportioning out the nominations. The percentage of Negroes on such boards or (especially) in judicial offices tended to run lower than the number of Negroes in legislative posts, for which Negroes run individually.

It is also true that no Negro has *ever* been elected to one of the key city-wide or county-wide executive positions, such as mayor, city clerk, or president of the Cook County Board. These are the positions with the greatest power and patronage.

In welfare agencies, where Negroes have token representation, they are virtually excluded from the key posts of executive director. Only five of the 135 directors of medium and of large welfare agencies were Negro.

Now, it was in the trade-union sector that the highest

percentage of Negroes had policy posts—13 percent. We asked several experts on the Chicago trade-union movement to list the number of Negroes among the 100 most powerful trade unionists in the area. Among the 100 people they named, the number of Negroes ranged from two to five. This did not surprise us, for it was compatible with our general knowledge of the number of Negroes with truly powerful posts in other sectors.

All in all, then, we would suggest the following rule of thumb: The actual power vested in Negro policy-makers is about one-third as great as the percentage of the posts they hold.

Thus when Negroes elected other Negroes to office, these officers tended to represent small constituencies. For example, the greatest number of Negroes in legislative posts came from relatively small districts that happen to have black majorities. Indeed, according to Cook County tradition, Negroes simply do not hold legislative posts in city, state or federal government *unless* they represent a district that is mostly black. No district with Negroes in the minority had a Negro representative, even when Negroes constituted the single largest ethnic group. And some districts with a Negro majority had a *white* representative.

Then too, the smaller the district, the more likely it would be homogeneous, and the greater the chances of its having a black majority that could return a Negro to office. In the Chicago area, consequently, Negroes were best represented on the City Council, which is based on 50 relatively small wards, each representing about 70,000 people; Negroes were represented most poorly in the U.S. House of Representatives, for which there are only nine rather large districts in Chicago, each representing about 500,000 people.

Most of the government policy-making posts that Negroes had been appointed to were in operations that had a large Negro clientele, if not a majority—as in the case of the Chicago public schools; or in operations that had largely Negro personnel, as in the case of the post office. On the appointed supervisory boards, in fact, those with as many as two Negro members were the Chicago Board of Education and the Board of Health, both of which serve very large numbers of Negroes.

This limiting of Negro policy-makers to Negro constituencies was quite as evident in the private sector. Three of the four banks with Negroes in policy-making posts were in Negro neighborhoods; and two were the smallest of the 102 banks we studied, and the other two were not much larger. The two insurance firms had mainly Negro clients, and were among the smallest of the 30 studied. In the voluntary organizations, the more they served Negroes, the higher the percentage of Negroes on their boards (although representation was by no means proportionate). Thus, the five Negro executive directors of welfare organizations we studied headed all-Negro constituencies: Three directed moderate-sized neighborhood settlements in the ghetto; one directed a virtually all-Negro hospital; and one directed an interracial agency that has traditionally had a Negro executive.

Still another way of limiting the power of Negro policy-makers, we discovered, was by "processing" them. Public and private institutions, as indicated, tend to have a token representation of Negroes. And many Negroes in these positions have totally identified with the traditional values and goals of the institution, regardless of what they mean to the mass of Negroes. Some of these Negro policy-makers, because of their small numbers and lack of an independent source of power, are neutralized. Others, if they are firm in representing the needs and outlook of the black community, are isolated. The two Negro members of the Chicago Board of Education represented these extremes. Mrs. Wendell Green, a longtime board member and the elderly widow of a former judge, had been the most diehard supporter of Benjamin Willis, the former schools superintendent, through all of his fights against the civil-rights movement. The other Negro— Warren Bacon, a business executive—sympathized with the campaign against inferior, segregated housing and, as a result, has been largely isolated on the board. He was rarely consulted on critical questions. His vote was usually cast with a small minority, and sometimes alone.

The fact is that the norms and traditions of *any* organization or enterprise limit the amount of power held by black policy-makers. It is no longer bold to assert that the major institutions and organizations of our society have an operational bias that is racist, even though their *official* policies may be the opposite. The Negro policy-maker in one of these institutions (or in a small black-controlled organization dependent upon these institutions, such as the head of a trade-union local) has a certain degree of conflict. If he goes along with the institution, from which he gains power and prestige, he ends up by implementing operations that restrict his minority group. Edward Banfield and James Q. Wilson have neatly pinpointed this dilemma in the political sphere:

Not only are few Negroes elected to office, but those who are elected generally find it necessary to be politicians first and Negroes second. If they are to stay in office, they must soft-pedal the racial issues that are of the most concern to Negroes as Negroes.

This pattern is seen in the failure of William Dawson, Cook County's one Negro congressman, to obtain many Presidential appointments or top federal civil-service posts for Negroes. Theoretically he is in a more strategic position to influence government operations than any other Chicago-based congressman, since he has 23 years' seniority and holds the important chairmanship of the Government Operations Committee. Yet in 1965 Negroes held only 2 percent of the top federal jobs in Chicago.

Any examination of the real power of Negroes in Chicago requires an examination of the strongest single organization in the Negro community—the Democratic Party. Wilson's study, *Negro Politics*, points out that the strength and cohesiveness of the Negro Democratic organization is largely dependent upon the strength of the total Cook County Democratic organization. The Negro organization is a "sub-machine" within the larger machine that dominates the city. The Negro sub-machine, however, has basically settled for lesser patronage positions and political favors, rather than using its considerable strength to try to make or change policy. Therefore, this Negro organization avoids controversial questions and seeks to avoid differences with the central organization on such vital issues as urban renewal and the schools.

In short, then, not only are Negroes underrepresented in the major policy-making positions in Cook County, but even where represented their actual power is restricted, or their representatives fail to work for the long-term interests of their constituency. It is therefore safe to estimate that Negroes really hold less than 1 percent of the effective power in the Chicago metropolitan area. Realistically, the power structure of Chicago is hardly less white than that of Mississippi.

From these figures it is clear that, at this time, Negroes in the Chicago area lack the power to make changes in the areas of housing, jobs and education. The basic subjugation of the black community, however, would not end if there were simply more Negroes in policy-making posts. We have seen the prevalence of tokenism, of whites' choosing Negro leaders who are conservative, of their boxing in Negro leaders who are proved to be liberal, of their giving these leaders less actual power than they give themselves.

Our analysis suggests that the best way to increase both the number *and* the power of Negro policy-makers is through unifying the black constituency. Access to policy-making positions could come through both the development of large, black-controlled organizations, and through getting Negroes into white-dominated organizations. If the constituency lacks its own clear set of goals and policies, however, things will surely remain the same. For success depends not just upon formal unity, but upon the nature of the goals set by the black community. In this situation, the overcoming of black powerlessness seems to require the development of a self-conscious community that has the means to determine its own interests, and the cohesiveness to command the loyalty of its representatives. We can safely predict that more and more Negroes will be moved into policy-making positions. The fundamental conflict, therefore, will take place between their cooptation into the established institutions and their accountability to a black constituency.

November 1968

FURTHER READING

Black Metropolis: A Study of Negro Life in a Northern Metropolis by St. Clair Drake and Horace Cayton, revised edition (New York & Evanston: Harper and Row, 1962).

Black Power, the Politics of Liberation in America by Stokely Carmichael and Charles V. Hamilton (New York: Random House, 1968).

Black Bourgeoisie by E. Franklin Frazier (Glencoe, Ill.: Free Press, 1957).

"The Web of Urban Racism" by Harold Baron in *Institutional Racism in America* edited by Louis Knowles and Kenneth Prewitt (Englewood Cliffs, N.J.: 1969).

Little Groups of Neighbors American Draft Boards

KENNETH M. DOLBEARE *and* JAMES W. DAVIS, Jr.

With a new Administration, a new Congress, and the prospect of a reduced need of soldiery, the reform of the Selective Service System may once again become a public issue. In 1967 the system received only a perfunctory review in Congress, despite (or, perhaps, because of) loud complaints from all sides and some provocative findings from a Presidential commission. In the last two years not much has changed. The problems are if anything worse:

1) There is an even greater surplus of manpower over needs, making even more important the manner of selecting the minority (about 45 percent of the eligible age group) who *are* required to serve.

This chapter is based on the authors' *Little Groups of Neighbors: The Selective Service System*, published by Markham Publishing Company, © 1968, all rights reserved by Markham Publishing Company, Chicago, Illinois.

2) Guaranteed deferments for those young men in college, frequently followed by occupational, Reserve or National Guard deferments, introduce a strong economic bias into conscription. (The lowest-income people do gain some compensation from the fact that so many of them fail the physical and mental examinations.) Therefore, the threat of induction hovers most compellingly over the sons of the working and lower-middle classes. In Wisconsin, the military-service experience of qualified men in some low-income, rural counties is 50 percent higher than qualified men in wealthy urban areas.

3) Finally, each of the nation's nearly 4,100 local boards has different standards and practices—so that the man who would be deferred in one area may be quickly drafted in another.

These facts were all well established in 1967, of course, when Congress brushed aside proposals for reforming the system. And it may be that the Vietnam War, the preferences of House Armed Services Committee Chairman L. Mendel Rivers, or the political artistry of Selective Service Director Lewis B. Hershey will serve again to prevent serious consideration of the anachronisms of the draft.

The major argument for retention of the system in its present form—and the argument that General Hershey has made since he acquired responsibility for conscription in the 1930s—is that the crucial act of selecting men for induction should be made through the discretionary judgments of local boards of part-time volunteers in each local community across the nation. These "little groups of neighbors," in General Hershey's oft-used phrase, must remain the foundation of the Selective Service System—because these men are repre-

sentative of their communities, they know who can best
be spared from the community (and therefore the need
for broad discretion in decision-making), and they are
known and trusted by their fellow citizens to the extent
that public acceptance of conscription itself rests on the
existence of local boards.

This is the way General Hershey put the matter in a
prepared budget presentation to the House Appropria-
tions Committee in 1966: "The ... functions [of
Selective Service] are carried on in the local boards
which are composed of little groups of neighbors on
whom is placed the responsibility to determine who is
to serve the nation in the Armed Forces and who is to
serve in industry, agriculture, and other deferred classifications." And later in 1966, in response to the House
Armed Services Committee's friendly queries about the
need for change in the system: "It would be essential to
avoid in any way interfering with the present decentralized approach of the system. . . . The decentralized, or
local board, or grass-roots operation of Selective Service
began with the First World War and demonstrated that
the nation would much more willingly support compul-
sory military service operated by their neighbors at
home. . . ."

But research conducted since 1967 shows con-
clusively that every major assumption made by General
Hershey and the Selective Service System concerning
local boards is wrong. The "little groups of neighbors"
that Selective Service and (apparently) Congress are so
attached to are by and large not "neighbors" in any
representative sense, they are not in contact with
registrants, they are not known or widely trusted by
local citizens (their discretionary powers are particularly
resented), and they are perhaps a principal reason for

public disapproval of conscription. Conducting conscription through the local-board system is costing Selective Service popular confidence and support; it is exaggerating the economic biases inherent in deferment policies, and it is creating the arbitrariness and lack of uniformity which are the hallmarks of the system. In short, only memories of turn-of-the-century rural America—and General Hershey's fear that change can mean only a return to the type of draft conducted during the Civil War—sustain the local-board principle.

Let us examine the findings in each major part of the "little groups of neighbors" argument.

The representativeness of local-board members. Early in 1967, the National Advisory Commission on Selective Service (the President's Commission, chaired by Burke Marshall) released data on the social characteristics of local-board members throughout the country. Even for such a devotedly backward-looking organization as Selective Service, it came as something of a surprise to find that 22 percent of all board members were over 70 years of age and nearly half were over 60. Two-thirds of all board members were veterans, and far more had their service experience in World War I—which ended 50 years ago—than saw service in the Korean War. The typical five-member draft board included three veterans, at least one of them from World War I; at least one member who was over 70; and no more than one member under 50. (In 1967 Congress responded to the system's superannuation by soberly enacting amendments limiting terms of service on local boards to 25 years, and requiring retirement at age 75. These amendments were not without effect, of course: Maine's Appeal Board, for example, lost four of its five members, ages 93, 81, 78 and 77. Yet the amendments did not give much impetus to a substantial turnover in membership.)

Board members were unrepresentative in other ways, too. In 1966 only 1.3 percent were Negroes, although Negroes constitute 11 percent of the male population and an even larger share of the armed forces. In four southern states with heavy concentrations of Negroes, there were no board members who were black; other southern and border states had only a few, and most northern cities had only token black membership. (These figures have been improved in the past two years, according to Selective Service, but the basic pattern still survives.) Occupationally, board members were drawn chiefly from such upper middle-class strata as professionals, managers and proprietors. Although half of the male labor force is employed in blue-collar jobs, only 9 percent of all board members reported that they were blue-collar workers.

States varied widely in the occupational makeup of their boards—apparently in response to the policies of state draft headquarters and to local political realities. New York City emphasizes lawyers—nearly one-third of all its board members are lawyers, even though registrants are legally prevented from bringing lawyers with them when they appear. (General Hershey says procedures are so simple that registrants don't have to be represented by counsel.) North Dakota avoids having lawyers on boards: In 1966, not one of its 213 board members was a lawyer. In some states (Florida and Pennsylvania among them) boards are heavily dominated by proprietors and managers; the highest percentage of blue-collar men (15 percent) is in Massachusetts, and the lowest (3 percent) in Washington.

Our own research in Wisconsin and elsewhere allows us to elaborate on the nature of board members' unrepresentativeness and the reasons for it. Age is a serious problem in Wisconsin, as it is nationally. Among the 81 percent of Wisconsin's 387 board members who answered our questionnaire, almost three times as many were over 60 as were under 45, and 26 percent were over 70. On the average, then, a Wisconsin local board would have two men who are retired from business (over 65) for each member whose job experience dates from World War II or after. Many men stay on their local boards long after they retire, and some actually join after retirement, in both cases apparently because they want to have something to do with their time. The job is not taxing, and they perceive it as important. Selective Service officials actually encourage long service, because it is not easy to find replacements and because long service makes life easier for the state headquarters: Experienced board members are more predictable, and require less guidance in times of stress than new men with new ideas.

Occupationally, board members are drawn from a special grouping within the middle class. Missing are the more mobile and higher-status occupations, like salesmen and physicians. Instead, board members are men with geographically fixed livelihoods—government employment, retail stores, farms, or family enterprises—suggesting that they have both long residence and a concern for the social and political management of the community. Vacancies in Wisconsin as in many other states are filled by having the remaining members nominate one of their acquaintances to the state headquarters, which passes the recommendation on to the Governor and thence to the President for appointment. Thus, the recruitment of new members is for the most part self-perpetuating. Occasionally, the state headquarters has to find a new man. In Wisconsin, this has created a remarkable overrepresentation of post-office employees, because the field man from state headquarters frequently begins his search by consulting the local postmaster. Whatever the route by which men reach their boards, the process only rarely reflects efforts toward representation of any kind on the boards.

If boards are therefore unrepresentative of their communities—or, perhaps more accurately, representative of only the social-control and political-control structures of their communities when the system was reestablished 20 years ago—consider how they look to their clientele, the registrants. To today's generation 18 to 25 years old—mobile, lacking their parents' experience with World War II, Korea, or Depression "hard times"; pressured by the Vietnam War; and only too aware of the pace of technological change—these "little groups of neighbors" are little more than a cruel joke. Selective Service requires that a registrant be subject to the board at which he registered at 18, despite any subsequent moves on his part to other locations and jobs around the country, so that often boards are not even "neighbors" in the geographical sense of the word. *Board members know their communities and who can best be spared for military service.* In some rural counties, where there are few registrants and there has been little change in the last 20 years, board members may in fact know their registrants and the needs of their communities. One could enter some reservations even here, though: We found some board members enthusiastic about their opportunity to support community norms by inducting men who fail to get a job in timely fashion, men who leave their wives, etc. But for the majority of registrants, who live in the nation's more urban areas, such intimacy of knowledge on the part of board members is wholly impossible.

Board members of such advanced ages, drawn so arbitrarily from such a narrow segment of the middle class, are unlikely either to have much of an idea of the needs of their communities or to know their registrants at all, let alone to know who can best be spared. In many cities, the jurisdiction of a board follows ancient ward or precinct lines or some other boundary equally irrelevant for purposes of defining social or economic units that might be "communities." Two or three square miles of apartment houses containing perhaps 20,000 registrants don't constitute a "community" with specific needs and priorities, nor is it likely that board members would know more than a tiny fraction of such a number of registrants. (Urban boards have 20,000 registrants on the average, though some have more than 50,000.)

Evidence from both local-board members and registrants indicates that board members are generally unfamiliar with their clients. Thus, we asked Wisconsin local-board members how often they had contact of *any* kind with *any* of their registrants. The results are:

Table 1: BOARD MEMBERS CONTACT WITH REGISTRANTS

	Frequent Contact	Occasional Contact	Rare or No Contact
Urban Board Members	3%	25%	72%
Small-city Members	15	48	37
Small-town Members	19	55	26

The majority of urban-board members rarely or never have contact with registrants, the majority of small-city members had occasional, rare or no contact; and the majority of small-town members had only occasional contact. Next, we asked a sample of University of Wisconsin students to name members of their local boards: Only a handful, even of rural residents, could name even one. And perhaps understandably, registrants showed a lack of trust in their boards. If you were to seek information from your local board, we asked the students, would you be willing to give your name? One-third of registrants in rural areas and one-half of urban registrants said No. Many registrants also seem to think that board members are chockful of bias and prejudice: When presented with hypothetical questions about their boards' criteria in selecting among equally qualified men for induction, nearly half of our respondents were convinced that race, class or occupational factors would control their boards' decision-making.

These findings suggest that local-board members, for the most part, neither know their "communities" nor their registrants—because their communities don't exist as such; because in any event they are too far detached from them; because there are too many registrants (many of whom have moved from the area); and because the contact between board members and registrants is usually slight, and often marked by fear and distrust on the part of registrants. Board members sometimes do receive and act upon bits of knowledge about their registrants, of course, but not always in the direction of a more rational decision process: The President's Commission reported that men who had moved out of their board's jurisdiction since age 18 were placed in 1-A classifications considerably more often than equally qualified men remaining in the jurisdiction!

Local boards are known and trusted by local citizens,

and they are the key to public acceptance of conscription. If possible, Selective Service's assumptions are even more mythical here than elsewhere. In September 1966, using the services of the University of Wisconsin's Survey Research Laboratory, we obtained responses from a sample of Wisconsin's adult population to a series of questions about the draft and the Selective Service System.

We discovered first that barely half the population was aware that the draft was conducted through local boards—despite almost daily publicity about the draft in the news media. A full 39 percent said flatly that they did not know who administered the draft; some associated it with units of local government; and only 52 percent gave responses that—with the most generous interpretation—we could define as indicating some knowledge about local boards. Of those who were aware of the existence of local boards, only one in ten could give the name of a member. And because half of the names given were females, while all board members were then male, these names may have been those of clerks. (No effort was made to verify the accuracy of the handful of names given.)

Next, we found that among those people who were aware of the existence of local boards, a narrow plurality thought that the local-board principle was not a good idea. As for those who had no prior knowledge about local-board administration, when acquainted with the practice, they said it was not a good idea by a ratio of about five to three. The combined sample delivered a clear plurality against local management of the draft.

Interestingly, there were sharp differences by class in people's attitudes toward the local-board principle.

Professionals, managers, proprietors, officials and farm-
ers—in short, those like board members themselves—
supported the local-board idea by sometimes more than
two-to-one ratios. Blue-collar workers and housewives
opposed local management by the same ratios.

Finally, we found that there was almost no relationship between people's attitudes toward local boards and
their attitudes toward conscription. For one thing,
many more people were aware of the existence of the
draft, a majority of them considering it to be fairly
administered. Those who considered the draft unfair
tended to be people with the most in the way of
financial outlay or education invested in a civilian
career, for whom military service was an unwanted
interruption. Blue-collar people, perhaps because service
was not such a comparatively bad alternative to their
other prospects, tended to think the draft was fair. But
the very people most convinced of the unfairness of the
draft itself (professionals, for example) were most likely
to be those who expressed the greatest confidence in
local boards, while the people who opposed the local-
board idea (i.e., blue-collar workers) were not adverse to
conscription.

There was only one important correlation between
people's attitudes toward local boards and their attitudes toward the fairness of the draft: Of those who
knew about local boards, those who believed that
boards "just followed orders from Washington" were
much more likely to think the draft was fair than those
who believed that local boards could "decide for
themselves" who should be drafted. Because this finding
flies so squarely in the face of the system's conviction
that discretion is necessary for local-board efficacy,
these data are worth presenting in full:

Table 2: ATTITUDES TOWARD THE DRAFT

	Local boards "Decide for themselves"	Local boards "Just follow orders from Washington"
The draft is fair	39%	62%
The draft is unfair	61	38
	100%	100%
	(Number: 67)	(Number: 148)

The implications of all these findings are clear: Local boards cannot be the source of public acceptance of conscription, for local boards are neither known nor approved—and not even the knowledgeable people approve of their discretionary powers. But local boards *may* be the price of acquiescence from that politically powerful segment of the middle class that itself mans and controls the local boards. In this case, of course, the local board system boils down to a cynical grant of power to the middle class to draft the sons of the working class in the least visible manner possible.

What do local boards contribute to Selective Service? From the evidence examined here, local boards seem to create antipathy in the majority of people and fear and distrust on the part of registrants. On the other hand, local boards seem to quiet any anxieties of those people who may be politically weighty—because such people are reassured that others like themselves run the boards. From the President's Commission Report and from our research—and from the daily observation of most citizens—eloquent testimony is available as to the lack of uniformity injected into conscription by the existence of so many legally autonomous local boards. Selective Service, perhaps because of its conviction about the necessity of local boards, makes a virtue out of this fact, arguing in effect that no two men in the nation are so similarly situated that they might reasonably expect to be similarly treated.

Not so readily obvious is the fact that local boards, by the mere fact of multiplying the number of jurisdictions on which induction calls must be made, both exacerbate nonuniformity and exaggerate the economic biases of national deferment policy. If there were only one (national) manpower pool from which all calls were made, local differences in percentages of men attending college or failing to meet induction standards would average out and conscription would be nationally uniform, calling similarly situated men from all over the nation at once.

The local-board principle, therefore, does definite harm—and very little in the way of benefit. What holds it up? How long can it endure as the central commitment of the American system of conscription? Our view is that, as a substitute for facts, there is nothing better than ideology—particularly when ideology may serve, as here, as a cloak for advantage.

Only the foolhardy are likely to venture forth against the assembled weight of the status quo of conscription and its mechanisms. Selective Service's local-board system is the beneficiary of a combination of an internally generated and thoroughly self-deluding conviction ("little groups of neighbors"), an all-encompassing decentralization ethic in and out of government, and a perhaps even more significant central core of sophisticated political achievement. In a 1967 Task Force Report, Selective Service triumphantly "rebutted" all the President's Commission's findings and proposals, chiefly because it did not question the basic premise that local boards were useful and essential. It defended their "achievements" without ever examining them.

Decentralization of government responsibilities commands support from many without regard for the specific consequences. National uniformity in the sharing of national burdens or benefits, though well established in such similar areas as Internal Revenue or Social Security or the Veterans' Administration, in regard to the draft still faces the accretions of decades of ideology and superstition. And because our public policies reflect the power distributions and proclivities of Congress more accurately than the merits of problems *or* the preferences of majorities of the people, and because those with the greatest political power are content with Selective Service, the local-board system—unfortunately—is likely to endure into the foreseeable future.

March 1969

FURTHER READING

The Draft: A Handbook of Facts and Alternatives edited by Sol Tax (Chicago: University of Chicago Press, 1967).

In Pursuit of Equity: Who Serves When Not All Serve? by the National Advisory Commission on Selective Service (Washington: U.S. Government Printing Office, 1967). This is the best single source of national data on the operations of the Selective Service.

Selective Service and American Society edited by Roger Little (New York: Russel Sage Foundation, 1969).

Selective Service and a Changing America by Gary L. Wamsley (Columbus, Ohio: Bobbs-Merrill, 1969).

Apartheid U.S.A.

THEODORE J. LOWI

The United States is over 100 years away from an official apartheid policy. Yet, after more than 20 years of serious involvement by the federal government in the "urban crisis," the social condition of American cities could be little worse if the concerned federal agencies had been staffed all those years by South African agents. A close look at the actual results of federal urban policies gives wonder how there remains any national legitimacy and why the crisis of the 1960s has not been more violent.

The crisis of the 1960s signaled the end of the era that began in the 1930s. Lyndon Johnson was the Herbert Hoover of this moment of change. As Hoover presided over the wreckage of the depression, Johnson presided over the wreckage of the New Deal. In both

This essay is a slightly revised version of a chapter in Theodore J. Lowi's *The End of Liberalism* published by W.W. Norton. ©W.W. Norton, 1969.

crises, the sincere application of established criteria began to yield unexpected, unintended and unacceptable results.

The New Deal was founded on the principle of positive government made possible—that is, acceptable to Americans—by a very special form of decentralization. Ideally, federal funds are to be passed to state and municipal administrators to deal with their problems as they see fit. The legislature is expected to set up a program without giving the administrator any guidance whatsoever for fear of intruding upon state or municipal autonomy. As K.C. Davis puts it, "Congress says, 'Here is a problem. Deal with it.' " The result we generally call enabling legislation.

The New Deal was expected to work effectively and without arbitrariness by putting the new programs in the best of all possible worlds: responsibility will be imposed upon central bureaucrats and decisions will be made miraculously in the public interest merely through the pulling and hauling of organized interests; central government expands; local influence expands as well; everybody gains. It is the providential "hidden hand" of Adam Smith applied to politics.

This neat process has been the prevailing public philosophy for the past generation. Panglossian political scientists describe it with overwhelming approval as pluralism. The Supreme Court has enshrined the essence of the New Deal in American jurisprudence as delegation of power. Most recently, political rhetoricians embrace it as creative federalism, maximum feasible participation and countervailing power. Thanks to the work of such unlikely comrades as Lyndon Johnson, Arthur Schlesinger, J.K. Galbraith, *Fortune* and the *Wall Street Journal*, the principle of decentralization through delegation became the consensus politics that celebrated the end of the New Deal era in 1968.

What follows is a simple case study of the implementation of the two major federal urban programs in a single city. The case goes far toward explaining why the national regime in the United States is no longer taken to be legitimate by so many black people and why this sense of illegitimacy was so likely to spread eventually to whites. Legitimacy, that elusive but vital underpinning of any stable regime, is that sense of the rightness of the general political order. It is that generalized willingness to view public error or corruption as the result of bad administration. There is probably no way practicably to measure legitimacy as such, but one can usually assess roughly the extent to which a regime is less legitimate today than yesterday—just as a doctor may not say precisely what a healthy body is but can know whether it is less healthy now than before.

In this spirit, one can fairly clearly detect a decline in the legitimacy of the regime by noting the rise of instances of repression of Left and Left-sounding activities; one can also detect it by noting the increasing number of political trials and political prisoners, and, more palpably still, the increased infiltration of Left organizations by paid informers. But other indications are not limited to the Left, as for example the increasing numbers of instances of defiance of federal laws—something Southerners have been leading the country in at least since 1954. One can therefore speak of problems of national legitimacy when he begins to sense a general unwillingness to submit political disputes to recognized channels of political settlement, when he sees mediation replaced by direct action.

This case suggests the extent to which the policies of the liberal state are producing its own downfall, and along with that the failure to achieve even a modicum of social justice. Also, in its perverse way, the case also illustrates the effectiveness of planning when governments do define their goals clearly and guide administrators firmly. Tragically the plan was for implementation of an evil policy, apartheid. But through the case perhaps liberals could learn a little something about how to plan for good ends.

Iron City is an urban-industrial area whose corporate boundary surrounds nearly 60,000 residents and whose true metropolitan area includes about 100,000. The history of the development plan of Iron City presents a single, well-documented case of the implementation of explicit racial goals. More than that, the nature of Iron City's official development plans and proposals upon which federal allocations were based serve to document beyond doubt the extraordinary permissiveness of federal urban policy.

The name of the city has been changed to protect the guilty. They are guilty as charged, but no more so than thousands of mayors, councilmen, planners, realtors and builders all over the country. The Iron City situation is extreme and unrepresentative, but it will soon be clear that it provides an ideal laboratory for discovering the nature and limitations of modern federal enabling legislation. Iron City is a southern city, and its development plan fostered racist goals, namely, apartheid, but in doing so its officials only stated the awful truth about the goals of land-use development plans in cities all over the country.

In 1950 over 20 percent of Iron City's population was Negro, and they did *not* live in a ghetto. There were

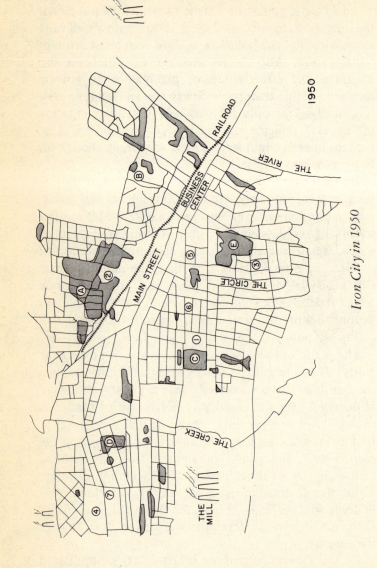

Iron City in 1950

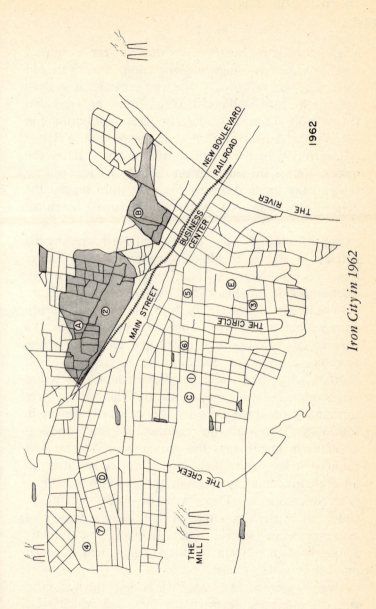

Iron City in 1962

1962

neighborhoods of Negroes in virtually every section of town. There was a narrow strip along the river, and there were several strips in the west central and western sections in easy walking distance from the steel and textile mills. There was a largely black neighborhood in the south central section, and there was a larger concentration in the north central section, "across the tracks." (Note the shadings on the map.) There was no Harlem; the implications of the very word suggest the nonsouthern origin of systematic housing discrimination.

Iron City's has been the typical Negro residential pattern in stable, middle-size southern cities. Rather than a single Negro section, there were interwoven neighborhoods of black and white. This patchwork pattern began in the 1920s with the slow but steady immigration of Negroes from outlying areas to the growing city. Access to industry and the needs of the wealthier whites for domestic servants made "close quarters" a desired condition. For example, the Negro neighborhoods east and north of The Circle were surrounded on three sides by the wealthiest homes in Iron City. But while the residents tolerated and encouraged in many ways the proximity of the races, it could not be said that Iron City constituted an integrated community. Each neighborhood was distinctly monochromatic. There were no black-white-black-white house patterns, although there were a number of instances when several Negro families lived directly across the street from or alley-to-alley with a larger number of white families.

Negroes seemed to accept their back-of-the-bus status and the questionable privileges they had which were unavailable to whites. Crimes committed within the race were not, as a rule, investigated or prosecuted with utmost vigor. Black bootleggers (legal sale of liquor has for years been forbidden in the county) had freer rein to cater to the blacks and the insatiably thirsty white middle class. The raising of a pig or a goat was usually allowed, in violation of public health regulations. The rents tended to run considerably lower. And merchants and newsboys were more permissive in granting or extending petty credit to Negroes. This was the dispersed and highly status-bound social situation as recently as 1950.

Early in that decade, however, most Southerners could see a racial crisis approaching, and for them the problems inherent in the residential pattern were immediately clear. In Iron City each of the major public schools was within walking distance of at least one strip of Negro housing and its complement of school-age children. The map serves to make this graphically clear.

Central High School (1 on the map) offered 9th-12th grade education to the white children who lived east of The Creek. Rebel High (4) served white children living west of The Creek, including some areas not shown on the map. Washington High School (2) taught both junior and senior high school grades (7th-12th) to Negro children from both the entire city and the surrounding county. Note the proximity of Negro neighborhoods, hence eligible children, to the white high schools. Most vulnerable to any impending court order for integration would be Central High, attended by virtually all of the children of upper-middle and middle-class families. Note also how far a good half of the Negro children commuted to Washington High and also how many of them actually crossed the paths to Rebel and Central in the course of their journey. The same problem existed for the junior high (3 and 7) and elementary schools (5, 6 and 7).

Into this situation stepped the Iron City Planning Commission in 1951. First, the commission analyzed housing, land uses, economic facilities and deterioration. In 1952 they produced a handsome and useful Master Plan, the emphasis of which was upon the need for measures ". . . for arresting beginning blight and correcting advanced blight." On the basis of the Master Plan, a more intensive investigation was ordered toward ultimate production of a Rehabilitation Plan to guide actual implementation and financing. The result of this careful study was a professionally designed, fully illustrated, three-color, glossy paper booklet entitled *Iron City Redevelopment*. The focus of this publication was three areas, designated A, B and E on the map, in which blight had made urban redevelopment necessary.

Upon closer scrutiny, however, the plan reveals itself less a scheme for urban renewal as much as a script for Negro removal. All of the projects proposed in the plan are explicit on this point. The underlying intent to create a ghetto is further highlighted by the inconsistencies between the design for Area E, which had relatively few Negroes, and that for Area A, which was predominantly Negro. The latter housing was as blighted as Area E, but, curiously, the standard of blighting was not applied. There the plan called for intensification of use rather than renewal.

The plan identified Area E as:

occupied by Negroes, but the number is too few to justify provisions of proper recreational, school and social facilities. . . . The opportunity to reconstitute the area as a residential district in harmony with its surroundings was the main reason for its selection as the number one redevelopment site.

The second, Area B, was chosen because "a relatively small amount of housing—standard and substandard—exists there"; therefore it would serve as a companion project to . . . [Area E] . . . thus affording home sites for those occupants of [Area E] who are not eligible for relocation in public housing or who, for reasons of their own, prefer single-family or duplex dwellings." Area A, as shown by the intensive survey and the maps published with the plan, contained as much dilapidated and blighted housing as Area E; but Area A was *not* designated an urban redevelopment area in the plan. Although "blighted and depreciating," it was the "center part of the area . . . growing as the focal point of Negro life." Along the main street of this area, extending into Area B, the plan proposed the building of an auditorium, a playfield and other public facilities "to serve [Iron City's] Negro community." Sites were inserted for the three Negro churches which would be removed by the redevelopment of Area E.

Before completion of *Iron City Redevelopment*, implementation projects had begun and were expanding as financing allowed. It was to be a showcase program, and enthusiasm ran high. The first steps, quite rationally, were to acquire housing for those families who were to be displaced. It was perfectly consistent with the city's view of these people that this housing would be public housing. There had been some public-housing projects built under depression legislation, but the only meaningful projects were those begun in 1952 under the Housing Act of 1949. On the map the letters A, B, C and D represent the actual locations of these projects. There was never any controversy over the racial distribution of the occupants. Projects A and B were 100 percent Negro; Projects C and D were 100 percent white. By 1955 they were completed and occupied.

Table 1: PUBLIC HOUSING PROJECTS IN IRON CITY

Project	Size (No. of Units)	% Negro in Project	Original Composition of Area	Development Cost
A	160	100	Negro	$1,491,000
B	224	100	Mixed	$2,491,000
C	146	0	Negro	$1,595,000
D	220	0	Negro	$2,300,000

Each public-housing project was placed carefully. Project A was built in the middle of the largest Negro area. Project B was built in a sparse area, about 50 percent Negro, but marked out in the plan as the area for future expansion of the Negro community. In the area around Project B, the plan proposed sites for the three new "colored churches" and the "colored auditorium."

Project C, an exclusively white project, was built literally on top of the Negro area around it. While it was relatively inexpensive and contained the fewest number of units, it occupied an eight-square-block area due to its design. According to the executive director of the Greater Iron City Housing Authority, it was "a rather unique design, known in the architectural trade as a crankshaft design, thus providing both front and rear courtyards." This project was cited professionally as an outstanding example of good design. And no wonder! Its maximum utilization of space, although a low-rent project, made it a combination public housing, urban renewal and Negro removal plan par excellence. Project D was also built on top of a blighted Negro neighborhood. While it was a relatively large project, it was not solely responsible for eliminating every Negro from the area, as was Project C.

Meanwhile, renewal of the central city was proceeding at a slower pace; it wasn't until 1956 that implementation projects were fully designed. Two areas, designated by the shaded areas around B and E on the map, were selected for intensive renewal. Most important was Area E, a 56-acre area relatively tightly packed with rickety frame houses, outside toilets, corn or potato plots and Negroes. In the official plan, Area E included the unconnected Negro neighborhood just north of The Circle, as well as the entire shaded area due east of The Circle. Area B was relatively sparsely populated, containing a few shacks which needed removing. In some of these shacks were white unemployables.

Within three years the two urban renewal projects were declared 100 percent accomplished. The results were indicated in the official report to the Urban Renewal Administration (see Table 2).

Table 2: COMPLETED URBAN RENEWAL
PROJECTS IN IRON CITY

Accomplishment	Activity	For Area E	For Area B
100%	Land Acquisition, No. of Parcels Acquired	168	39
100%	No. of Families Relocated	176	24
100%	No. of Structures Demolished (Site Clearance)	236	33

In Area E every trace of Negro life was removed. As the executive director of the Greater Iron City Housing Authority put it, "In this project, all of the then-existing streets were vacated and a new land use map was developed." One entirely new street was put in, several of the narrow lanes (e.g., Saint James' Alley) were covered over, and through-connectors were built for a dead-end street or two.

All of Area E has now become prime property. One large supermarket, several neighborhood businesses, and two apartment complexes are operating on renewal land purchased from the authority. To serve the 95 percent white area, an elementary school was constructed, as a consolidation of schools No. 5 and No. 6 which no longer exist. Its large playground and lighted ball field occupy most of the eastern sector of Area E. The renewal effort resulted in an equally impressive campus for the nearby junior high, No. 3. But most of the area was zoned for single family residences, and, as of 1968, the boom in construction of houses in the $25,000-$40,000 range was still in progress.

Area B now enjoys a new elementary school with a field house, lighted ball field, tennis court and playground. The city also built a swimming pool here, but it and the original municipal pool on The River were closed for several years to avoid integration of public facilities. Moreover, though redevelopment sites had been set aside in Area B for the three churches demolished in the redevelopment of Area E, each of the congregations chose locations elsewhere in the Negro community. Similarly, most of the relocating Negroes rejected Area B in favor of Area A, even though it was more densely populated and blighted. Except for the 224 units of new public housing, Area B remains underutilized. Furthermore, the major part of Area B extends north of Project B toward the mountain, where *Iron City Redevelopment* reports that although some of the terrain is steep, much of it is gently rolling and well drained. . . . In most southern cities there is a scarcity of vacant land located close to schools and churches and shopping districts and served by city utilities and transportation, land that is suitable and desirable for expansion of Negro neighborhoods or creation of new ones. [Area B] is such an area.

Apparently the Negroes do not agree, and most of the area remains a graded, but raw, expanse of red southern earth on the side of the mountain. This was the one part of the plan that went wrong; this was the voluntary part, not financed by federal agencies.

Yet, as a whole, the plan was an overwhelming success. Well before the 1960 census the large Negro contingent in Area E had been reduced to 5.1 percent of the entire census tract, and this was comprised of a few shanties behind the bottling works and the western edge of the area along The River. In Area C the removal process immediately around Central High was completed with Public Housing Project C. After 1960 some 10 percent of the area was still nonwhite, but this was drying up still further. Removal from Area D was approaching totality. By 1964 removal from all areas west of The Creek was given further assistance by the completion of one federally supported artery running east-west through the city and the inauguration of Iron City's portion of the new north-south Interstate Highway. That brought the nonwhite proportion in the western sectors of the city down to about 3 percent of the total population of those areas.

This is how the situation stood by the end of 1967: west of The Creek and north of Main Street (all around Area D), there remained six Negro families. When a nearby textile mill was closed down some years before, they, as employees, were given the right to buy their houses, and they have chosen to remain. West of The Creek and south of Main Street (the area including The Mill), fewer than 5 percent of the housing units were occupied by Negroes. Virtually every one of these houses is located in isolated and sparse sections along The Creek and behind The Mill, where one can still plant a plot of sorghum, catch a catfish, and, undisturbed, let a 1948 Chevrolet corrode into dust. Closer to the center of things, east of The Creek and south of Main Street, the 1960 distribution of Negroes continues to be reduced. Every last shack is gone from Area E and the entire central section of the white city. Three small pockets remain in the western portion near Area C, and that is all that remains in all of the white city. The last remaining Negro neighborhood of any size, a group of shanties running along The River south of Main Street, was removed by the construction of a City Hall-Police Department-YMCA complex. Area B remains completely nonwhite and underdeveloped. Area A now fills the entire triangle pointing north. It is a ghetto.

The plan enjoyed strong consensus among officials and white citizens. It enjoyed at least the acquiescence and tacit consent of the Negroes whose landlords, in any case, were white. Consensus or not, the plan would have had little chance of success without outside financial assistance. That assistance came, abundantly, from federal programs. And, most importantly, the federal personnel who allocated these funds, and still do, also had access to all the project plans, including the Master Plan and the Renewal Plan. Despite Iron City's open approach to apartheid—nothing was kept secret—federal assistance was never in question. Relative to the population of Iron City and the size of its annual public sector budget, federal aid was quite substantial— amounting to 20 percent of the municipal budget for a few years. What we have seen here is an honest, straightforward job of federally sponsored physical and social planning. And the results were dramatic. Perhaps only New Haven, Connecticut, a city famous for its redevelopment, has had a higher per capita success ratio.

Direct federal assistance for public housing in Iron City amounted to slightly over $280,000 for the single fiscal year 1966. Each year since the completion of the four projects the city received a similar amount. This varying figure cannot be broken down among the four projects because it is computed on the basis of the "development costs" given above and granted as a lump sum. The Public Housing (recently changed to Housing Assistance) Administration of Housing and Urban Development (HUD) is authorized by law to grant *each year* to any housing authority the difference between expenses (governed by development costs) and income from public housing. Such a subsidy arrangement enabled authorities like Iron City's to borrow from private banks and to refinance through sale of relatively cheap Housing Authority bonds. What is even more significant is that, under the formula, Iron City is authorized to receive a maximum grant of nearly $305,000 per annum. It is a point of pride at the Greater Iron City Housing Authority that the full amount available under the law was never needed or requested. At a minimum estimate of $250,000 per year, federal grants to help carry the public housing have amounted to $3,000,000. And federal public housing grants are never-ending. Each year the total to Iron City goes up another $250,000 or more.

Federal assistance for urban renewal, as differentiated from housing assistance, was another indispensable part of the plan. Between 1957 and 1961, by which time virtually everything but land disposition was completed, Iron City received just short of $1,600,000 from the federal government under the urban redevelopment laws. This amounts to an additional subsidy of $400,000 per annum.

The federal housing assistance was at least $300,000 for each year between 1954 or 1955 and 1957. Together with the urban renewal allotments, the total was at least $700,000 during the years of peak planning activity, 1957-1962. This money is the key to the plan's success.

But to this we must also add the resources made available through various other federal agencies. Federal highway assistance added an undetermined amount for new arteries and, incidentally, forced Negroes to move from the western edge of Iron City. The Federal Housing Authority and the Veterans Administration help to finance the lovely homes being built in Area E. It has not been possible to determine whether federal community facilities funds helped remove Negroes from The River where the new City Hall complex now stands. Nor has it been possible to determine if the local banks balked at extending FHA and VA home owner credit to Negroes seeking to build on the mountain side north of Area B. Answers would affect the meaning of the case only marginally.

First, the case bears out what many people have been saying for two decades, that slum removal meant Negro removal. But it goes further. It supports the even more severe contention that the ultimate effects of federal urban policies have been profoundly conservative or separatist, so much so as to vitiate any plans for positive programs of integration through alteration of the physical layout of cities.

Second, it supports the general thesis that a policy of delegation of powers without rule of law will ultimately come to ends profoundly different from those intended by the most libertarian and humanistic of sponsors. Moreover, it supports the unfashionable contention that some of the most cherished instruments of the liberal state may be positively evil—and that a criterion by which this evil can be predicted is the absence of public and explicit legislative standards by which to guide administrative conduct.

Third, the case of Iron City, especially the explicit nature of its racial policy, shows precisely how and why federal policy is ill equipped to govern the cities directly. The permissiveness of federal enabling legislation could do no greater harm to the social future of the cities than if harm were intended. The present disorder in the cities is explained properly by the failure of government and politics, rather than by the inferiority of Negro adjustment. The case demonstrates how national legitimacy can be tarnished to the degree that it is loaned to the cities for discretionary use and how the crisis of public authority is inevitable as long as a political process unguided by law climaxes in abuses such as those catalogued in Iron City. In sum, it helps show why liberal government based on current principles of delegation cannot achieve justice.

Every Negro in Iron City knew what was happening. Every Negro in Chicago and New York and Cleveland and Detroit knows the same about his city too. But since northern Negroes are not as docile, does that mean that federal imperium was used completely differently outside the South? True, planning authorities would never so deliberately pursue such obviously racial planning. It is also true that few social plans could be as relatively extensive or as successful as Iron City's. Nonetheless, it is undeniable that misuse of federal programs in ways indistinguishable in principle from the Iron City misuse has been widespread.

Martin Anderson, for example, estimated in 1964 that about two-thirds of all displacements resulting from urban renewal were Negro, Puerto Rican, or some other minority group. In public housing the record is even more somber. First, because the pattern is even clearer, and second, because these projects stand as ever-present symbols of the acts of discrimination by which they were created.

A study by Bernard Weissbrourd for the Center for the Study of Democratic Institutions concluded that " . . . most cities have followed a deliberate program of segregation in public housing. . . ." Until July 1967, many housing administrators followed a rule of "free choice" allowing eligible tenants to wait indefinitely for an apartment, which allowed them also to decline a vacancy on racial grounds. Still more recently it was revealed that the Chicago Housing Authority, with the full knowledge of federal agencies, cleared all proposed public housing sites with that member of the Board of Aldermen whose ward would be affected. Thus, while the whole story cannot be told from official statistics, we may conclude what every urban Negro knows—Iron City is not unique.

According to HUD reports of 1965, only three of New York City's 69 public housing projects were officially listed as all nonwhite or all white in occupancy; but ten of Philadelphia's 40 projects were all nonwhite, and 21 of Chicago's 53, five of Detroit's 12, four of Cleveland's 14, and all of Dallas' ten projects were listed as either all nonwhite or all white. The rest of reality is hidden, because the Public Housing Administration defines an "integrated project" as one in which there are "white and more than one nonwhite, including at least one Negro family." Not only does this system of reporting make it impossible to determine the real number of truly integrated projects, it also serves to maintain local racial policies and prejudices.

The Civil Rights Act of 1965 was supposed to have put an end to such practices, but there is little evidence that it can or will improve the situation in public housing in particular or city housing in general. It was not until July of 1967 that the rule of "free choice" was replaced with a "rule of three," a plan whereby an applicant must take one of the first three available units or be dropped to the bottom of the eligible lists. All of this is undeniable testimony that the practices all along had constituted a "separate but equal" system of federally supported housing.

In June 1967, three years after the 1964 Civil Rights Act and after strenuous efforts by the Johnson Administration, two of Detroit's five segregated projects became "integrated" when one white family moved into each of two totally black projects. At the same time, at least 11 of New York's projects were classified as "integrated" when, in fact, fewer than 15 percent of the units were occupied by families of some race other than the race of the 85 percent majority in that project.

For 33 years the Federal Housing Authority has insured over $110 billion of mortgages to help whites escape, rather than build the city. This confession was made when the FHA instituted a *pilot* program to increase FHA support for housing finance in "economically unsound" areas. And it took the belated 1967 directive on public housing to get them to do that much. These remedial steps came five years after President Kennedy's famous "stroke of the pen" decision aimed at preventing discrimination in publicly supported housing and three years after the first applicable Civil Rights Act. Yet no such legislation or executive decisions can erase the stigma of second-class citizenship placed upon the residents of federal housing programs. Nor can more skillful administration of essentially separatist programs remove the culpability of federal participation in the American local government policy of apartheid. Rather, all of these efforts merely suggest that remedies and correctives are never going to help bad organic laws, because bad organic laws are, quite literally, congenitally defective.

Perhaps it is better to have no new public housing than to have it on the Iron City pattern and at the expense of national legitimacy. With the passing of the Housing Act of 1968 and union agreements to build modular units off-site, some will surely argue that the answers lie in the proper expansion of public housing. But unless steps are taken to prevent the duplication of the patterns reviewed here, more will hardly yield better. Other writers and officials have proposed various solutions. President Johnson suggested creating semi-public corporations to finance public low-cost housing, while Senator Charles Percy would offer incentives to private corporations. These proposals focus on the details of financing and offer further examples of the confusion shared by liberals today concerning forms of law versus essentially technocratic forms of administration for achievement of simple, ordinary justice. Regardless of the means of financing, these programs will produce no lasting social benefit without the rule of law that states unmistakably what administrators can and cannot do, what is to be forbidden, and what is to be achieved. That is the moral of the Iron City story.

February 1970

FURTHER READING

The Death and Life of Great American Cities by Jane Jacobs (New York: Modern Library, 1969).

The Zoning Game by Richard F. Babcock (Madison, Wis.: University of Wisconsin Press, 1966).

The Federal Bulldozer by Martin Anderson (Cambridge, Mass.: MIT Press, 1964).

The City Is the Frontier by Charles Abrams (New York: Harper & Row, 1965).

Who Governs? by Robert A. Dahl (New Haven: Yale University Press, 2nd ed. 1967).

Dagger in the
Heart of Town:
Mass. Planners and Cambridge Workers

GORDON FELLMAN
BARBARA BRANDT *and* ROGER ROSENBLATT

The building of highways has become a nationwide controversy, surrounded by charges that congressmen, federal highway officials and state engineers are "mortgaged to the road gang," that rural highways blight the natural beauty they are meant to render accessible and that urban highways are "white men's roads through black men's bedrooms." Engineers argue that constantly increasing automobile traffic must be accommodated by newer and wider freeways, and so they continue in their drive to construct 42,500 miles of interstate highway that must be completed by 1974 in order to benefit from the federal government's payment of 90 percent of the construction cost. Simultaneously, local highway opponents ranging from poor blacks to nature-lovers, from upper-class whites to the workingclass children of European immigrants, have managed, at this writing, to delay the construction of highways in over two dozen cities around the nation.

In Cambridge, Massachusetts, there exists an urban road controversy that may be a classic. This city of 95,000 houses Harvard University, the Massachusetts Institute of Technology (MIT) and a sizeable number of families of middle-class professionals, along with a large ethnically mixed working-class population. For almost a dozen years now, a combination of local residents, city, state and federal politicians, neighborhood priests and volunteer city-planners have succeeded in holding off construction of the Inner Belt, a proposed eight-lane freeway slated to cut through a heavily populated working-class residential area, uprooting about 5,000 people and bisecting the city.

For the past four years, a team of sociological observers has followed the development of antihighway protest in Cambridge. We have talked to, surveyed and even participated in the everyday activities of some of the 5,000 or so residents of the Brookline Street-Elm Street area due to be destroyed by the proposed Inner Belt.

As highway-planners themselves admit, urban high-ways are the most difficult, expensive and heartrending to build. For, despite the benefits of improved trans-portation the highway is expected to bring, there is also the cost of relocating hundreds or thousands of families (who are often low-income and black and, therefore, especially hard to relocate). Through our firsthand observation of the day-to-day life of the people of Brookline and Elm streets in Cambridge, combined with statistical data gleaned during the summer of 1967 from a survey, we have been able to construct a detailed and revealing picture of the Brookline-Elm people and some understanding of the ramifications of constructing a highway through an area like this. Although the Cambridge situation has some unique features, in many ways what we learned here is applicable to many neighborhoods elsewhere.

The proposed Brookline-Elm Street location for the Inner Belt in Cambridge is not a natural pathway of the city. Instead, it cuts through the heart of a densely settled section, taking a wide strip where approximately 1,300 families (about 5,000 people) live and another 3,000 work.

The Brookline-Elm area is the kind of crowded tree-sparse, frame-house neighborhood that leads cosmopolitan city-dwellers or sophisticated suburbanites to wrinkle their noses in disgust. But the cause of the disgust is more one of taste than of objective unattractiveness or disrepair. Overstuffed chairs with lace doilies on the arms and backs, gardens with an old rubber tire—scalloped and painted white—encircling a geranium, clothes lines strung on a wide porch or between poles in a backyard, fake brick or shingled asbestos siding, flowered wallpaper and crowded knickknack shelves are not the cup of tea of the upper-middle class.

But in contrast to the sometimes littered streets and the sometimes run-down exteriors on the one-, two- and three-family homes and the small apartment buildings, the interiors are spotless. Amateur carpenters and handymen abound among working husbands and housewives, homeowners and tenants alike. They seem to be endlessly engaged in painting and papering projects, installing new kitchen cabinets, building on porches or additional rooms or remodeling bathrooms.

Since Brookline-Elm is located midway between

Harvard and MIT, the number of students settling in the old apartments is continually increasing (students represented about 5 percent of the population in 1967 according to our study). A number of landlords have found it profitable to raise rents, driving out the older tenants, then to modernize the apartments and charge exorbitant rents which only several students living together can afford.

A small number of other academic and professional people also live in the large-roomed frame houses or the relatively inexpensive apartments in the area, but most residents are members of typical working-class families— the husband employed at a nearby candy factory, book bindery or electronics plant, the wife full time at home or working part time also at a factory, as a sales clerk or as a nurse or nurse's aide. About three-quarters of the population have no formal education beyond high school (more than half are not high school graduates). Almost half the men and one-third of the working women hold unskilled or semiskilled jobs (the remainder of the men usually hold skilled jobs or are on welfare or pensions). Eighty-five percent of the residents report having combined family incomes below $7,500, and the average family income in this neighborhood is between $3,000 and $5,000 per year.

Living close to members of one's ethnic group is desired by many first- and second-generation Americans, and Brookline-Elm is an area of primary settlement for newcomers. Almost one-third of the residents are immigrants, another large group are the children of immigrants, and widely various ethnic enclaves dot the densely populated area—Portuguese, Lithuanian, Puerto Rican—along with scatterings of Negro residents (both native-born and West Indian, who together make up about 15 percent of the population), Canadians, Irish, Italians, Greeks, Poles, Armenians and about one-quarter of miscellaneous "old American" stock. The neighborhood is perhaps unique in that there is absolutely no evidence of intergroup friction or hostility.

A number of the foreign-born residents still speak their native languages and have social dealings primarily with others of their group who live next door or down the street; they patronize ethnic stores nearby, join the ethnic clubs in the area and attend ethnic churches. Almost exactly half the population is Roman Catholic (another third is Protestant, the remainder are Greek Orthodox, Jewish or have no religious affiliation), and over one-third of the residents—mainly Irish and Italians—attend two large Catholic churches whose congregations will be reduced by half if the Inner Belt is constructed.

About one-fourth of the residents dislike the area and would like to leave, although most cannot afford to. This group includes some short-term residents such as students, academics, professionals and a number of young working-class families. They are the more mobile; their eyes are fixed on the move upward and outward—to the suburbs or a "better" part of Cambridge, to California where there is the possibility of higher paying electronics work, to "the country" or to another university.

The majority of Brookline-Elm residents, however, display the family-centered and locally based life style common in many working-class communities. Almost half the residents have lived in the area more than ten years; over a third have lived here more than 20 years. Most are pleased with their home and neighborhood and like the schools and the convenience to transportation and shopping. Despite a few complaints, mainly about lack of recreational facilities for children, the majority do not want to move.

Like working-class people anywhere, the Brookline-Elm residents are not "joiners." Except for the PTA, to which slightly over half of the families with children in school belong, but in which almost none are active, over three-fourths of the residents belong to no clubs or organizations and do not take part in any community activities except for attending church, which most do at least once in a while, and voting in state, city and national elections, which 70 percent claim to do. Most of their social life is spent at home, with nearby friends and, most characteristically, with relatives.

As the middle class commonly sees the world, a "family" means a married couple and their dependent children, living far from grandparents and other relatives. In working-class culture, however, the basic family unit is often more extensive than that—a whole host of brothers, sisters, uncles, aunts, grandparents, grandchildren and cousins who live nearby and constitute a large portion, if not the main part, of the social life of their members. In the Brookline-Elm area, over half the residents have relatives in Cambridge other than their immediate family, and almost half the residents live within walking distance of relatives. A typical case is a woman whose widowed mother lives next door, whose married daughter lives two blocks away and whose son lives near enough to stop each morning to see his mother on the way to work. Many residents said they moved to this area in order to be near members of their family; over one-quarter of the people interviewed said they visit with relatives every day, and over half report that they see their relatives at least once a week. While middle-class people commonly strive to escape this kind of thing, working-class people often define such closeness as "natural" and extremely important in their lives.

Nearby friends are also part of the social landscape of the lives of Brookline-Elm people. A large majority have friends within walking distance and visit them at least once weekly. This is especially important for housewives; virtually none have access to a car during the day.

Leisure and work life are also locally based. In usual working-class fashion, leisure time for many residents consists of home repairs and remodeling, visiting with nearby relatives and friends or going to stores or a bar or restaurant in the nearby Central Square business area. Most residents are also employed close to their homes (over one-fifth of those interviewed mentioned nearness to work as another reason for moving to the neighborhood), and one-quarter of the people who live here are able to walk to work, which is twice the average in all of Massachusetts for people who walk to work. Only half the families own cars; and only 40 percent of the residents, which is much less than the national average, drive to work. The remainder take conveniently located public transportation. Most people in the area shop for groceries in the immediate vicinity; half buy their clothing and furniture in Central Square, and almost half use local doctors and dentists.

Economic considerations are part of what attracts people to Brookline-Elm and holds them there. In addition to its convenience to shopping, work places and transportation, it is still, despite skyrocketing rents, one of the least expensive parts of Cambridge. Half our sample considered the rents they paid "below average" (typical rent in 1967 was $55 per month). The home owners, who make up about one-fifth of the residents, and most of whom own their homes fully, generally paid less than $8,000 for their property when they bought it years ago. (Their labor and the market have of course raised property values since then.) The meager income of some multiple-unit home owners is supplemented by, if not completely dependent on, rentals.

It is this area, unique in some ways, in others typical of any working-class part of America, that is scheduled for demolition with the construction of the eight-lane Inner Belt road.

The most direct and obvious social cost of an urban highway—one that is apparent to highway planners as well as those affected by their work—is relocation. Before 1968, federal law simply required that home owners dislocated by federally aided highways be reimbursed for the "fair market value" on their house, a figure clearly open to controversy, and that tenants receive a couple of hundred dollars moving expense. The 1968 Federal Aid Highway Act now provides that all those to be dislocated, whether owners or tenants, be offered the choice of "decent, safe, and sanitary housing" *before* they are moved out, that no federal-aid projects may be approved unless enough such housing is available and that relocation housing must be within the financial means of those displaced. In addition, home owners are to be given up to $5,000 over market value, if necessary, to help them purchase a new dwelling, and tenants are to be paid up to $1,500, if necessary, for renting or buying a new home. This remuneration is more generous than what came before. How adequate or satisfying it will prove to be is anyone's guess.

In view of the current shortage of low-cost housing in Cambridge and greater Boston (a situation familiar to many metropolitan areas), it is unlikely that many

Brookline-Elm residents, if they have to move, can find replacement housing near their old neighborhood. This would mean increased expenses—not only for rent but also for transportation to work, to relatives and perhaps to shopping, all of which add sizeable hardships to the lives of people of very modest incomes. Relocation in a sprawling suburb, or in another urban section even two or three miles from the old neighborhood, will cause difficulties, particularly for the 50 percent of the population without cars and for the many older residents who cannot drive. The problem of finding new housing for the sizeable proportion of black and white low-income residents will be particularly acute.

Both home owners and tenants frequently put much time and effort into the upkeep of their homes—inside and out—and their gardens. A quarter of the residents have spent over $1,000 on repairs and remodeling from the time they moved into their house or apartment. Particularly for men and women like these, who rarely find status and meaning in their work life or in community or political affairs, the physical dwelling itself is a source of feelings of self-worth and pride, a place where the environment can be mastered, especially if one is a home owner.

Residents worry whether the road will come through; they agonize over whether to shingle anew their house, over whether to buy new carpeting or cupboards or not to buy. Many said that they or their landlords had halted repairs in expectation that the Belt would come. A number of residents told us that local banks refused to lend them home-repair funds. Such apprehensions about investments no doubt contribute in large measure to the rundown appearance of some houses. We also found many instances in which an absentee landlord had let the exterior of his building run down, but the tenants had kept the interiors of their own apartments in good condition.

State highway officials have suggested relocating Brookline-Elm residents into high-rise apartments built over the highway. From the residents' point of view, and for objective reasons as well, there are a number of objections to this solution.

1) One has less control over one's physical environment in a modern high-rise apartment building than in older buildings or in one's own home.

2) Correctly or not, working-class people identify high-rise apartments for their income group with public housing, which is anathema to them for many reasons.

3) The one familiar experience with housing over highways, the George Washington Bridge apartments in New York City, indicates that traffic noises and fumes make the lower two or three floors of such buildings difficult or impossible to rent and even a dozen or more floors unpleasant to live in.

4) The most likely federal programs for financing such housing could not possibly provide for as many low-income families as would need to relocate in the new air-rights buildings; allowed rent schedules are not low enough and rent supplement programs are not yet sufficient for a subsidy solution to the problem.

5) Most of the people we interviewed would not like that kind of housing for a host of reasons ranging from esthetics to the difficulty entailed in supervising children (one cannot supervise a child playing on the ground ten stories below).

6) At least three to four years would elapse between the time of leaving existing housing and moving to new air-rights structures. Families are not going to live in

tents in the interim, and few, if any, would be willing to consider an initial move from Brookline-Elm as "temporary."

7) The planner usually assumes that the social unit to relocate is the "nuclear family"—the parents with dependent children. As we have explained, while this assumption may be correct with regard to the more mobile middle class, it betrays ignorance of the social patterns and life styles of working-class people.

This raises the question of a large group of people whose lives are ordinarily ignored by highway and renewal planners—the "survivors." In a middle-class area, the "survivors" are those living directly adjacent to a newly built expressway, who may receive some financial compensation for the incovenience of the traffic, with its accompanying noise, fumes and vibrations. In a working-class area like Brookline-Elm, however, the survivors include the people on adjoining streets and blocks whose friends and relatives had to move away, or whose work places, businesses, churches and other community facilities were destroyed by construction of the road. Hacking a neighborhood into two chunks was a main objection to the location of the hotly contested Interstate 40 in Nashville, Tennessee.

Another result of the construction of massive expressways in cities is a peculiar segmentation of the city. Frequently, as in Washington, D.C., highways are built on the informal boundary line between wealthier areas and poor—often black—neighborhoods, thereby turning what was formerly a potentially passable social barrier into an impassable concrete wall. In Cambridge, the Inner Belt, if located on Brookline and Elm streets, would serve to separate the MIT area from much of the low-income Central Square section and would offer a boundary up to which MIT would expand. (Some local politicians speculate that MIT favors the Brookline-Elm route for this reason.)

As one might expect, there has been citizen opposition to the highway, but—in view of the vehemence with which most Brookline-Elm residents decry the road—protest has been surprisingly mild and small-scale.

News of a possible Inner Belt first became common knowledge in 1948. The Brookline-Elm designation for the Cambridge part of the Belt was suggested by the Cambridge city planner in 1958 and officially recommended by the state highway department in 1962. Prior to 1965, however, highway opponents did not have to take the threat of the Belt too seriously because a state law passed in 1961 allowed nine cities, including Cambridge, veto power over any proposed road. (The Cambridge City Council has always officially opposed *all* belt routes through Cambridge, and the city planner who first recommended the Brookline-Elm alignment no longer works for Cambridge.) But in August 1965 the veto was rescinded. Within a matter of weeks, a citizens' antihighway group—Save Our Cities (SOC)— was begun through the joint efforts of an elderly labor organizer and a young housewife, both living in the Brookline-Elm area. At the same time, a small group of young academics and professionals in city-planning and related technical and social science disciplines, none of them personally affected by the road, came together to seek alternatives to the Brookline-Elm route, in order to lower the figure of 1,300 homes that would be taken by the Brookline-Elm alignment. The planners published in the weekly Cambridge paper a series of articles discussing the Belt, the neighborhoods it would cut through and the possibility of alternate routes. From then on, residents and outsiders in SOC joined with the volunteer planners to push alternatives to the Brookline-Elm route. In late 1965 one priest from each of the two large Roman Catholic churches near the Belt route also joined the protest group. The two priests, the labor organizer, the housewife and several of the volunteer planners thereafter provided formal and tactical leadership to the citizen protest.

SOC sponsored a rally at the state capitol in October 1966 and organized a residents' trip to Washington to see Senators Edward Kennedy and Edward Brooke in May 1967. The volunteer planners worked on several alternate route designs, all of them variations of those mentioned above; sponsored an antiroad petition signed by over 500 prominent Harvard and MIT faculty members, including John Kenneth Galbraith and Daniel Patrick Moynihan; and worked with the city council in negotiations with state highway officials over restudy of the Brookline-Elm and alternate routes.

From 1966 to 1968 the citizens' group held public meetings at neighborhood churches and schools once or twice each month. The 60 or 70 people who usually came were informed of the latest anti-Belt activities, offered the opportunity to ask questions or make statements and continually urged by the neighborhood leaders to write protest letters to federal and state officials. About ten of the people at each meeting were interested nonresidents, students and local politicians.

SOC meetings typically combine detailed technical discussions by planners, heated exhortations by neighborhood leaders to citizen action anywhere from letter-writing to civil disobedience and political analysis tempered with religious allusions on the part of the priests. The audience regularly gives heartfelt testimony about how someone was born in the home he now lives in and about how he would have to be dragged out by the state highway engineers before he would move and about how the only way to defeat the Belt is by more people coming to these meetings and by writing more letters and calling more talk shows. Such remarks invariably are followed by enthusiastic applause. At meetings near election time, there are the additional features of a series of emotional speeches by candidates for various state and local offices, usually about how the Belt is "all politics" and how the Brookline-Elm people had been "sold down the river" by certain politicians and institutions (who always remain nameless).

Yet, in the eyes of many residents, highways are projects designed for the public good; this perception, combined with their characteristically strong respect for governmental authority, restrains their tendency to express hostility and resentment toward the Belt and its champions. Nevertheless, almost 80 percent of those interviewed knew that alternate routes had been suggested, and almost two-thirds felt that the road could well be put somewhere else. Many residents also expressed the cynical belief that then Governor John A. Volpe, whose large construction firm has been headed by his brother since Volpe entered public life, stood to gain personally by construction of the Belt he so loudly advocated. (The Volpe Construction Company, incidentally, built the office building in Washington, D.C., that houses the Department of Transportation, which ex-Governor Volpe now heads.)

Neighborhood folklore is traditionally hostile to both Harvard and MIT for reasons including the expansion problem and its effect on rent levels and on neighborhood character. It is particularly bitter towards MIT,

which has announced public opposition to three alternate routes, all of which skirt or cut through its
property and which might take one or more university
buildings, depending on final engineering details. "Tech-
nolgoy" (as the residents call it) is suspected of wielding
behind-the-scenes influence to keep these alternates
from being seriously considered by highway officials.

Despite the residents' generally strong feelings against
moving, however, and their frequent cynical view that
"politics" was behind the choice of the route that will
displace them, most have done little or nothing to
oppose the road. Our interviews show that only about
one-third of all the residents have ever attended any
meetings about the highway. Of the residents who
attended SOC protest meetings, most did so "in order to
find out more about the Belt." Many people attended
one or two meetings, then stayed at home grumbling,
"You never find out anything"—that is, whether or not
the Belt will definitely go through. Only a small number
of those who attended SOC meetings did so explicitly to
learn about other anti-Belt actions; these were mainly
older home owners, who constituted a hard core that
attend meetings month after month. About 30 percent
of the people interviewed posted a "Beat the Belt" sign
or a "Cambridge is a city, not a highway" sign on their
homes; 15 percent wrote to officials; and about 5 or 6
percent of the population took part in the State House
rally.

Most residents believed that the efforts of the protest
were doomed to failure. Perhaps, they said, highway
opponents would manage to hold off the road a while
longer. The negotiating and politicking for restudies by
a combination of city, state and federal politicians, the
priests and SOC neighborhood leaders and the volunteer

planners have so far managed to delay a final decision, and the latest restudy will extend into 1971. But ultimately, said 90 percent of the residents, the road will go through.

This finding is perhaps the most significant of all. It points to widespread feelings of political apathy, impotence and despair that characterize the working-class people along Brookline-Elm and beyond. The typical working-class man or woman accepts, respects and obeys the system. He does what a good citizen should (70 percent of the people we interviewed claimed to vote in state, city and national elections), but he does not feel like an active participant in it; rather, he feels himself essentially acted upon by the system.

Like many working-class people, the residents refer to themselves as the "little people": in their own words, they are "of a common class, people that aren't up in politics. [We] work from one payday to the next." They are the "underdog," "not the degree people," "the average wage-earner," "the lowest," "the kind that can be pushed around. . . . We're the little people."

True, they respect society's institutions and vote in elections, but their bitterness and sense of impotence come out in other ways. "Do you think you have more influence on the government than most people?" residents were asked in a context separate from the Belt issue. A tenth felt that they had more influence; another tenth, that they had less influence; one-third said, "I have the same amount of influence as everyone else" (but many then clarified it—"*no one* has any influence"); and 45 percent—almost half—said, "I have no influence at all." When we asked Brookline-Elm residents if they felt that any level of government was more responsive to citizen appeal than others, about half felt that no level was more responsive, and slightly less answered that city government was more responsive. Later we inquired whether the person being interviewed felt that individuals had any say over what went on in Cambridge; almost two-thirds felt that individuals have little or no say over local government, and half felt that individuals have no say at all.

It is these feelings of silent impotence which are likely, with forced relocation that will deprive many Brookline-Elm people of most of the financial and emotional bases of their sense of stability and self-worth, to turn into a deepening bitterness and anger. It must be stressed that this anger and bitterness will spread among many "little people" not directly affected by this highway but whose convictions that people like themselves have no power over government decisions are confirmed with construction of the highway and forced relocation of the working-class residents. And it is to such people, who know they can be forced to move for a highway that will, in their eyes, only help suburbanites get into downtown Boston a little faster, that right-wing demagogues such as George Wallace speak (at least in the absence of a Robert Kennedy). Their appeals to the "forgotten Americans" who are pushed around by the "intellectuals" and "eggheads" in government bureaucracies tap a raw nerve among the many hard-working, law-abiding working-class and lower-middle-class people throughout America who themselves, or whose friends and relatives, have been made to move for similar highway and urban renewal projects. (The report of the National Commission on Urban Problems, headed by Senator Paul H. Douglas, estimates that for an 11-year period ending in 1968, approximately 330,000 families were displaced by highway construction.)

The Massachusetts state highway department once characterized the Brookline-Elm protest forces as "a handful of cranks." This epithet contains two deeper implications that should be made explicit and discussed: one, that only a small number of people oppose the road; and two, that the opponents to the road are not citizens with a valid complaint that deserves a fair hearing.

The fallacy in the first assumption is obvious. We have just seen the widespread and bitter sense of political alienation and impotence that characterizes the large majority of Brookline-Elm residents. The fact that hundreds of people do not attend every SOC meeting, and that thousands did not come marching on the State House, does not mean that the residents by and large are in favor of the road. On the contrary, the largest portion dread the coming of the highway and resent and fear the public agencies that will throw them out of their homes. But the all-pervading sense of their own smallness in public affairs and belief in their total lack of influence over the government deter most residents from wasting their valuable time and energy and their emotional strength; it is all too likely they will fail anyway. (It must also be pointed out that many low-income people do not take part in community affairs because they are so involved in the day-to-day struggle just to get along.)

The second implication, that the highway opponents are not citizens worthy of consideration but "cranks," combines a number of important but usually unseen issues.

The highway builder claims to be speaking for majority values when he seeks to build a highway to accommodate more and more cars on an ever-speedier trip downtown. In this view, highway opponents are just a bunch of crackpots standing in the way of "progress."

But the Brookline-Elm protestors stand for another value the majority holds dear: the right of each person to live without interference in his own home. Yet they have been unsuccessful in pushing this idea among the general public, and particularly among highway planners.

This is where social class considerations enter. Working-class people feel inadequate to criticze highway designs even though they may strongly oppose them. The world of bureaucracy, technical studies and professional certification is extremely intimidating to a factory worker who may not even have graduated from high school. Therefore, on the unusual occasion when the working-class neighborhood group does meet with middle-class bureaucrats to press its case, it probably enters that meeting from a position of weakness, doubting the legitimacy of its position. To an important extent, the upper-middle-class assumption that technical arguments are more "real" than emotional ones shakes the working-class people's faith in their own case. Many believe, probably, that "experts," by virtue of their training, take all possibilities into consideration and emerge with the wisest possible choice. The working-class person who is cowed by presumed "expert" wisdom at the same time that he feels himself and people like him unfairly treated is no more a contradiction than the middle-class planner or official who preaches the rhetoric of equality and democracy while simultaneously mocking working-class protestors.

From the highway officials' point of view, the working-class petitioners appear to be seen as a bunch of loud, emotional women and rough-spoken, poorly educated men who possess an uninspired way of life that is easily transportable from one frame three-decker to another with little or no harm; they are not seen as a coherent group with a cherished life style rooted in a specific area and with a culture worth preserving. This suggests that, like everyone else, government officials respond to plans and counterplans not only on the merits of the plan but also according to *who* proposes and supports them. If the residents alone went to government highway planners, as deferential petitioners (the characteristic mode of most SOC actions), their pleas would simply be ignored. The various higher status, technically and politically more sophisticated allies who came to the aid of the Brookline-Elm people had an advantage in fighting the highway in that, first of all, highway officials instinctively take them more seriously inasmuch as both government planners and middle-class advocates for the residents "speak the same language." Second, middle-class professionals are now as cowed by authority or intimidated by higher education as are working-class people.

But "who" may be interpreted on another level; that is, if the person approaching the government agency speaks from a base of power, then, regardless of his education or style of dress and speech, he will be taken seriously.

In one sense, the political impotence characterizing the working-class residents of Brookline-Elm may be seen as subjective: they are powerless because most of them believe that they are powerless. But in another sense the working-class people of Brookline-Elm are objectively correct in their assessment of themselves as powerless.

Our political system works on the principle of corporate barter: interest groups represent manufacturers and workers, banks, retailers, universities, realtors, construction firms and the like; but in the area threatened by the highway, there is no "natural" institution that can represent the threatened people to governmental planning agencies.

Labor unions do not concern themselves with this kind of issue. The Catholic church encompasses a significant proportion of the population, and some of the protest leadership has arisen from the clergy of these two churches, with the formerly covert, now overt, approval of Boston's Richard Cardinal Cushing. Yet two active priests bring only themselves into the controversy, not fellow priests or their congregations or the political weight of the church. A few people do belong to political and ethnic-based clubs located in the area, but these clubs attract only a small part of the population and play no role in the Inner Belt controversy, although the very existence of some may directly depend on its outcome. Local, state and national politicians take up the cause of Brookline-Elm residents, but they do so as elected representatives of an unorganized constituency. To say that such representation is adequate in a democracy is to suggest that consumers, since they have elected representatives in government, are as influential on government as manufacturers and retailers. Only a high-school civics text (and maybe a few college ones) would argue that case.

We suggest that there is at this point in history a rarely recognized but much needed role in the planning process. The role is that of a person savvy enough to have some idea of what goes on at both sides of the planning process, who is able to transmit the procedures and assumptions of the planners to the subjects of the planning process and vice versa. In other words, this political broker or middleman would help less politically sophisticated citizens understand that planners are moved not by pleas but by counterplans backed by power and would help the public authorities understand the life styles and goals of the people whose lives they intend to affect.

At the same time, it is to be hoped that the education and the role of the government planner will be expanded in order to avoid such social catastrophes as the construction of the Inner Belt down Brookline and Elm streets. As planners come more and more to recognize the inseparability of physical and social considerations in planning, they may see education and organization of citizens as part of the planning process. And as urban neighborhoods organize, whether to govern school districts, organize community development corporations or protect themselves from highway and urban renewal plans made without their interests in mind, they may become viable political institutions. It may be well for a society to consider encouraging this development, rather than discouraging it, as is likely to be the case.

Urban highways generate at least as much new traffic to their sites as they take off the city streets, add to already polluted air and continue to rob cities of valuable land for parking lots and still more highways as auto travel downtown becomes easier. Maybe it would make more sense to stop trying to find humane relocation procedures for potential displaced persons and instead take their dignity in their neighborhoods and their growing political disaffection as sufficient reason, in combination with the social and ecological harm caused by ever-increasing auto traffic, for defining "progress" in terms other than those of ribbons of concrete and speed of private automobile travel.

September 1970

FURTHER READING

"Neighborhood Protest of an Urban Highway" by Gordon Fellman in the *Journal of the American Institute of Planners* (March 1969).

"Grieving for a Lost Home" by Marc Fried in *The Urban Condition* edited by Leonard J. Duhl (New York: Basic Books, 1963).

"Some Sources of Residential Satisfaction in Our Urban Slums" by Marc Fried and Peggy Gleicher in the *Journal of the American Institute of Planners* (November 1961).

"The Human Implications of Current Redevelopment Relocation Planning" by Herbert Gans in the *Journal of the American Institute of Planners* (February 1959).

The Urban Villagers by Herbert Gans (Glencoe, Ill.: The Free Press, 1962).

Death and Life of Great American Cities by Jane Jacobs (New York: Vintage Books, 1961).

"The Interest in Rootedness: Family Relocation and an Approach to Full Indemnity" by Ernest Norton Tooby in *Stanford Law Review* (April 1969).

Amphetamine Politics on
Capitol Hill

JAMES M. GRAHAM

The American pharmaceutical industry annually manufactures enough amphetamines to provide a month's supply to every man, woman and child in the country. Eight, perhaps ten, billion pills are lawfully produced, packaged, retailed and consumed each year. Precise figures are unavailable. We must be content with estimates because until 1970, no law required an exact accounting of total amphetamine production.

Amphetamines are the drug of the white American with money to spend. Street use, contrary to the popular myths, accounts for a small percentage of the total consumption. Most of the pills are eaten by housewives, businessmen, students, physicians, truck drivers and athletes. Those who inject large doses of "speed" intravenously are but a tiny fragment of the total. Aside from the needle and the dose, the "speed freak" is distinguishable because his use has been branded as illegal. A doctor's signature supplies the ordinary user with lawful pills.

All regular amphetamine users expose themselves to varying degrees of potential harm. Speed doesn't kill, but high sustained dosages can and do result in serious mental and physical injury, depending on how the drug is taken. The weight-conscious housewife, misled by the opinion-makers into believing that amphetamines can control weight, eventually may rely on the drug to alter her mood in order to face her monotonous tasks. Too frequently an amphetamine prescription amounts to a synthetic substitute for attention to emotional and institutional problems.

Despite their differences, all amphetamine users, whether on the street or in the kitchen, share one important thing in common—the initial source of supply. For both, it is largely the American pharmaceutical industry. That industry has skillfully managed to convert a chemical, with meager medical justification and considerable potential for harm, into multi-hundred million dollar profits in less than 40 years. High profits, reaped from such vulnerable products, require extensive, sustained political efforts for their continued existence. The lawmakers who have declared that possession of marijuana is a serious crime have simultaneously defended and protected the profits of the amphetamine pill-makers. The Comprehensive Drug Abuse Prevention and Control Act of 1970 in its final form constitutes a victory for that alliance over compelling, contrary evidence on the issue of amphetamines. The victory could not have been secured without the firm support of the Nixon Administration. The end result is a national policy which declares an all-out war on drugs which are *not* a source of corporate income. Meanwhile, under the protection of the law, billions of amphetamines are overproduced without medical justification.

Hearings in the Senate

The Senate was the first house to hold hearings on the administration's bill to curb drug abuse, the Controlled Dangerous Substances Act (S-3246). Beginning on September 15, 1969 and consuming most of that month, the hearings before Senator Thomas Dodd's Subcommittee to Investigate Juvenile Delinquency of the Committee on the Judiciary would finally conclude on October 20, 1969.

The first witness was John Mitchell, attorney general of the United States, who recalled President Nixon's ten-point program to combat drug abuse announced on July 14, 1969. Although that program advocated tighter controls on imports and exports of dangerous drugs and promised new efforts to encourage foreign governments to crack down on production of illicit drugs, there was not a single reference to the control of domestic manufacture of dangerous drugs. The president's bill when it first reached the Senate placed the entire "amphetamine family" in Schedule III, where they were exempt from any quotas and had the benefit of lesser penalties and controls. Hoffman-LaRoche, Inc. had already been at work; their depressants, Librium and Valium, were completely exempt from any control whatsoever.

In his opening statement, Attorney General Mitchell set the tone of administrative policy related to amphetamines. Certainly these drugs were "subject to increasing abuse"; however, they have "widespread medical uses" and therefore are appropriately classed under the administration guidelines in Schedule III. Tight-mouthed John Ingersoll, director of the Bureau of Narcotics and Dangerous Drugs (BNDD), reaffirmed the policy, even though a Bureau study over the last year (which showed that 92 percent of the amphetamines and barbiturates in the illicit market were legitimately manufactured) led him to conclude that drug companies have "lax security and recordkeeping." The answer, therefore, lay in tighter inventory requirements and in new registration procedures, which are incorporated in the bill.

Senator Dodd was no novice at dealing with the pharmaceutical interests. In 1965 he had steered a drug-abuse bill through the Senate with the drug industry fighting every step of the way. Early in the hearings he recalled that the industry "vigorously opposed the passage of (the 1965) act. I know very well because I lived with it, and they gave me fits and they gave all of us fits in trying to get it through." He would need all the fortitude he could muster in the months to come, for the industry once again was ready to protect its interest and its profits.

The medical position on amphetamine use was first presented by the National Institute of Mental Health's Dr. Sidney Cohen, a widely recognized authority on drug use and abuse. He advised the subcommittee that 50 percent of the lawfully manufactured pep pills were diverted at some point to illicit channels. Some of the pills, though, were the result of unlawful manufacture as evidenced by the fact that 33 clandestine laboratories had been seized in the last 18 months.

Dr. Cohen recognized three categories of ampheta-mine abuse, all of which deserved the attention of the government. First was their "infrequent ingestion" by students, businessmen, truck drivers and athletes. Second were those people who swallowed 50–75 milligrams daily without medical supervision. Finally, there were the speed freaks who injected the drug intravenously over long periods of time. Physical addiction truly occurs, said Dr. Cohen, when there is prolonged use in high doses. Such use, he continued, may result in malnutrition, prolonged psychotic states, heart irregularities, convulsions, hepatitis and an even chance of sustained brain damage.

As the hearings progressed, the first two classes of abusers described by Dr. Cohen would receive less and less attention, while the third category—the speed freaks—would receive increasing emphasis. The amphetamine industry was not at all unhappy with this emphasis. In fact, they would encourage it.

This strategy, while diverting attention away from the problems of prescription amphetamine use, raised a troubling question: Who was supplying the high-dosage user?

Ingersoll had already said that BNDD statistics indicated that only 8 percent of illicit speed was illegally manufactured. Thomas Lynch, attorney general of California, testified that his agents had in 1967 successfully negotiated a deal for one-half million amphetamine tablets with a "Tijuana Café man." Actual delivery was taken from a California warehouse. All of the tablets seized originated with a Chicago company which had not bothered to question the authenticity of the retailer or the pharmacy. Prior to the 1965 hearings, the Food and Drug Administration completed a ten-year study involving 1,658 criminal cases for the illegal sale of amphetamines and barbiturates. Seventy-eight percent of all convictions involved pharmacists, and of these convictions 60 percent were for illicit traffic in amphetamines.

Absurd, responded the executive director of the

National Association of Boards of Pharmacy. His figures showed that while there were over 100,000 pharmacists in the country, only 153 licenses (or 2.95 per year per state) were revoked in the last four years.

The pharmacists were not the source of illicit diversion, according to the National Association of Retail Druggists (NARD) and the National Association of Chain Drug Stores. Indeed, NARD had conducted an extensive educational program combating drug abuse for years, and, as proof of it, introduced its booklet, "Never Abuse—Respect Drugs," into the record. Annual inventories were acceptable for Schedule I and II drugs, NARD continued, but were unwarranted for the remaining two schedules which coincidently included most of their wares—unwarranted because diversion resulted from forged prescriptions, theft and placebo (false) inventories.

The amphetamine wholesalers were not questioned in any detail about diversion. Brief statements by the National Wholesale Druggists Association and McKesson Robbins Drug Co. opposed separate inventories for dangerous drugs because they were currently comingled with other drugs. Finally, the massive volume of the drugs involved—primarily in Schedule III—was just too great for records to be filed with the attorney general.

The representative of the prescription drug developers was also not pressed on the question of illicit diversion. Instead, the Pharmaceutical Manufacturers' Association requested clarifications on the definitional sections, argued for formal administrative hearings on control decisions and on any action revoking or suspending registration, and endorsed a complete exemption for over-the-counter nonnarcotic drugs.

With some misgivings, Carter-Wallace Inc. endorsed

the administration bill providing, of course, the Senate would accept the president's recommendation that meprobamate not be subjected to any control pending a decision of the Fourth Circuit as to whether the drug had a dangerously depressant effect on the central nervous system. On a similar special mission, Hoffman-LaRoche Inc. sent two of its vice-presidents to urge the committee to agree with the president's recommendation that their "minor tranquilizers" (Librium and Valium) remain uncontrolled. Senator Dodd was convinced that both required inclusion in one of the schedules. The Senator referred to a BNDD investigation which had shown that from January 1968 to February 1969, three drug stores were on the average over 30,000 dosage units short. In addition, five inspected New York City pharmacies had unexplained shortages ranging from 12 to 50 percent of their total stock in Librium and Valium. Not only were the drugs being diverted, but Bureau of Narcotics information revealed that Librium and Valium, alone or in combination with other drugs, were involved in 36 suicides and 750 attempted suicides.

The drug company representatives persisted in dodging or contradicting Dodd's inquiries. Angry and impatient, Senator Dodd squarely asked the vice-presidents, "Why do you worry about putting this drug under control?" The response was as evasive as the question was direct: There are hearings pending in HEW, and Congress should await the outcome when the two drugs might be placed in Schedule III. (The hearings had begun in 1966; no final administrative decision had been reached and Hoffman-LaRoche had yet to exercise its right to judicial review.)

In the middle of the hearings, BNDD Director Ingersoll returned to the subcommittee to discuss issues raised chiefly by drug industry spokesmen. He provided the industry with several comforting administrative interpretations. The fact that he did not even mention amphetamines is indicative of the low level of controversy that the hearings had aroused on the issue. Ingersoll did frankly admit that his staff had met informally with industry representatives in the interim. Of course, this had been true from the very beginning.

The president of the American Pharmaceutical Association, the professional society for pharmacists, confirmed this fact: His staff participated in "several" Justice Department conferences when the bill was being drafted. (Subsequent testimony in the House would reveal that industry participation was extensive and widespread.) All the same, the inventory, registration and inspection (primarily "no-knock") provisions were still "unreasonable, unnecessary and costly administrative burden(s)" which would result in an even greater "paper work explosion."

For the most part, however, the administration bill had industry support. It was acceptable for the simple reason that, to an unknown degree, the "administration bill" was a "drug company bill" and was doubtless the final product of considerable compromise. Illustrative of that give-and-take process is the comparative absence of industry opposition to the transfer of drug-classification decision and research for HEW to Justice. The industry had already swallowed this and other provisions in exchange for the many things the bill could have but did not cover. Moreover, the subsequent windy opposition of the pill-makers allowed the administration to boast of a bill the companies objected to.

When the bill was reported out of the Committee on the Judiciary, the amphetamine family, some 6,000 strong, remained in Schedule III. Senator Dodd apparently had done some strong convincing because Librium, Valium and meprobamate were now controlled in Schedule III. A commission on marijuana and a declining penalty structure (based on what schedule the drug is in and whether or not the offense concerned trafficking or possession) were added.

Senate Debate—I

The Senate began consideration of the bill on January 23, 1970. This time around, the amphetamine issue would inspire neither debate nor amendment. The energies of the Senate liberals were consumed instead by unsuccessful attempts to alter the declared law enforcement nature of the administration bill.

Senator Dodd's opening remarks, however, were squarely directed at the prescription-pill industry. Dodd declared that the present federal laws had failed to control the illicit diversion of lawfully manufactured dangerous drugs. The senator also recognized the ways in which all Americans had become increasingly involved in drug use and that the people's fascination with pills was by no means an "accidental development": "Multihundred million dollar advertising budgets, frequently the most costly ingredient in the price of a pill, have, pill by pill, led, coaxed and seduced post-World War II generations into the 'freaked-out' drug culture. . . . Detail men employed by drug companies propagandize harried and harassed doctors into pushing their special brand of palliative. Free samples in the doctor's office are as common nowadays as inflated fees." In the version adopted by the Senate, Valium, Librium and meprobamate joined the amphetamines in Schedule III.

Hearings in the House

On February 3, 1970, within a week of the Senate's passage of S-3246, the House began its hearings. The testimony would continue for a month. Although the Senate would prove in the end to be less vulnerable to the drug lobby, the issue of amphetamines—their danger and medical justification—would be aired primarily in the hearings of the Subcommittee on Public Health of the Committee on Interstate and Foreign Commerce. The administration bill (HR 13743), introduced by the chairman of the parent committee, made no mention of Librium or Valium and classified amphetamines in Schedule III.

As in the Senate, the attorney general was scheduled to be the first witness, but instead John Ingersoll of the BNDD was the administration's representative. On the question of amphetamine diversion, Ingersoll gave the administration's response: "Registration is. . . the most effective and least cumbersome way" to prevent the unlawful traffic. This coupled with biennial inventories of all stocks of controlled dangerous drugs and the attorney general's authority to suspend, revoke or deny registration would go a long way in solving the problem. In addition, the administration was proposing stronger controls on imports and exports. For Schedules I and II, but not III or IV, a permit from the attorney general would be required for exportation. Quotas for Schedules I and II, but not III or IV, would "maximize" government control. For Schedules III and IV, no approval is required, but a supplier must send an advance notice on triple invoice to the attorney general in order to export drugs such as amphetamines. A prescription could be filled only five times in a six-month period and thereafter a new prescription would be required, whereas previously such prescriptions could be refilled as long as a pharmacist would honor them.

The deputy chief counsel for the BNDD, Michael R. Sonnenreich, was asked on what basis the attorney general would decide to control a particular drug. Sonnenreich replied that the bill provides one of two ways: Either the attorney general "finds *actual street abuse* or an interested party (such as HEW) feels that a drug should be controlled." (Speed-freaks out on the street are the trigger, according to Sonnenreich; lawful abuse is not an apparent criterion.) He further emphasized that although scientific opinions would be sought and considered, the decision rested with the attorney general alone.

The registration fee schedule would be reasonable ($10.00—physician or pharmacist; $25.00—wholesalers; $50.00—manufacturers). However, the administration did not want a formal administrative hearing on questions of registration and classification, and a less formal rule-making procedure was provided for in the bill.

Returning to the matter of diversion, Sonnenreich disclosed that from July 1, 1968 to June 30, 1969 the BNDD had conducted full-scale compliance investigations of 908 "establishments." Of this total, 329 (or about 36 percent) required further action, which included surrender of order forms (162), admonition letters (38), seizures (36) and hearings (31). In addition to these full-scale investigations, the Bureau made 930 "visits." (It later came to light that when the BNDD had information that a large supply of drugs was unlawfully being sold, the Bureau's policy was to warn those involved and "90 percent of them do take care of this

matter.") Furthermore, 574 robberies involving dangerous drugs had been reported to the Bureau.

Eight billion amphetamine tablets are produced annually, according to Dr. Stanley Yolles, director of the
National Institute of Mental Health, and although the
worst abuse is by intravenous injection, an NIMH study
found that 21 percent of all college students had taken
amphetamines with the family medicine cabinet acting
as the primary source—not surprising in light of the
estimate that 1.1 billion prescriptions were issued in
1967 at a consumer cost of $3.9 billion. Of this total,
178 million prescriptions for amphetamines were filled
at a retail cost of $692 million. No one knew the
statistics better than the drug industry.

Representing the prescription-writers, the American
Medical Association also recognized that amphetamines
were among those drugs "used daily in practically every
physician's armamentarium." This casual admission of
massive lawful distribution was immediately followed
by a flat denial that physicians were the source of "any
significant diversion." Any such charge was "premature
and not fully substantiated."

The next witness was Donald Fletcher, manager of
distribution protection, Smith Kline & French Laboratories, one of the leading producers of amphetamines.
Fletcher, who was formerly with the Texas state police,
said his company favored "comprehensive controls" to
fight diversion and stressed the company's "educational
effort." Smith Kline & French favored federal registration and tighter controls over exports (by licensing the
exporter, *not* the shipment). However, no change in
present record-keeping requirements on distribution,
production or inventory should be made, and full
hearings on the decisions by the attorney general should

be guaranteed. Without any particular emphasis, Fletcher suggested that HEW have final authority on scientific and medical decisions.

The committee did not ask the leading producer of amphetamines a single question about illicit diversion. Upon conclusion of the testimony, subcommittee Chairman John Jarman of Oklahoma commented, "Certainly, Smith Kline & French is to be commended for the constructive and vigorous and hard-hitting role that you have played in the fight against drug abuse."

Dr. William Apple, executive director of the American Pharmaceutical Association (APhA), was the subject of lengthy questioning and his responses were largely typical. Like the entire industry, the APhA was engaged in a massive public education program. Apple opposed the inventory provisions, warning that the cost would be ultimately passed to the consumer. He was worried about the attorney general's power to revoke registrations ("without advance notice") because it could result in cutting off necessary drugs to patients.

Apple admitted organizational involvement "in the draft stage of the bill" but all the same, the APhA had a "very good and constructive working relationship" with HEW. Apple argued that if the functions are transferred to Justice, "We have a whole new ball game in terms of people. While some of the experienced people were transferred from HEW to Justice, there are many new people, and they are law-enforcement oriented. We are health-care oriented." Surely the entire industry shared this sentiment, but few opposed the transfer as strongly as did the APhA.

Apple reasoned that since the pharmacists were not the source of diversion, why should they be "penalized by costly overburdensome administrative requirements." The source of the drugs, Apple said, were either clandestine laboratories or burglaries. The 1965 Act, which required only those "records maintained in the ordinary course of business" be kept, was sufficient. Anyway, diversion at the pharmacy level was the responsibility of the pharmacists—a responsibility which the APhA takes "seriously and [is] going to do a better job [with] in the future."

Congress should instead ban the 60 mail-order houses which are not presently included in the bill. (One subcommittee member said this was a "loophole big enough to drive a truck through.") The corner druggist simply was not involved in "large-scale diversionary efforts."

There was universal agreement that amphetamines are medically justified for the treatment of two very rare diseases, hyperkinesis and narcolepsy. Dr. John D. Griffith of the Vanderbilt University School of Medicine testified that amphetamine production should be limited to the needs created by those conditions: "A few thousand tablets [of amphetamines] would supply the whole medical needs of the country. In fact, it would be possible for the government to make and distribute the tablets at very little cost. This way there would be no outside commercial interests involved." Like a previous suggestion that Congress impose a one cent per tablet tax on drugs subject to abuse, no action was taken on the proposal.

The Pharmaceutical Manufacturers' Association (PMA) was questioned a bit more carefully in the House than in the Senate. PMA talked at length about its "long and honorable history" in fighting drug abuse. Its representative echoed the concern of the membership over the lack of formal hearings and requested that a representative of the manufacturing interests be appointed to the Scientific Advisory Committee. Significantly, the PMA declined to take a position on the issue of transfer from HEW to Justice. The PMA endorsed the administration bill. PMA Vice-president Brennan was asked whether the federal government should initiate a campaign, similar to the one against cigarettes, "to warn people that perhaps they should be careful not to use drugs excessively." Brennan's response to this cautious suggestion is worth quoting in full:

> I think this is probably not warranted because it would have the additional effect of giving concern to people over very useful commodities. . . . There is a very useful side to any medicament and to give people pause as to whether or not they should take that medication, particularly those we are talking about which are only given by prescription, I think the negative effect would outweigh any sociological benefit on keeping people from using drugs.

The very next day, Dr. John Jennings, acting director of the Food and Drug Administration (FDA), testified that amphetamines had a "limited medical use" and their usefulness in control of obesity was of "doubtful value." Dr. Dorothy Dobbs, director of the Marketed Drug Division of the FDA further stated that there was now no warning on the prescriptions to patients, but that the FDA was proposing that amphetamines be labeled indicating among other things that a user subjects himself to "extreme psychological dependence" and the possibility of "extreme personality changes. . . [and] the most severe manifestation of amphetamine intoxication is a psychosis." Dr. Dobbs thought that psychological dependence even under a physician's prescription was "quite possible."

Congressman Claude Pepper of Florida, who from this point on would be the recognized leader of the anti-amphetamine forces, testified concerning a series of hearings which his Select Committee on Crime had held in the fall of 1969 on the question of stimulant use. Pepper pointed out that each year eight billion amphetamines were lawfully produced, and, according to the BNDD—80 percent of the amphetamines seized in 1968 were part of that lawful production.

Pepper's committee had surveyed medical deans and health organizations on the medical use of amphetamines. Of 53 responses, only one suggested that the drug was useful "for *early* stages of a diet program." (Dr. Sidney Cohen of NIMH estimated that 99 percent of the total legal prescriptions for amphetamines were ostensibly for dietary control.) Pepper's investigation also confirmed a high degree of laxness by the drug companies. A special agent for the BNDD testified that by impersonating a physician, he was able to get large quantities of amphetamines from two mail-order houses in New York. One company, upon receiving an order for 25,000 units, asked for further verification of medical practice. Two days after the agent declined to reply, the units arrived. Before Pepper's committee, Dr. Cohen of NIMH testified that amphetamines were a factor in trucking accidents due to their hallucinatory effects.

Dr. John D. Griffith from Vanderbilt Medical School, in his carefully documented statement on the toxicity of amphetamines, concluded "amphetamine addiction is more widespread, more incapacitating, more dangerous and socially disrupting than narcotic addiction." Considering that 8 percent of all prescriptions are for amphetamines and that the drug companies make only one-tenth of one cent a tablet, Dr. Griffith was not

surprised that there was so little scrutiny by manufacturers. Only a large output would produce a large
profit. Dr. Griffith testified flatly that "making these
drugs available for the treatment of obesity and depression has proved to be quite harmful to the public."

Treatment for stimulant abuse was no easier than for
heroin addiction and was limited to mild tranquiliza-
tion, total abstinence and psychiatric therapy. But,
heroin has not been the subject of years of positive
public "education" programs nor has it been widely
prescribed by physicians or lawfully produced. A health
specialist from the University of Utah pointed out that
the industry's propaganda had made amphetamines:
"One of the major ironies of the whole field of drug
abuse. We continue to insist that they are good drugs
when used under medical supervision, but their greatest
use turns out to be frivolous, illegal and highly
destructive to the user. People who are working in the
field of drug abuse are finding it most difficult to
control the problem, partly because they have the
reputation of being legal and good drugs."

The thrust of Pepper's presentation was not obvious
from the questioning that followed, because the subcommittee discussions skirted the issue. Pepper's impact
could be felt in the subsequent testimony of the
executive director of the National Association of Boards
of Pharmacy. The NABP objected to the use of the
word "dangerous" in the bill's title because it "does
little to enhance the legal acts of the physician and
pharmacist in diagnosing and dispensing this type of
medication." (The Controlled Dangerous Substances
Act would later become the Comprehensive Drug Abuse
Prevention and Control Act of 1970.)

As in the Senate hearings, Ingersoll of the BNDD

returned for a second appearance and, this time, he was the last witness. Ingersoll stated that he wished "to place. . . in their proper perspective" some "of the apparent controversies" which arose in the course of testimony. A substantial controversy had arisen over amphetamines, but there was not a single word on that subject in Ingersoll's prepared statement. Later, he did admit that there was an "overproduction" of amphetamines and estimated that 75 percent to 90 percent of the amphetamines found in illicit traffic came from the American drug companies.

Several drug companies chose to append written statements rather than testifying.

Abbott Laboratories stated that it "basically" supported the administration bills and argued that because fat people have higher mortality rates than others, amphetamines were important to the public welfare, ignoring the charge that amphetamines were not useful in controlling weight. Abbott then argued that because their products were in a sustained-release tablet, they were "of little interest to abusers," suggesting that "meth" tablets per se cannot be abused and ignoring the fact that they can be easily diluted.

Eli Lilly & Co. also endorsed "many of the concepts" in the president's proposals. They as well had "participated in a number of conferences sponsored by the [BNDD] and. . . joined in both formal and informal discussions with the Bureau personnel regarding" the bill. Hoffman-LaRoche had surely watched, with alarm, the Senate's inclusion of Librium and Valium in Schedule III. They were now willing to accept all the controls applying to Schedule III drugs, including the requirements of record-keeping, inventory, prescription limits and registration as long as their "minor tranquilizers" were not grouped with amphetamines. Perhaps, the company suggested, a separate schedule between III and IV was the answer. The crucial point was that they did not want the negative association with speed and they quoted a physician to clarify this: "If in the minds of my patients a drug which I prescribe for them has been listed or branded by the government in the same category as 'goofballs' and 'pep pills' it would interfere with my ability to prescribe. . . and could create a mental obstacle to their. . . taking the drug at all."

When the bill was reported out of committee to the House, the amphetamine family was in Schedule III, and Hoffman—LaRoche's "minor tranquilizers" remained free from control.

Debate in the House - I

On September 23, 1970, the House moved into Committee of the Whole for opening speeches on the administration bill now known as HR 18583. The following day, the anti-amphetamine forces led by Congressman Pepper carried their arguments onto the floor of the House by way of an amendment transferring the amphetamine family from Schedule III into Schedule II. If successful, amphetamines would be subject to stricter import and export controls, higher penalties for illegal sale and possession and the possibility that the attorney general could impose quotas on production and distribution. (In Schedule III, amphetamines were exempt from quotas entirely.) Also, if placed in Schedule II, the prescriptions could be filled only once. Pepper was convinced from previous experience that until quotas were established by law the drug industry would not voluntarily restrict production.

Now the lines were clearly drawn. The House hearings had provided considerable testimony to the effect that massive amphetamine production coupled with illegal diversion posed a major threat to the public health. No congressman would argue that this was not the case. The House would instead divide between those who faithfully served the administration and the drug industry and those who argued that Congress must act or no action could be expected. The industry representatives dodged the merits of the opposition's arguments, contending that a floor amendment was inappropriate for such "far reaching" decisions.

"Legislating on the floor. . . concerning very technical and scientific matters," said subcommittee member Tim Lee Carter of Kentucky, "can cause a great deal of trouble. It can open a Pandora's box" and the amendment which affected 6,100 drugs "would be disastrous to many companies throughout the land."

Paul G. Rogers of Florida (another subcommittee member) stated that the bill's provisions were based on expert scientific and law-enforcement advice, and that the "whole process of manufacture and distribution had been tightened up." Robert McClory of Illinois, though not a member of the subcommittee, revealed the source of his opposition to the amendment:

> Frankly. . . there are large pharmaceutical manufacturing interests centered in my congressional district. . . . I am proud to say that the well-known firms of Abbott Laboratories and Baxter Laboratories have large plants in my [district]. It is my expectation that C. D. Searl & Co. may soon establish a large part of its organization [there]. Last Saturday, the American Hospital Supply Co. dedicated its new building complex in Lake

County. . . where its principal research and related operations will be conducted.

Control of drug abuse, continued McClory, should not be accomplished at the cost of imposing "undue burdens or [by taking] punitive or economically unfair steps adversely affecting the highly successful and extremely valuable pharmaceutical industries which contribute so much to the health and welfare of mankind."

Not everyone was as honest as McClory. A parent committee member, William L. Springer of Illinois, thought the dispute was basically between Pepper's special committee on crime and the subcommittee on health and medicine chaired by John Jarman of Oklahoma. Thus phrased, the latter was simply more credible than the former. "There is no problem here of economics having to do with any drug industry."

But economics had everything to do with the issue according to Representative Jerome R. Waldie of California: "The only opposition to this amendment that has come across my desk has come from the manufacturers of amphetamines." He reasoned that since the House was always ready to combat crime in the streets, a "crime that involved a corporation and its profits" logically merits equal attention. Waldie concluded that the administration's decision "to favor the profits [of the industry] over the children is a cruel decision, the consequences of which will be suffered by thousands of our young people."

Pepper and his supporters had compiled and introduced considerably evidence on scientific and medical opinions on the use and abuse of amphetamines. It was now fully apparent that the evidence would be ignored because of purely economic and political considerations. In the closing minutes of debate, Congressman Robert Giaimo of Connecticut, who sat on neither committee, recognized the real issue: "Why should we allow the legitimate drug manufacturers to indirectly supply the [sic] organized crime and pushers by producing more drugs than are necessary? When profits are made while people suffer, what difference does it make where the profits go?"

Pepper's amendment was then defeated by a voice vote. The bill passed by a vote of 341 to 6. The amphetamine industry had won in the House. In two days of debate, Librium and Valium went unmentioned and remained uncontrolled.

Debate in the Senate - II

Two weeks after the House passed HR 18583, the Senate began consideration of the House bill. (The Senate bill, passed eight months before, continued to languish in a House committee.) On October 7, 1970, Senator Thomas Eagleton of Missouri moved to amend HR 18583 to place amphetamines in Schedule II. Although he reiterated the arguments used by Pepper in the House, Eagleton stated that his interest in the amendment was not solely motivated by the abuse by speed freaks. If the amendment carried, it would "also cut back on abuse by the weight-conscious housewife, the weary long-haul truck driver and the young student trying to study all night for his exams."

The industry strategy from the beginning was to center congressional outrage on the small minority of persons who injected large doses of diluted amphetamines into their veins. By encouraging this emphasis, the drug companies had to face questioning about illicit diversion to the "speed community," but they were able to successfully avoid any rigorous scrutiny of the much larger problem of lawful abuse. The effort had its success. Senator Thomas J. McIntyre of New Hampshire, while noting the general abuse of the drugs, stated that the real abuse resulted from large doses either being swallowed, snorted or injected.

Senator Roman Hruska of Nebraska was not suprisingly the administration and industry spokesman. He echoed the arguments that had been used successfully in the House: The amendment seeks to transfer between 4,000 and 6,000 products of the amphetamine family; "some of them are very dangerous" but the bill provides a mechanism for administrative reclassification; administration and "HEW experts" support the present classification and oppose the amendment; and, finally, the Senate should defer to the executive where a complete study is promised.

It would take three to five years to move a drug into Schedule II by administrative action, responded Eagleton. Meanwhile amphetamines would continue to be "sold with reckless abandon to the public detriment." Rather than placing the burden on the government, Eagleton argued that amphetamines should be classed in Schedule II and those who "are making money out of the misery of many individuals" should carry the burden to downgrade the classification.

Following Eagleton's statement, an unexpected endorsement came from the man who had steered two drug control bills through the Senate in five years. Senator Dodd stated that Eagleton had made "a good case for the amendment." Senator John Pastore was sufficiently astonished to ask Dodd pointedly whether he favored the amendment. Dodd unequivocally affirmed his support. Dodd's endorsement was clearly a turning point in the Senate debate. Hruska's plea that the Senate should defer to the "superior knowledge" of the attorney general, HEW and BNDD was met with Dodd's response that, if amphetamines were found not to be harmful, the attorney general could easily move them back into Schedule III. In Schedule II, Dodd continued, "only the big powerful manufacturers of these pills may find a reduction in their profits. The people will not be harmed." With that, the debate was over and the amendment carried by a vote of 40 in favor, 16 against and 44 not voting.

Dodd may have been roused by the House's failure, without debate, to subject Librium and Valium to controls, which he had supported from the beginning. Prior to Eagleton's amendment, Dodd had moved to place these depressants in Schedule IV. In that dispute, Dodd knew that economics was the source of the opposition: "It is clearly evident . . . that [the industry] objections to the inclusion of Librium and Valium are not so much based on sound medical practice as they are on the slippery surface of unethical profits." Hoffman-LaRoche annually reaped 40 million dollars in profits—"a tidy sum which [they have] done a great deal to protect." Senator Dodd went on to say that Hoffman-LaRoche reportedly paid a Washington law firm three times the annual budget of the Senate subcommittee staff to assure that their drugs would remain uncontrolled. "No wonder," exclaimed Dodd, "that the Senate first, and then the House, was overrun by Hoffman-LaRoche lobbyists," despite convincing evidence that they were connected with suicides and attempted suicides and were diverted in large amounts into illicit channels.

By voice vote Hoffman-LaRoche's "minor tranquilizers" were brought within the control provisions of Schedule IV. Even Senator Hruska stated that he did not oppose this amendment, and that it was "very appropriate" that it be adopted so that a "discussion of it and decision upon it [be] made in the conference."

The fate of the minor tranquilizers and the amphetamine family would now be decided by the conferees of the two houses.

In Conference

The conferees from the Senate were fairly equally divided on the issue of amphetamine classification. Of the eleven Senate managers, at least six were in favor of the transfer to Schedule II. The remaining five supported the administration position. Although Eagleton was not appointed, Dodd and Harold Hughes would represent his position. Hruska and Strom Thurmond, both of whom had spoken against the amendment, would act as administration spokesmen.

On October 8, 1970, before the House appointed its conferees, Pepper rose to remind his colleagues that the Senate had reclassified amphetamines. Although he stated that he favored an instruction to the conferees to support the amendment, he inexplicably declined to so move. Instead, Pepper asked the conferees "to view this matter as sympathetically as they think the facts and the evidence they have before them will permit." Congressman Rogers, an outspoken opponent of the Pepper amendment, promised "sympathetic understanding" for the position of the minority.

Indeed, the minority would have to be content with that and little else. All seven House managers were members of the parent committee, and four were members of the originating subcommittee. Of the seven, only one would match support with "sympathetic understanding." The other six were not only against Schedule II classification, but they had led the opposition to it in floor debate: Jarman, Rogers, Carter, Staggers and Nelsen. Congressman Springer, who had declared in debate that economics had nothing to do with this issue, completed the House representation. Not a single member of Pepper's Select Committee on Crime was appointed as a conferee. On the question of reclassification, the pharmaceutical industry would be well represented.

Hoffman-LaRoche, as well, was undoubtedly comforted by the presence of the four House subcommittee conferees: The subcommittee had never made any attempt to include Valium and Librium in the bill. On that question, it is fair to say that the Senate managers were divided. The administration continued to support no controls for these depressants.

At dispute were six substantive Senate amendments to the House bill: Three concerned amphetamines, Librium and Valium; one required an annual report to Congress on advisory councils; the fifth lessened the penalty for persons who gratuitously distributed a small amount of marijuana; and the sixth, introduced by Senator Hughes, altered the thrust of the bill and placed greater emphasis on drug education, research, rehabilitation and training. To support these new programs, the Senate had appropriated $26 million more than the House.

The House, officially, opposed all of the Senate amendments.

From the final compromises, it is apparent that the Senate liberals expended much of their energy on behalf of the Hughes amendment. Although the Senate's proposed educational effort was largely gutted in favor of the original House version, an additional 25 million dollars was appropriated. The bill would also now require the inclusion in state public health plans of "comprehensive programs" to combat drug abuse, and the scope of grants for addicts and drug-dependent persons was increased. The House then accepted the amendments on annual reports and the possession charge for gratuitous marijuana distributors.

The administration and industry representative gave but an inch on the amphetamine amendment: Only the liquid injectible methamphetamines, speed, would be transferred to Schedule II. All the pills would remain in Schedule III. In the end, amphetamine abuse was restricted to the mainlining speed freak. The conference report reiterated the notion that further administrative action on amphetamines by the attorney general would be initiated. Finally, Librium and Valium would not be included in the bill. The report noted that "final administrative action" (begun in 1966) was expected "in a matter of weeks." Congress was contented to await the outcome of those proceedings.

Adoption of the Conference Report

Pepper and his supporters were on their feet when the agreement on amphetamines was reported to the House on October 14, 1970. Conferee Springer, faithful to the industry's tactical line, declared that the compromise is a good one because it "singles out the worst of these substances, which are the liquid, injectable methamphetamines and puts them in Schedule II." If amphetamine injection warranted such attention, why, asked Congressman Charles Wiggins, were the easily diluted amphetamine and methamphetamine pills left in

Schedule III? Springer responded that there had been "much discussion," yes and "some argument" over that issue, but the conferees felt it was best to leave the rest of the amphetamine family to administrative action.

Few could have been fooled by the conference agreement. The managers claimed to have taken the most dangerous and abused member of the family and subjected it to more rigorous controls. In fact, as the minority pointed out, the compromise affected the least abused amphetamine: Lawfully manufactured "liquid meth" was sold strictly to hospitals, not in the streets, and there was no evidence of any illicit diversion. More importantly, from the perspective of the drug manufacturers, only five of the 6,000-member amphetamine family fell into this category. Indeed, liquid meth was but an insignificant part of the total methamphetamine, not to mention amphetamine, production. Pepper characterized the new provision as "virtually meaningless." It was an easy pill for the industry to swallow. The Senate accepted the report on the same day as the House.

Only Eagleton, the sponsor of the successful Senate reclassification amendment, would address the amphetamine issue. To him, the new amendment "accomplish[ed] next to nothing." The reason for the timid, limpid compromise was also obvious to Eagleton: "When the chips were down, the power of the drug companies was simply more compelling" than any appeal to the public welfare.

A week before, when Dodd had successfully classified Librium and Valium in the bill, he had remarked (in reference to the House's inaction): "Hoffman-LaRoche, at least for the moment, have reason to celebrate a singular triumph, the triumph of money over con-

science. It is a triumph. . . which I hope will be
shortlived."

The Bill Becomes Law

Richard Nixon appropriately chose the Bureau of
Narcotics and Dangerous Drugs offices for the signing of
the bill on November 2, 1970. Flanked by Mitchell and
Ingersoll, the president had before him substantially the
same measure that had been introduced 15 months
earlier. Nixon declared that America faced a major crisis
of drug abuse, reaching even into the junior high
schools, which constituted a "major cause of street
crime." To combat this alarming rise, the president now
had 300 new agents. Also, the federal government's
jurisdiction was expanded: "The jurisdiction of the
attorney general will go far beyond, for example,
heroin. It will cover the new types of drugs, the
barbiturates and amphetamines that have become so
common *and are even more dangerous because of their
use"* (author emphasis).

The president recognized amphetamines were "even
more dangerous" than heroin, although he carefully
attached the qualifier that this was a result "of their
use." The implication is clear: The president viewed
only the large dosage user of amphetamines as an
abuser. The fact that his full statement refers only to
abuse by "young people" (and not physicians, truck
drivers, housewives or businessmen) affirms the implication. The president's remarks contained no mention of
the pharmaceutical industry, nor did they refer to any
future review of amphetamine classification. After a
final reference to the destruction that drug abuse was
causing, the president signed the bill into law.

January 1972

Life in Appalachia
The Case of
Hugh McCaslin

ROBERT COLES

Hugh McCaslin is unforgettable. He has red hair and, at 43, freckles. He stands six feet four. As he talked to me about his work in the coal mines, I kept wondering what he did with his height down inside the earth.

Once he must have been an unusually powerful man; even today his arms and legs are solid muscle. The fat he has added in recent years has collected in only one place, his waist, both front and back.

> I need some padding around my back; it's hurt, and I don't think it'll ever get back right. I broke it bad working, and they told me at first they'd have it fixed in no time flat, but they were wrong. I don't know if they were fooling themselves, or out to fool me in the bargain. It's hard to know *what's* going on around here—that's what I've discovered these last few years.
>
> I'll tell you, a man like me, he has a lot of time

to think. He'll sit around here, day upon day, and what else does he have to keep his mind on but his thoughts? I can't work, and even if I could, there's no work to do, not around here, no sir. They told me I'm 'totally incapacitated,' that's the words they used. They said my spine was hurt, and the nerves, and I can't walk and move about the way I should. As if I needed them to tell me!

Then they gave me exercises and all, and told me I was lucky, because even though I wasn't in shape to go in the mines, I could do anything else, anything that's not too heavy. Sometimes I wonder what goes on in the heads of those doctors. They look you right in the eye, and they're wearing a straight face on, and they tell you you're sick, you've been hurt digging out coal, and you'll never be the same, but you're really not so bad off, because your back isn't so bad you can't be a judge, or a professor, or the president of the coal company or something like that, you know.

Once Hugh McCaslin (not his real name) asked me to look at an X-ray taken of his back and his shoulders—his vertebral column. He persuaded the company doctor to give him the X-ray, or so he said. (His wife told me that he had, in fact, persuaded the doctor's secretary to hand it over, and tell her boss—if he ever asked—that somehow the patient's "file" had been lost.) He was convinced that the doctor was a "company doctor"—which he assuredly was—and a "rotten, dishonest one." Anyway, what did *I* see in that X-ray? I told him that I saw very little. I am no radiologist, and whatever it was that ailed him could not be dramatically pointed out on an X-ray, or if it could I was not the man to do it. Well, yes, he did know that, as a matter of fact:

I got my nerves smashed down there in an

accident. I don't know about the bones. I think there was a lot of pressure, huge pressure on the nerves, and it affected the way I walk. The doctor said it wasn't a fracture on a big bone, just one near the spine. He said it wasn't 'too serious,' that I'd be O.K., just not able to go back to work, at least down there.

Then, you see, they closed down the mine itself. That shows you I wasn't very lucky. My friends kept telling me I was lucky to be alive, and lucky to be through with it, being a miner. You know, we don't scare very easy. Together, we never would talk about getting hurt. I suppose it was somewhere in us, the worry; but the first time I heard my friends say anything like that was to me, not to themselves. They'd come by here when I was sick, and they'd tell me I sure was a fortunate guy, and God was smiling that day, and now He'd be smiling forever on me, because I was spared a *real* disaster, and it was bound to come, one day or another. It kind of got me feeling funny, hearing them talk like that *around my bed*, and then seeing them walk off real fast, with nothing to make *them* watch their step and take a pain pill every few hours.

But after a while I thought maybe they did have something; and if I could just recover me a good pension from the company, and get my medical expenses all covered—well, then, I'd get better, as much as possible, and go fetch me a real honest-to-goodness job, where I could see the sun all day, and the sky outside, and breathe our air here, as much of it as I pleased, without a worry in the world.

But that wasn't to be. I was dumb, real dumb,

and hopeful. I saw them treating me in the hospital, and when they told me to go home I thought I was better, or soon would be. Instead, I had to get all kinds of treatments, and they said I'd have to pay for them, out of my savings or somewhere. And the pension I thought I was supposed to get, that was all in my mind, they said. They said the coal industry was going through a lot of changes, and you couldn't expect them to keep people going indefinitely, even if they weren't in the best of shape, even if it did happen down in the mines.

Well, that's it, to make it short. I can't do hard work, and I have a lot of pain, every day of my life. I might be able to do light work, desk work, but hell, I'm not fit for anything like that; and even if I could, where's the work to be found? Around here? Never in a million years. We're doomed here, to sitting and growing the food we can and sharing our misery with one another.

My brother, he helps; and my four sisters, they help; and my daddy, he's still alive and he can't help except to sympathize, and tell me it's a good thing I didn't get killed in that landslide and can see my boys grow up. He'll come over here and we start drinking. You bet, he's near 80, and we start drinking, and remembering. My daddy will ask me if I can recollect the time I said I'd save a thousand dollars for myself by getting a job in the mines and I say I sure can, and can he recollect the time he said I'd better not get too greedy, because there's bad that comes with good in this world, and especially way down there inside the earth.

He will take a beer or two and then get increasingly

angry. His hair seems to look wilder, perhaps because he puts his hands through it as he talks. His wife becomes nervous and tries to give him some bread or crackers, and he becomes sullen or embarrassingly direct with her. She is trying to "soak up" his beer. She won't even let it hit his stomach and stay there a while. She wants it back. He tells her, "Why don't you *keep* your beer, if you won't let it do a thing for me?"

They have five sons, all born within nine years. The oldest is in high school and dreams of the day he will join the army. He says he will be "taken" in, say, in Charleston or Beckley—in his mind, any "big city" will do. He will be sent off to California or Florida or "maybe New York" for basic training; eventually he will "land himself an assignment—anywhere that's good, and it'll be far away from here, I do believe that." Hugh McCaslin becomes enraged when he hears his son talk like that; with a few beers in him he becomes especially enraged:

That's the way it is around here. That's what's happened to us. That's what they did to us. They made us lose any honor we had. They turned us idle. They turned us into a lot of grazing sheep, lucky to find a bit of pasture here and there. We don't *do* anything here anymore; and so my boys, they'll all want to leave, and they will. But they'll want to come back, too—because this land, it's in their bones going way back, and you don't shake off your ancestors that easy, no sir.

My daddy, he was born right up the road in this here hollow, and his daddy, and back to a long time ago. There isn't anyone around here we're not kin to somehow, near or far. My daddy was the one supposed to leave for the mines. He figured he could make more money than he could dream about, and it wasn't too far to go. He went for a while, but some years later he quit. He couldn't take it. I grew up in a camp near the mine, and I'd still be there if it wasn't that I got hurt and moved back here to the hollow. Even while we were at the camp we used to come back here on Sundays, I remember, just like now they come here on weekends from Cincinnati and Dayton and those places, and even from way off in Chicago. I can recall the car we got; everybody talked about it, and when we'd drive as near here as we could— well, the people would come, my grandparents and all my uncles and aunts and cousins, and they'd look and look at that Ford, before they'd see if it was *us*, and say hello to us. I can recollect in my mind being shamed and wanting to disappear in one of those pockets, where my daddy would keep his pipes. My mother would say it wasn't they didn't want to see us, but the Ford, it was real special to them, and could you blame them for not looking at us?

That was when things were really good. Except that even then I don't think we were all that contented. My mother always worried. Every day, come 3 or so in the afternoon, I could tell she was starting to worry. Will anything happen? Will he get hurt? Will they be coming over soon, to give me some bad news? (No, we had no telephone, and neither did the neighbors.) It got so we'd come home from school around 2 or so, and just sit there with her, pretending—pretending to do things, and say things. And then he'd come in, every time. We could hear his voice coming, or his steps, or the door, and we'd all loosen up—and pretend again, that there was nothing we'd worry about, because there wasn't nothing *to* worry about.

One day—I think I was seven or eight, because I was in school, I know that—we had a bad scare. Someone came to the school and told the teacher something, whispered it in her ear. She turned into a sheet, and she looked as though she'd start crying. The older kids knew what had happened, just from her looks. (Yes, it was a one-room schoolhouse, just like the one we have here, only a little bigger.) They ran out, and she almost took off after them, except for the fact that she remembered us. So she turned around and told us there that something bad had happened down in the mines, an explosion, and we should go home and wait there, and if our mothers weren't there—well, wait until they got home.

But we wanted to go with her. Looking back at it, I think she worried us. So she decided to take us, the little ones. And I'll tell you, I can remember that walk with her like it was just today. I can see it, and I can tell you what she said, and what we did, and all. We walked and walked, and then we came through the woods and there they were, all of a sudden before our eyes. The people there, just standing around and almost nothing being said between them. It was so silent I though they'd all turn around and see us, making noise. But, you see, we must have stopped talking, too, because for a while they didn't even give us a look over their shoulders. Then we come closer, and I could hear there was noise after all: The women were crying, and there'd be a cough or something from some of the miners.

That's what sticks with you, the miners wondering if their buddies were dead or alive down there. Suddenly I saw my father, and my mother. They were with their arms about one another—real unusual—and they were waiting, like the rest.

Oh, we got home that night, yes, and my daddy said they were gone—they were dead and we were going away. And we did. The next week we drove here in our Ford, and I can hear my daddy saying it wasn't worth it, money and a car, if you die young, or you live but your lungs get poisoned, and all that, and you never see the sun except on Sundays.

But what choice did he have? And what choice did I have? I thought I might want to do some farming, like my grandfather, but there's no need for me, and my grandfather couldn't really keep more than himself going, I mean with some food and all. Then I thought it'd be nice to finish school, and maybe get a job someplace near, in a town not a big city. But everything was collapsing all over the country then, and you'd be crazy to think you were going to get anything by leaving here and going out there, with the lines standing for soup—oh yes, we heard on the radio what it was like all over.

It could be worse, you say to yourself, and you resolve to follow your daddy and be a miner. That's what I did. He said we had a lousy day's work, but we got good pay, and we could buy things. My daddy had been the richest man in his family for a while. In fact, he was the only man in his family who had any money at all. After the family looked over our Ford, they'd give us that real tired and sorry look, as though they needed some help real bad, and that's when my daddy would hand out the dollar bills, one after the other. I can picture it right now. You feel rich, and you feel real kind.

Hugh McCaslin's life wouldn't be that much better even if he had not been seriously hurt in a mine accident. The miners who were his closest friends are now unemployed, almost every one of them. They do not feel cheated out of a disability pension, but for all practical purposes he and they are equally idle, equally bitter, equally sad. With no prompting from my psychiatric mind he once put it this way:

They talk about depressions in this country. I used to hear my daddy talk about them all the time, depressions. It wasn't so bad for my daddy and me in the thirties, when the Big One, the Big Depression, was knocking everyone down, left and right. He had a job, and I knew I was going to have one as soon as I was ready, and I did. Then when the war come, they even kept me home. They said we were keeping everything going over here in West Virginia. You can't run factories without coal. I felt I wouldn't mind going, and getting a look at things out there, but I was just as glad to stay here, I guess. I was married, and we were starting with the kids, so it would have been hard. My young brother, he went. He wasn't yet a miner, and they just took him when he was 18, I think. He come back here and decided to stay out of the mines, but it didn't make much difference in the end, anyway. We're all out of the mines now around here.

So, you see it's *now* that *we're* in a depression. They say things are pretty good in most parts of the country, from what you see on TV, but not so here. We're in the biggest depression ever here: We have no money, and no welfare payments, and we're expected to scrape by like dogs. It gets to your mind after a while. You feel as low as can be, and nervous about everything. That's what a depression does, makes you dead broke, with a lot of bills and the lowest spirits you can ever picture a man having. Sometimes I get up and I'm ready to go over to an undertaker and tell him to do something with me real fast.

I have spent days and nights with the McCaslin family, and Hugh McCaslin doesn't always feel that "low," that depressed, that finished with life. I suppose it can be said that he has "adapted" to the hard, miserable life he faces. At times he shouts and screams about "things," and perhaps in that way keeps himself explicitly angry rather than sullen and brooding. His friends call him a "firebrand," and blame his temper on his red hair. In fact, he says what they are thinking, and need to hear said by someone. They come to see him, and in Mrs. McCaslin's words, "get him going." They bring him homemade liquor to help matters along.

The McCaslins are early risers, but no one gets up earlier than the father. He suffers pain at night; his back and his legs hurt. He has been told that a new hard mattress would help, and hot baths and aspirin. He spends a good part of the night awake—"thinking and dozing off and then coming to, real sudden-like, with a pain here or there." For a while he thought of sleeping on the floor, or trying to get another bed, but he could not bear the prospect of being alone:

My wife, Margaret, has kept me alive. She has some of God's patience in her, that's the only way

I figure she's been able to last it. She smiles when things are so dark you'd think the end has come. She soothes me, and tells me it'll get better, and even though I know it won't I believe her for a few minutes, and that helps.

So he tosses and turns in their bed, and his wife has learned to sleep soundly but to wake up promptly when her husband is in real pain. They have aspirin and treat it as something special—and expensive. I think Hugh McCaslin realizes that he suffers from many different kinds of pain; perhaps if he had more money he might have been addicted to all sorts of pain-killers long ago. Certainly when I worked in a hospital I saw patients like him—hurt and in pain, but not "sick" enough to require hospitalization, and in fact "chronically semi-invalids." On the other hand, such patients had tried and failed at any number of jobs. We will never know how Hugh McCaslin might have felt today if he had found suitable work after his accident, or had received further medical care. Work is something a patient needs as he starts getting better, as anyone who works in a "rehabilitation unit" of a hospital well knows. Hugh McCaslin lacked medical care when he needed it, lacks it today, and in his own words needs a "time-killer" as much as a pain-killer. His friends despair, drink, "loaf about," pick up a thing here and there to do, and "waste time real efficiently." So does he—among other things, by dwelling on his injured body.

He dwells on his children, too. There are five of them, and he wants all of them to leave West Virginia. Sometimes in the early morning, before his wife is up, he leaves bed to look at them sleeping:

I need some hope, and they have it, in their young age and the future they have, if they only get the hell out of here before it's too late. Oh, I like it here, too. It's pretty, and all that. It's peaceful. I'm proud of us people. We've been here a long time, and we needed real guts to stay and last. And who wants to live in a big city? I've been in some of our cities, here in West Virginia, and they're no big value, from what I can see, not so far as bringing up a family. You have no land, no privacy, a lot of noise, and all that. But if it's between living and dying, I'll take living; and right here, right now, I think we're dying—dying away, slow but sure, every year more and more so.

He worries about his children in front of them. When they get up they see him sitting and drinking coffee in the kitchen. He is wide-awake and hungrier for company than he knows. He wants to learn what they'll be doing that day. He wants to talk about things, about the day's events and inevitably a longer span of time, the future: "Take each day like your life hangs on it. That's being young, when you can do that, when you're not trapped and have some choice on things." The children are drowsy, but respectful. They go about dressing and taking coffee and doughnuts with him. They are as solicitous as he is. Can they make more coffee? They ask if they can bring him anything—even though they know full well his answer: "No, just yourselves."

Mrs. McCaslin may run the house, but she makes a point of checking every decision with her husband. He "passes on" even small matters—something connected with one of the children's schoolwork, or a neighbor's coming visit, or a project for the church. She is not sly and devious; not clever at appearing weak but "manipulating" all the while. She genuinely defers to her husband, and his weakness, his illness, his inability to find work—and none of those new medical, social, or psychological "developments" have made her see fit to change her ways. Nor is he inclined to sit back and let the world take *everything* out of his hands. As a matter of fact, it is interesting to see how assertive a man and a father he still is, no matter how awful his fate continues to be. He is *there*, and always there—in spirit as well as in body. I have to compare him not only with certain Negro fathers I know, who hide from welfare workers and flee their wives and children in fear and shame and anger, but also with a wide range of white middle-class fathers who maintain a round-the-clock absence from home (for business reasons, for "social" reasons), or else demonstrate a much-advertised "passivity" while there. Hugh McCaslin, as poor as one can be in America, not at all well-educated, jobless, an invalid, and a worried, troubled man, nevertheless exerts a strong and continuing influence upon everyone in his family. He is, again, *there*—not just at home, but very much involved in almost everything his wife and children do. He talks a lot. He has strong ideas, and he has a temper. He takes an interest in all sorts of problems—not only in those that plague Road's Bend Hollow:

My daddy was a great talker. He wasn't taken in by the big people who run this country. He didn't read much, even then when he was young, but he had his beliefs. He said we don't give everyone a break here, and that's against the whole purpose of the country, when it was first settled. You know, there are plenty of people like him. They know how hard it is for a working man to get his share—to get *anything*. Let me tell you, if we had a chance, men like me, we'd vote for a different way of doing things. It just isn't right to use people like they're so much dirt, hire them and fire them and give them no respect and no real security. A few make fortunes and, the rest of us, we're lucky to have our meals from day to day. That's not right; it just isn't.

I tell my boys not to be fooled. It's tough out there in the world, and it's tough here, too. We've got little here except ourselves. They came in here, the big companies, and bled us dry. They took everything, our coal, our land, our trees, our health. We died like we were in a war, fighting for those companies—and we were lucky to get enough money to bury our kin. They tell me sometimes I'm bitter, my brothers do, but they're just as bitter as I am—they don't talk as much, that's the only difference. Of course it got better here with unions and with some protection the workers got through the government. But you can't protect a man when the company decides to pull out; when it says it's got all it can get, so goodbye folks, and take care of yourselves, because we're moving on to some other place, and we just can't do much more than tell you it was great while it lasted, and you helped us out a lot, yes sir you did.

He does not always talk like that. He can be quiet for long stretches of time, obviously and moodily quiet. His wife finds his silences hard to bear. She doesn't know what they will "lead to." Every day she asks her husband whether there is anything "special" he wants to eat—even though they both know there isn't much they can afford but the daily mainstays—bread, coffee, doughnuts, crackers, some thin stew, potatoes, home-made jam, biscuits. Mrs. McCaslin defers to her husband, though; one way is to pay him the courtesy of asking

him what he wants. I have often heard them go back
and forth about food, and as if for all the world they
were far better off, with more choices before them:

Anything special you want for supper?

No. Anything suits me fine. I'm not too hungry.

Well, if that's it then I'd better make you hungry
with something special.

What can do that?

I thought I'd fry up the potatoes real good
tonight and cut in some onions. It's better than
boiling, and I've got some good pork to throw in.
You wait and see.

I will. It sounds good.

He hurts and she aches for him. His back has its "bad
spells," and she claims her own back can "feel the pain
that goes through his." They don't touch each other
very much in a stranger's presence, or even, I gather,
before their children, but they give each other long
looks of recognition, sympathy, affection, and sometimes anger or worse. They understand each other in
that silent, real, lasting way that defies the gross labels
that I and my kind call upon. It is hard to convey in
words—theirs or mine—the subtle, delicate largely un-
spoken, and continual *sense of each other* (that is the
best that I can do) that they have. In a gesture, a glance,
a frown, a smile they talk and agree and disagree.

I can tell what the day will be like for Hugh
when he first gets up. It's all in how he gets out of
bed, slow or with a jump to it. You might say we
all have our good days and bad ones, but Hugh has
a lot of time to give over to his moods, and around
here I guess we're emotional, you might say.

I told her that I thought an outsider like me might
not see it that way. She wanted to know what I meant,

and I told her: "They call people up in the hollow 'quiet,' and they say they don't show their feelings too much to each other, let alone in front of someone like me."

"Well, I don't know about that," she answered quickly, a bit piqued. "I don't know what reason they have for that. Maybe they don't have good ears. We don't talk *loud* around here, but we say what's on our mind, straightaway, I believe. I never was one for mincing on words, and I'll tell anyone what's on my mind, be he from around here or way over on the other side of the world. I do believe we're cautious here, and we give a man every break we can, because you don't have it easy around here, no matter who you are; so maybe that's why they think we're not given to getting excited and such. But we do.

I went back to Hugh. Did she think he was more "emotional" than others living nearby?

Well, I'd say it's hard to say. He has a temper, but I think that goes for all his friends. I think he's about ordinary, only because of his sickness he's likely to feel bad more than some, and it comes out in his moods. You know, when we were married he was the most cheerful man I'd ever met. I mean he smiled all the time, not just because someone said something funny. His daddy told me I was getting the happiest of his kids, and I told him I believed he was right, because I'd already seen it for myself. Today he's his old self sometimes, and I almost don't want to see it, because it makes me think back and remember the good times we had.

Oh, we have good times now, too; don't mistake me. They just come rare, compared to when times were good. And always it's his pain that hangs over us; we never know when he'll be feeling right, from day to day.

But when he's got his strength and there's nothing ailing him, he's all set to work, and it gets bad trying to figure what he might do. We talk of moving, but we ask ourselves where we'd go to. We don't want to travel a thousand miles only to be lost in some big city and not have even what we've got. Here there's a neighbor, and our kin, always. We have the house, and we manage to scrape things together, and no one of my kids has ever starved to death. They don't get the food they should, sometimes, but they eat, and they like what I do with food. In fact they complain at church. They say others don't brown the potatoes enough, or the biscuits. And they like a good chocolate cake, and I have that as often as I can.

When Hugh is low-down he doesn't want to get out of bed, but I make him. He'll sit around and not do much. Every few minutes he'll call my name, but then he won't really have much to say. I have those aspirin, but you can't really afford to use them all the time.

When he feels good, though, he'll go do chores. He'll make sure we have plenty of water, and he'll cut away some wood and lay it up nearby. He'll walk up the road and see people. He has friends, you know, who aren't sick like him, but it doesn't do them much good around here to be healthy. They can't work any more than Hugh can. It's bad, all the time bad.

We find our own work, though, and we get paid in the satisfaction you get. We try to keep the house in good shape, and we keep the road clear all year round. That can be a job come winter.

A lot of the time Hugh says he wished he could read better. He'll get an old magazine—the *Reader's Digest*, or the paper from Charleston—and he'll stay with it for hours. I can see he's having a tough time, but it keeps him busy. He tells the kids to remember his mistakes and not to make them all over again. Then they want to know why he made them. And we're off again. He talks about the coal companies and how they bribed us out of our 'souls,' and how he was a fool, and how it's different now. When they ask what they'll be doing with their reading and writing, it's hard to give them an answer without telling them to move. You don't want to do that, but maybe you do, too. I don't know.

Hugh fought the television. He said it was no good, and we surely didn't have the money to get one. You can get them real cheap, though, second-hand, and there's a chance to learn how to fix it yourself, because some of the men who come back from the army, they've learned how and they'll teach you and do it for you if you ask them. We had to get one, finally. The kids, they said everyone else didn't have the money, any more than we did, but somehow they got the sets, so why couldn't we? That started something, all right. Hugh wanted to know if they thought we could manufacture money. So they wanted to know how the others got their sets. And Hugh said he didn't know, but if they would go find out, and come tell him, why then he'd show them that each family is different, and you can't compare people like that.

Well, then they mentioned it to their uncle—he works down there in the school, keeping it in order, and he's on a regular salary, you know, and lives as good as anyone around here, all things told, I'd say. So he came and told us he'd do it, get a set for us, because the kids really need them. They feel left out without TV.

That got Hugh going real bad. He didn't see why the radio wasn't enough, and he wasn't going to take and take and take. He wanted help, but not for a TV set. And then he'd get going on the coal companies, and how we got that radio for cash, and it was brand-new and expensive, but he was making plenty of money then. And he didn't want to go begging, even from kin. And we could just do without, so long as we eat and have a place to sleep and no one's at our door trying to drive us away or take us to jail.

Finally I had to say something. I had to. It was one of the hardest things I've ever had to do. He was getting worse and worse, and the kids they began to think he was wrong in the head over a thing like TV, and they didn't know why; they couldn't figure it out. He said they wouldn't see anything but a lot of trash, and why should we let it all come in here like that? And he said they'd lose interest in school, and become hypnotized or something, and he'd read someplace it happens. And he said gadgets and machines, they come cheap, but you end up losing a lot more than you get, and that was what's happening in America today.

Now, the kids could listen for so long, and they're respectful to him, to both of us, I think you'll agree. They'd try to answer him, real quiet, and say it wasn't so important, TV wasn't, it was just there to look at, and we would all do it and have a good time. And everyone was having it, but that didn't mean that the world was changing, or that you'd lose anything just because you looked at a picture once in a while.

And finally, as I say, I joined in. I had to—and I sided with them. I said they weren't going to spend their lives looking at TV, no sir, but it would be O.K. with me if we had it in the house, that I could live with it, and I think we could all live with it. And Hugh, he just looked at me and didn't say another word, not that day or any other afterwards until much later on, when we had the set already, and he would look at the news and listen real careful to what they tell you might be happening. He told me one day, it was a foolish fight we all had, and television wasn't any better or worse than a lot of other things. But he wished the country would make more than cheap TVs. 'We could all live without TV if we had something more to look forward to,' he said. I couldn't say anything back. He just wasn't feeling good that day, and to tell the truth TV is good for him when he's like that, regardless of what he says. He watches it like he used to listen to his radio, and he likes it better than he'd ever admit to himself, I'm sure.

On Sundays they go to church. Hugh says he doesn't much believe in "anything," but he goes; he stays home only when he doesn't feel good, not out of any objection to prayer. They all have their Sunday clothes, and they all enjoy getting into them. They become new and different people. They walk together down the hollow and along the road that takes them to a Baptist church. They worship vigorously and sincerely, and with a mixture of awe, bravado, passion, and restraint that leaves an outside observer feeling, well—skeptical, envious, surprised, mystified, admiring and vaguely nostalgic. I think they emerge much stronger and more united for the experience, and with as much "perspective," I suppose, as others get from different forms of contemplation, submission, and joint participation. Hugh can be as stoical as anyone else, and in church his stoicism can simply pour out. The world *is* confusing, you see. People have *always* suffered, good people. Somewhere, somehow, it is not all for naught—but that doesn't mean one should raise one's hopes too high, not on this earth.

After church there is "socializing," and its importance need not be stressed in our self-conscious age of "groups" that solve "problems" or merely facilitate "interaction." When I have asked myself what "goes on" in those "coffee periods," I remind myself that I heard a lot of people laughing, exchanging news, offering greetings, expressing wishes, fears, congratulations and condolences. I think there is a particular warmth and intensity to some of the meetings because, after all, people do not see much of one another during the week. Yet how many residents of our cities or our suburbs see one another as regularly as these "isolated" people do? Hugh McCaslin put it quite forcefully: "We may not see much of anyone for a few days, but Sunday will come and we see everyone we want to see, and by the time we go home we know everything there is to know." As some of us say, they "communicate efficiently."

There is, I think, a certain hunger for companionship

that builds up even among people who do not feel as "solitary" as some of their observers have considered them. Particularly at night one feels the woods and the hills close in on "the world." The McCaslins live high up in a hollow, but they don't have a "view." Trees tower over their cabin, and the smoke rising from their chimney has no space at all to dominate. When dusk comes there are no lights to be seen, only their lights to turn on. In winter they eat at about 5 and they are in bed about 7:30 or 8. The last hour before bed is an almost formal time. Every evening Mr. McCaslin smokes his pipe and either reads or carves wood. Mrs. McCaslin has finished putting things away after supper and sits sewing—"mending things and fixing things; there isn't a day goes by that something doesn't tear." The children watch television. They have done what homework they have (or are willing to do) before supper. I have never heard them reprimanded for failing to study. Their parents tell them to go to school; to stay in school; to do well in school—but they aren't exactly sure it makes much difference. They ask the young to study, but I believe it is against their "beliefs" to say one thing and mean another, to children or anyone else.

In a sense, then, they are blunt and truthful with each other. They say what they think, but worry about how to say what they think so that the listener remains a friend or—rather often—a friendly relative. Before going to bed they say good-night, and one can almost feel the reassurance that goes with the greeting. It is very silent "out there" or "outside."

Yes, I think we have good manners [Hugh McCaslin once told me]. It's a tradition, I guess, and goes back to Scotland, or so my daddy told me. I tell the kids that they'll know a lot more than I do when they grow up, or I hope they will; but I don't believe they'll have more consideration for people—no sir. We teach them to say hello in the morning, to say good morning, like you said. I know it may not be necessary, but it's good for people living real close to be respectful of one another. And the same goes for the evening.

Now, there'll be fights. You've seen us take after one another. That's O.K. But we settle things on the same day, and we try not to carry grudges. How can you carry a grudge when you're just this one family here, and miles away from the next one? Oh, I know it's natural to be spiteful and carry a grudge. But you can only carry it so far, that's what I say. Carry it until the sun goes down, then wipe the slate clean and get ready for another day. I say that a lot to the kids.

Once I went with the McCaslins to a funeral. A great-uncle of Mrs. McCaslin's had died at 72. He happened to be a favorite of hers and of her mother. They lived much nearer to a town than the McCaslins do, and were rather well-to-do. He had worked for the county government all his life—in the Appalachian region, no small position. The body lay at rest in a small church, with hand-picked flowers in bunches around it. A real clan had gathered from all over, as well as friends. Of course it was a sad occasion, despite the man's advanced age; yet even so I was struck by the restraint of the people, their politeness to one another, no matter how close or "near kin" they were. For a moment I watched them move about and tried to block off their subdued talk from my brain. It occurred to me that, were they dressed differently and in a large manor home, they might very much resemble English gentry at a reception. They were courtly people; they looked it and acted it. Many were tall, thin and close-mouthed. A few were potbellied, as indeed befits a good lusty duke or duchess. They could smile and even break out into a laugh, but it was always noticeable when it happened. In general they were not exactly demonstrative or talkative, yet they were clearly interested in one another and had very definite and strong sentiments, feelings, emotions, whatever. In other words, as befits the gentry, they had feelings but had them under "appropriate" control. They also seemed suitably resigned, or philosophical—as the circumstances warranted. What crying there was, had already been done. There were no outbursts of any kind, and no joviality either. It was not a wake.

A few days later Hugh McCaslin of Road's Bend Hollow talked about the funeral and life and death:

He probably went too early, from what I hear. He was in good health, and around here you either die very young—for lack of a doctor—or you really last long. That's the rule, though I admit we have people live to all ages, like anywhere I guess. No, I don't think much of death, even being sick as I am. It happens to you, and you know it, but that's O.K. When I was a boy I recall my people burying their old people, right near where we lived. We had a little graveyard, and we used to know all our dead people pretty well. You know, we'd play near their graves, and go ask our mother or daddy about who this one was and what he did, and like that. The other way was through the Bible: Everything was written down on pieces of paper inside the family Bible. There'd be births and marriages and deaths, going way back, I guess as far back as the beginning of the country. I'm not sure of the exact time, but a couple of hundred years, easy.

We don't do that now—it's probably one of the biggest changes, maybe. I mean apart from television and things like that. We're still religious, but we don't keep the records, and we don't bury our dead nearby. It's just not that much of a *home* here, a place that you have and your kin always had and your children and theirs will have, until the end of time, when God calls us all to account. This here place—it's a good house, mind you—but it's just a place I got. A neighbor of my daddy's had it, and he left it, and my daddy heard and I came and fixed it up and we have it for nothing. We worked hard and put a lot into it, and we treasure it, but it never was a *home*, not the kind I knew, and my wife did. We came back to the hollow, but it wasn't like it used to be when we were kids and you felt you were living in the same place all your ancestors did. We're *part* of this land, we were here to start and we'll probably see it die, me or my kids will, the way things are going. There will be no one left here and the stripminers will kill every good acre we have. I thought of that at the funeral. I thought maybe it's just as well to die now, if everything's headed in that direction. I guess that's what happens at a funeral. You get to thinking.

June 1968

FURTHER READING

Night Comes to the Cumberlands by Harry M. Caudill (Boston: Little Brown, 1963).

Stinking Creek by John Fetterman (New York: E.P. Dutton, 1967).

Yesterday's People by Jack A. Weller (Lexington, Ky.: University of Kentucky Press, 1965).

Invisible
Migrant Workers

DOROTHY NELKIN

Early last summer, the soft earth of a California peach orchard yielded the bodies of 25 nameless murder victims. Their anonymity was made less astonishing by the discovery that all the dead men were migrant farm workers—a group whose isolation from society is well known. Indeed, the accounts of the lives of migratory workers from *Grapes of Wrath* to *Harvest of Shame* have described these people as invisible to the rest of American society. But are they invisible even to each other? Was there no one to miss the slain men? Surely no group can be so alienated as to accept murder rather than call the police—or can it?

To discover just what social forces could account for the namelessness of migrant faces, a four-year partici-pant-observation study was made of black migrant farm workers in the northeastern United States. The findings suggest that migrant invisibility is systematic—that it is controlled by mechanisms both from within and with-out the migrant group.

Though the migrant worker may live in a camp five months out of a year, his communication with the permanent community is kept at a minimum. First, he is often physically isolated. Camps are usually located in out-of-the-way sites several miles from the nearest town. And since most migrants were brought North on a bus by a crew leader, they rarely have their own means of transportation. If community facilities near camps are used there are often separate stores and laundromats so that migrants are segregated from local residents. Other more subtle barriers also separate the migrants from local populations. For example, the illegal sale of alcohol in camps is not only ignored, but sometimes encouraged in the hope that the migrants will drink in camp rather than in the town bars.

Sodus Village is the center of one such agricultural area; there are 50 labor camps in the township with facilities for housing about 1,000 workers. Many of their employers live in the village, which has a popula-tion of 1,233 of age 14 or over. Even though migrants use the town laundromats and gas stations, shop in the stores and drink at the local bar, a random sampling of the townspeople showed that over two-thirds had no direct contact with the workers. Nearly 10 percent said they had never noticed a labor camp nearby. Even among the majority who were aware of the camps, having noticed them from the highway, knowledge of life within the camps was vague or nonexistent. Despite their physical presence in the community they are not a part of it. The migrant is an outsider, an element to be dealt with as a problem.

An agricultural community may have church or lay

groups concerned with migrant welfare. Their interest ranges broadly from prayer and indignation to the management of day schools and child-care centers. Old clothes, money and transportation services are often provided when there are people with the energy and ability to organize collections. It was found, however, that the clergy were more interested in social action programs than were their parishioners. One minister had been working with migrants for several years and, despite a highly conservative parish consisting largely of growers, devoted considerable energy to providing social services in nearby labor camps. His parishioners had not complained about his activities with the migrant workers, but they did not volunteer to participate personally in his programs. Torn between his desire to help the migrants and his obligations to his parish, he hesitated to spend much time on migrant-worker problems. When asked if his parishioners would mind if migrants came to the church, he replied that the question never came up. Since there was absolutely no social contact between the two groups, the migrants would "just not be interested in coming." He strongly asserted that migrants "do better in their own situation," and that he would not consider encouraging a migrant to attend services in his church. His activities consisted primarily of showing films and bringing athletic equipment to the camp. But the migrants were apathetic toward his efforts, and he felt that he had failed to accomplish anything of significance. Totally frustrated, he was waiting for mechanization to solve the problem by drying up the migrant labor stream.

The habit of ignoring controversial or disturbing problems in a community is seldom a conscious one but may surface during a crisis. In one agricultural area, a migrant child-care center was about to close in the middle of the summer because the public-school building in which it was located was no longer available. A local minister was under pressure to find an alternate location. When asked about the possibility of using his Sunday-school building, he said it would be impossible since there was a very small septic tank and the system would be ruined if more people used the toilets. He finally admitted, however, that the vestry was more liberal than the parishioners, who were quite willing to supply old clothes as long as the migrants remained in their camps; caring for their children on church property was another matter.

The success of other agencies concerned with migrant welfare has been similarly limited. State and federally sponsored antipoverty programs have been organized to change the migrant labor situation, but social workers have had difficulty in communicating with their clients and arousing interest in the programs provided. Social workers tend to assume that the value of their offerings is self-evident, that they need only bring what they think is necessary into the camps, and the migrants will welcome them. They are often dismayed to discover this is not the case. There are a number of possible reasons for this breakdown in communications: the attitude of migrants commonly labeled apathy, the irrelevance of the particular program offered and the fear that outsiders are only introducing one more exploitative mechanism.

A more important factor in the failure of most programs, however, is that client invisibility is built into the sponsoring organizations themselves. The experience of one social-work organization will serve as an example. Though its stated purpose was to improve conditions for migrants and to enable them to deal knowledgeably and effectively with society, agency staff members indicated that they were perpetually frustrated by lack of rapport with migrants in the camps they visited. The director of this agency knew little about his clients and seldom visited the camps in which his program operated, working instead through subordinate field instructors. In spite of his limited activity in the field, he ran the program in a centralized and authoritarian manner, and the field instructors, who had day-to-day familiarity with the camps, often found themselves disagreeing with his decisions.

For the most part, field instructors occupied their time playing with children and showing films, many of which were inappropriate to the audience. For example, one oil-company advertisement exalted the American farmer and pictured him as a national hero, fair and blond, driving his tractor across the many acres of his farm. Another was a sex education film originally developed for a middle-class school audience.

Field instructors were constrained by the centralization of decision-making in the organization and by inadequate preparation for work with migrants. Training sessions had been conducted by teachers who had experience in industrial personnel work, but who had no knowledge of problems peculiar to the migrant system. Thus, much energy was deflected to handling problems within the organization itself.

This agency and others are hampered by their dependence on local authorities. They must adjust their activities more to established community interests than to the migrants who make few conspicuous demands. Thus, their primary goals become the avoidance of disruption and the maintenance of a level of satisfaction which will minimize demands. At the same time they must make sure that educational programs, health care and other activities do not interfere with the harvest.

National or statewide church organizations occasionally employ social workers to deal with migrant labor problems. They select personnel who will work quietly, offering services that will keep the migrants happily ensconced in the camps. One social worker regularly tried to call attention to problems in the camp. His organization disapproved, and he was eventually asked to submit his resignation.

Other programs have been hampered by the insensitivity of social workers themselves, some of whom have been observed conducting themselves in camps as if their clients were not there. One such worker talked to a friend while showing movies one evening. He was unaware that their conversation was interfering with the sound track. The viewers, distracted by the voices, kept looking back, but the two men continued to talk in a normal tone until the end of the film. In another case, a social worker invited a researcher to see some migrant rooms. When knocking produced no response from the occupant of one room, he went in anyway. He asked another woman if he could show her room to the observer but had opened the door and was inside before she had a chance to answer. The woman said nothing. It did not occur to him that his actions were an invasion of privacy and later, oblivious to the people nearby, he declared that this was his favorite camp because "people are very friendly and there is never any threat of trouble."

Even genuinely concerned volunteers find themselves constrained by community pressures. One woman had written a letter to the welfare department concerning incidents in which migrants were refused medical attention. When inspectors were sent to investigate the matter, delegations of concerned citizens visited her home to ask her to retract her statements. Other outspoken volunteers have been effectively controlled by their organizations and reassigned to innocuous jobs. One black social worker described by his co-workers as "not very well liked here" was under pressure from colleagues who feared he would "cause trouble." He had been critical of interminable meetings and of other social workers who avoided going to the camps. In the camps, however, where he distributed Social Security cards and dispensed information about jobs and events outside the camp, observers noted that he was more effective and had closer rapport with the migrants than had any of the other social workers. He eventually left the organization.

Because they find it difficult to work without an organizational base and equally difficult to work within the existing ones, many of the most concerned and active people drop out of migrant work altogether. For most social work activities are directed only toward making the migrant situation more bearable and not to changing it—films and old clothes are brought to the camps, women are trained to prepare surplus food and people are taught their rights *as migrants*. These activities are indeed important, but only help migrants adapt more efficiently to their present circumstances. Relatively few programs in the North are specifically directed toward training people for jobs out of the migrant labor stream. The experience of participants and observers alike in the study provides a strong indication that the invisibility of migrants is built into the very institutions created to deal with them.

Migrant invisibility is evident in the recruitment process itself. Arrangements for recruiting agricultural labor are handled through the farm labor division of the state employment services. For example, the grower makes his manpower needs known in the early spring and contracts are negotiated with crew leaders via the Farm Labor Service in Florida to transport a specified number of workers North on a specified date. Here the responsibility of the employment service and often of the grower ends. The migrant himself in involved only when he is signed up by the crew leader, who acts as intermediary throughout the season. Growers provide camps and work sites, but many prefer to leave all dealings with the migrants themselves to the crew leaders. For example, 67 percent of 119 migrants interviewed had never been directly supervised by a grower. This avoidance of contact is often maintained at the expense of efficiency.

The crew leader system, developed from the delegation of employment responsibility, perpetuates migrant invisibility. It is the crew leader who assumes all responsibility, not only for recruitment and work supervision, but also for the sustenance of his crew, the policing of the camp, transportation and the provision of other services normally provided by a community. However, he is not accountable to outside authorities for these maintenance activities and may even have a stake in concealing how they are carried out—a point suggested by the threats made against farm workers who agree to testify before an investigating committee.

The desire of growers to minimize public awareness of their labor camps was apparent in the no trespassing signs found at the entrance of many camps, the difficulties encountered by VISTA volunteers who found themselves barred from some camps and problems in attempting to place students in camps for research purposes. One grower, who is in fact active on several migrant service committees, contends that the condition of migrants has greatly improved, but the problem now is that there are far too many social agencies involved. According to this grower, social workers do not recognize that migrants have different cultural backgrounds and that "they do not need the same things we do." From his perspective, most social work activities are destructive because they create unfavorable publicity. The growers' position is understandable in light of their vested interest in leaving things as they are. The subtle pervasiveness of this tendency is better illustrated by groups whose self-interest is less obvious.

Government inspectors are responsible for deciding whether or not migrant camps meet minimum standards. The main inspection occurs prior to the season, before the occupants of the camp arrive. Subsequent inspections, if they occur at all, are cursory. There are complex structural problems in the current system of inspection in New York State which hamper its effectiveness. The New York State Joint Legislative Committee Report in 1967 noted that local county health officers were not adequately enforcing the state sanitary code. "It is the opinion of this Committee that the County health officers and their assistants are too close to the leadership structure in the county, where the migrants are non-voters and have no representation in the power structure of these counties." As members of the local community, inspectors are often friends of growers and see them regularly the year round which may make it more difficult for them to enforce regulations. One inspector asserted in an interview that there was no exploitation in labor camps and that most migrants have too many expectations. He suggested that a large, self-contained labor camp be built with complete service facilities, including stores, clinics and child-care centers. This would avoid scattering people in tenant houses and small camps throughout agricultural communities. While such an arrangement might be convenient in terms of the availability of services, it is a solution that would further reduce migrant visibility.

Although enforcement problems are ubiquitous, legislation concerning labor camps places the burden of responsibility on the individual inspector. A content analysis of the New York State Health Code introduced in March 1968 reveals that in 16 items, the decision on the acceptability of a given condition is left to the discretion of the permit-issuing official. Other aspects of this legislation, intended to improve the situation, reveal an ignorance of the social realities in the camps and demonstrate the dangers of piecemeal improvement of a fundamentally poor situation. The vagueness of the earlier legislation had given the migrant a certain degree of independence from the crew leader. For example, because he was allowed to cook food in his room, he could avoid paying for prepared meals. Ironically, the new legislation, intended to improve fire safety, set minimum standards for cooking areas and left no alternative but to buy meals from the crew leader, thereby reinforcing his control. The intended solution of one problem only served to exacerbate another.

Camp conditions were the focus of a crisis that occurred when an organizer convinced a migrant to discuss the problems of farm labor on the radio. He described the decrepit buildings, the lack of sufficient water supply and the inadequate cooking and bathroom facilities. Despite the fact that the program was broadcast on an FM station with relatively few listeners, the publicity was sufficient to arouse not only local growers, but also community groups ostensibly concerned with improving just those conditions criticized. The next morning the grower, an inspector and the crew leader questioned the migrant who had appeared on the program and asked him to leave the camp. He went to town to rent a trailer, but later when he returned for his clothes, he was discouraged from leaving by the grower who feared further publicity.

One irate official at the government employment office complained that such publicity calls attention only to the worst camps, while ignoring all the positive changes in the migrant situation. The organizer, he felt, was interfering in what was none of his business. A church volunteer criticized the organizer, saying that he had angered a lot of people by intruding too aggressively; this would do more harm than good, for it would be damaging to social work programs in the area. The migrant who participated in the broadcast was spoken of with disdain ("He brought his own Beautyrest mattress north"), suggesting that he was not a real migrant because he showed concern with his own comfort.

A more serious incident revealed the extent and consequences of the invisibility of the migrant laborers. During the summer of 1966, a group of migrants in an agricultural community marched into town as a protest against their conditions, and fear of a riot was expressed. The event shocked community officials who had assumed that the migrants were well satisfied with the circumstances in which they lived. "Why," said the mayor, "they walked by here on the road and I waved to them and they laughed and smiled . . . real happy, you know." And the wife of the police chief noted, "this place is a paradise compared to what they are used to living in. Of course you or I wouldn't want to live that way, but I believe they like it fine."

Such a total lack of communication with the migrants is not entirely the fault of the community. The migrants themselves, as an outgroup subject to external pressures, control their visibility for purposes of protection in somewhat the same way as gypsies have developed subtle and complex mechanisms for maintaining a mystique of obscurity. Gypsies know back roads and inconspicuous gathering places, employ a private language and use decoys and facades such as fortune-telling; the latter diverts attention from what they consider to be the really important aspects of their culture. Invisibility permits autonomy and limits interference.

Migrants too are concerned primarily with self-protection. Living in the North for only part of the year and unfamiliar with many physical and social aspects of their environment, they feel isolated and alien. One articulate individual described his discomfort. In the South he knew where he could go and what he could do without getting into trouble; in the North he was never certain and he never knew what people were thinking. "Here people don't know where they stand and they are self-conscious all the time."

A second incentive for controlling visibility lies in the migrant's lack of autonomy. Control comes from outside the group and from such unpredictable sources as the weather and "the Man." Invisibility allows a sense of independence: "I don't drink. I mind my own business. It depends on how you act. If you're careful there'll be no trouble."

Finally, it is often pragmatically convenient to be invisible. Families needing income from their children's labor, for example, must be sensitive to their visibility when inspectors come to the fields.

Children working illegally often disappear from view as soon as state-government license plates are spotted. In one case, researchers using state vehicles found that their cars had to be relicensed or many people in the camps would disappear upon their arrival.

In many cases, crew leaders conceal overcrowded camp conditions. In one camp, approved for 86 occupants, there were 120 people, a discrepancy never noticed until a count was required for purposes of allocating government food during a time when there was no work. When the situation of overcrowding became visible, the crew leader with a logic clear only to himself eliminated 34 names, claiming that exactly 86 people were eligible. In effect he was able to make more than one-fourth of his crew disappear.

Certain aspects of migrant behavior correspond strikingly to the process of information control that Erving Goffman has described as "stigma management." To maintain invisibility in Goffman's terms, it is necessary to avoid any action which might violate the expectations of others. This is an important group norm in migrant camps. There is considerable pressure to avoid arguing with a farmer or supervisor regardless of provocation. When one man spoke back to a farmer in a mildly facetious manner, he was immediately rebuked by the group for acting in this unexpected and therefore conspicuous fashion. Similarly, there are normative sanctions against picking too rapidly or too slowly. One must not stand out by working apart from the group and thereby possibly calling attention to the pace of others. Norms against ratebusting are of course not unique to this group, but they are particularly salient in this case because of the limited channels through which individuals may achieve mobility.

Similarly, group norms tend to level participants, to put down those who want to assume leadership. The outside society which perceives migrants as an undifferentiated group reinforces this leveling tendency and thus perpetuates stagnation.

Field researchers were struck by the dual personality exhibited by many migrants who assumed a meek demeanor in the presence of white people, but who were aggressive among their peers. To remain inconspicuous, these migrants had learned to assume different styles of behavior that meshed with the expectations of others. Thus, they manage the information that others receive about them.

A visitor to a migrant camp will often find himself next to a juke box turned up to full volume or faced with other means to limit communication, such as garbled accents, hand over mouth or silence. When not confronted directly, migrants maintain invisibility by simply avoiding outsiders.

Since there are few visitors, migrants remain unseen simply by staying in the camps. Certain people, primarily older workers, chose to stay out of town even when a ride was available. Younger people appeared less concerned, but when they did go to town they avoided unfamiliar areas. Once in the public eye, normative constraints against calling attention to the group were in operation. One young shoplifter was warned repeatedly, "don't cause trouble." Migrants hesitated to enter stores. In one case, a man who tried on a pair of shoes was afraid not to buy them. Although he did not want the shoes, he felt it would be less conspicuous to buy them than to leave without a purchase. A group of migrants on a truck being serviced at a garage would not ask for the key to the rest room, nor would they go into the station to buy soda.

The reluctance to call on outside authority is another symptom of the desire to maintain invisibility. Police are rarely requested to manage internal problems. Since migrants tend to distrust police authority, crew leaders prefer to maintain control themselves. When a police inquiry does take place, it is usually at the instigation of outsiders. For example, one man alienated several people in his camp and, afraid they would beat him, fled the camp. Local white residents who were concerned by his presence in their neighborhood initiated a police inquiry.

The police prefer to avoid involvement: A police officer, interviewed about his investigation of a fight between two migrants that occurred in the town, said that he instructed a group of migrants who had observed the fight to take care of the problem. "These are your people, you take care of them." They obliged by driving the men back to the camp. The officer claimed that he like to avoid arresting migrants since it would keep them out of work. He preferred to ignore incidents and just to "quiet things down." Those migrants who do want police protection resent such an attitude, though they have come to expect it.

Migrant invisibility, then, is fostered both by the migrants themselves in an effort to adapt to their particular circumstances as well as by employers and social work groups and poverty organizations seeking to improve the situation. Groups seeking change share the preconception that while there are many problems, there are no alternatives to present arrangements. Solutions to problems are seen to lie in small, non-structural changes. The primary concern is to avoid disturbing incidents which might in any way threaten the existing system. The tendency is to isolate migrants, to keep them in the camps where there is minimum visibility and limited contact with the outside community.

To render the migrant visible would expose the depths of the problem and certainly jeopardize the interests of those who have a stake in the system as it presently operates. Open acknowledgement of the existence of a social situation that is dissonant with basic social values would call these conditions into question. As long as the migrant remains out of sight, he is also out of mind. Disturbance may be minimized, but the obvious question remains: Can an invisible problem be resolved?

April 1972

FURTHER READING

On the Season: Aspects of the Migrant Labor System, by Dorothy Nelkin (New York State School of Industrial and Labor Relations, Cornell University, publication no. 8, November 1970).

Migrant: Agricultural Workers in America's Northeast, by William H. Friedland and Dorothy Nelkin (New York: Holt, Rinehart & Winston, September 1971).

"Our Invisible Poor" by Dwight MacDonald in *Poverty in America* edited by Ferman, Kornbluh and Haber, revised edition (Ann Arbor: University of Michigan Press, 1968).

The Slaves We Rent, by Truman Moore (New York: Random House, 1965).

Why Employment-Agency Counselors Lower their Clients' Self-Esteem

THOMAS M. MARTINEZ

There are more than 5,000 private employment agencies in the United States, and their numbers increase about 15 percent per year. The "job counselors" working for these agencies fill millions of positions annually—90 percent in white-collar, salaried jobs. Private employment agencies are thus a major force in our national employment picture.

But the fact is that many job counselors are hired as a species of salesman, and they are seldom expert in any other role; the business of the agency may not be obtaining jobs, but obtaining fees; and the counseling services may consist, in large part, of manipulating the applicant to lower his sense of his own worth, thus making it easier for the counselor to place the applicant in a job and obtain a fee.

During the summer of 1964 I worked as a counselor for a private agency in a large Midwestern city. As a participant observer I gathered material for this study, focusing on how the counselor attempts to manipulate the applicant's definition of himself to make it easier to place him in a job quickly; and how the agency itself selects and shapes the personalities of its counselors.

The whole process starts with the job opening. A few of these openings are called in by the interested companies—usually the jobs are for some specialists the company is having difficulty in hiring. But the majority of the openings are obtained when the counselors call the companies, ostensibly to stimulate interest in the qualifications of some particular applicant or applicants. During the call, the counselor inquires about other possible personnel needs. Here is a sample presentation, used by my agency to teach its counselors how to "sell":

> Sir, my name is ———. I'm with the ——— department of ——— Agency. I don't know what you have open, but I'm calling in regards to a ——— [title of position, like "industrial engineer"] who has ——— years of experience, ——— education, and is [married or unmarried]. He is presently [employed or unemployed] and available for an interview [give possible time].
>
> If the employer expresses a desire to see the applicant, then obtain the following information: the salary paid for the position and their policy on the fee (who pays, the employer or the applicant?). If the employer does not want to commit himself on the salary, ask him the highest and the lowest he will pay for that position.

Unlike the applicants themselves, counselors looking for openings generally bypass personnel departments, especially in the smaller companies, and go straight to the executives involved. The executives know more about the specific jobs; they do the actual hiring; and they do not feel so threatened by employment agencies as do the personnel managers. After all, in theory, if a personnel manager were doing his job properly, employment agencies might not be necessary.

Applicants are recruited by four basic methods:

1) Over 70 percent come in voluntarily, in answer to ads.

2) Some are referred to the agency by a particular counselor or friend.

3) A few are solicited from names obtained from other applicants or friends.

4) In a very few cases, an alert counselor recruits the potential employer (personnel manager, vice-president) himself as an applicant for some other position.

Those who come to the agency on their own are the most eager, and the most willing, to be manipulated.

To the private agency, the applicant is a commodity— he has "market value." And the agency tries to manipulate him to make him more easily handled and more easily sold.

As the typical applicant enters the glass doors of the twelfth-floor office, he meets a female receptionist. She asks him, "Have you ever been here before?" If he has not, she hands him a five-by-eight-inch background-information card. Hastily, she tells him to take a seat in the area to which she points, to fill out the card, and to return it to her as soon as he is finished.

Within 60 seconds after the applicant returns his card to the receptionist, one of the department managers whom the receptionist summoned rushes to her desk and takes the card. The manager reads the applicant's name aloud. As he approaches his caller, the manager thrusts his hand forward as an invitation to shake. The manager shakes his hand once, briefly but firmly, gives his name, then says, "Follow me," and makes a sharp turn.

The manager walks hurriedly and the applicant is usually racing to catch up. He stops at one of the counselor's desks and introduces the applicant to the counselor he will be working with.

The counselor repeats the firm, brief handshake and tells him to sit down in the chair next to his desk. The seat on the visitor's chair is four inches lower than the seat on the counselor's chair. This tends to make the counselor psychologically "above" his visitor. Like the patient on the couch interacting with his psychoanalyst or the defendant with the judge, the applicant has to lift his head in order to speak with his counselor.

The applicant, in short, enters into a setting that provides specific instructions about what he is to do. Once he has complied he has, in effect, agreed to the agency's right to determine his behavior, and to make arrangements for him and about him. Contractual rights and obligations have been indicated, and he has, in effect, accepted them. As Erving Goffman has pointed out, "to move one's body in response to a slight request, let alone to a command, is partly to grant the legitimacy of the other's line of action."

Next, the interview. Individual counselors vary in method, but the goal is always the same: to control the applicant. The degree of that control is measured by the extent of compliance. In my agency, the process even had a name: "conditioning." The counselor seeks to establish his authority, and to control, or at least profoundly influence, the applicant's image of himself. The counselor must accomplish both of these goals; if he does not, he cannot properly control the applicant.

The general prestige and aura of the agency—its location, furnishings, busy and alert counselors—all help elicit favorable first impressions from the job-seeker. Then—sometimes subtly, sometimes harshly—the counselor quickly lets the job-seeker know that he is in the presence of an expert, and the only way he can get a good job is to cooperate fully and, in effect, do what he is told.

Techniques for obtaining the applicant's faith and obedience vary. One successful counselor had been an industrial engineer for nine years before coming to the agency, and continually invoked his experience: "I know, because I was an industrial engineer myself." Another successful counselor invoked his years of successful experience in employment work—his techniques had gotten so many placements for so many people over so many years that how could their efficacy be doubted?

The age of the counselors is another factor in controlling applicants, especially older, professionally trained ones. Many of these applicants, in fact, seem to feel the need of a kind of Freudian father-figure; they are uncomfortable with counselors much younger than they are.

In several cases, for example, job-seekers called the agency in response to newspaper ads. Over the telephone, they seemed eager to find out what was available. The counselor, age 22, made appointments with them to come to the agency.

Soon after meeting with their counselor, who was fairly successful in conditioning applicants, the applicants' attitude changed from one of ready cooperation to reservation—a reverse conditioning. In each case, the job-seekers were more than 20 years older than the counselor. The applicants probably felt that the younger man was incapable of advising them on an important decision. In these cases, applicant control was impossible. (Sometimes the manager would perceive this and keep older applicants away from young counselors.)

Probably the most important factor that influences conditioning is brought to the agency by the applicant himself—his self-image, his belief in what he is and what he is worth. Most of the applicants at my agency were professional and technical workers with a lot of formal training. They therefore tended to regard themselves highly, to consider their skills valuable. They would not take just any positon. They strongly resisted such ideas as a possible cut in pay, or moving to another city. So the counselor's first job was to psychologically cut these applicants down to size.

The counselor begins by determining how highly the applicant regards himself—by asking him to list and rate his skills (even though the counselor already has his background-information card), and testing his reaction to hypothetical job offers. The applicant usually exaggerates his skills—probably because of what Harry Stack Sullivan called the "need for high self-esteem"; because of his desire to impress the counselor; and because he wants to obtain a job that offers the rewards usually given to highly qualified employees. Once the counselor is sure of this exaggeration, he sets to work.

First, he tells the applicant about other men in his field who are more qualified in education and experience, but are making less money. Even if the applicant already seems to have a low enough opinion of himself, this putting down may be done anyway, to make *certain* that he retains no secret thoughts about his elevated worth.

Second, the applicant is told that, at present, his field is overcrowded. Good jobs are scarce because too many good men with the same skills are unemployed. In a buyer's market, sellers cannot be choosy.

If the applicant does not accept the counselor's view of him, the counselor has two other courses. He may trade applicants with another counselor, who might have better luck; or he can "show" the applicant by sending him out to be interviewed for a couple of jobs he is definitely underqualified for. Both courses are sometimes necessary for proper "conditioning."

Another major factor (besides self-definition) that influences conditioning is the applicant's actual work experience. The two factors interrelate in making the applicant susceptible to the counselor's authority, as is shown in the table.

FOUR KINDS OF JOB APPLICANTS

		Work Experience	
		HIGH	LOW
	HIGH	1	2
Self-esteem			
	LOW	3	4

1) Applicant 1 has high self-esteem and years of experience in his field. He is usually the most difficult to condition. Generally he is already employed, making satisfactory wages and reasonably satisfied; he is likely to have been recruited personally by the counselor, and not to have come in spontaneously. But if he is successfully conditioned, he can be easily placed.

2) Applicant 2 regards himself highly, but has little or no relevant work experience. He is difficult to condition, but not so difficult as applicant 1. He is likely to be young, and a recent graduate. Typically, counselors

regard him as a nuisance; in conditioning, they emphasize his inexperience, and try to sell him on the future opportunities of a particular job, ignoring its lowly-paid present.

3) Of the four, the easiest to condition, the real money-maker, is the applicant with much experience and a low estimation of his worth—applicant 3. Very likely he wants to change employers, and is willing to accept lower wages. His reasons vary: he may want greater opportunity for advancement; he may want better working conditions and associates; he may have been laid off, or out of work because of sickness, or he recently moved to this part of the country for personal reasons more important to him than extra income.

4) Applicant 4, with little self-esteem or experience, is the easiest to condition, but no so easy as applicant 3 to place. Like applicant 2, also without experience, he is likely to be a recent graduate. Again like applicant 2, he is frequently put in a trainee position. Often the counselor actually constructs a career for him, thereby molding his self-conception.

Ideally, the counselor should vary his techniques for each applicant; but, because he has a natural desire to keep using what has worked in the past, and because it is easier to make applicants adapt to him than vice versa, many counselors use the same techniques—modified only as to degree—for everyone. This is called the "universal approach."

One very successful counselor specialized in placing highly trained structural engineers and designers. Yet he would systematically tear down each new applicant—ripping apart his self-image piece by piece. Applicants often became angry, voices rose, and politeness disappeared. But after the applicant was sufficiently frustrated and depressed, the counselor would indicate that there might still be hope—and start to put the image back together again into a more acceptable, controllable form. In effect he said: "You aren't worth much to industry, but I may be able to do something for you anyway." For him this approach worked, and he wouldn't change it. He said that he couldn't afford to "lose a placement" (have an applicant refuse a job offer) because of inadequate conditioning.

Friendship between counselor and applicant is, of course, taboo. "Friendship breeds compassion," and compassion has no home in the private employment agency. A counselor who is a friend could cater to an applicant's wishes—and might even reverse the relationship, becoming the buyer instead of the seller.

My department manager told several stories to demonstrate the dangers of friendship. For instance:

One counselor did not obtain the applicant's signature on the contract because he was a friend. (The signature is the guarantee that he will pay the fee if the position he accepts calls for it.) The applicant appealed to their friendship as sufficient guarantee. The young man was sent to an interview for a job, and the terms of the agreement with the employer were that the "applicant pays fee." He was offered the job and accepted. Informed of this by the employer, the counselor called his friend to congratulate him. And when the counselor asked when he would come in to pay his fee, his friend, the applicant, told him to "jump in the lake."

Of course, the counselor may, as a matter of technique or control, want to appear sincere or friendly. The selling techniques are often informal and seemingly friendly—applicant and counselor call each other by first names. The counselor wants to lead the applicant the way he wants him to go, while letting the applicant think he is getting what *he* wants. But the counselor is usually dissembling.

The way counselors select and condition applicants is built into the way the counselors themselves are selected and conditioned. The counselor-applicant may be solicited by ads stressing salesmanship: "We are looking for aggressive, young men to start as trainees to become employment counselors. This is selling at a high level with large commissions. . . ." Or, department managers may select them from among job applicants who seem to have the requisite salesmanship qualities. Little else seems required.

The initial screening of new counselors is similar to the initial interview with the applicant. Here is the experience of one counselor who responded to the agency's advertisement:

I called the agency and asked to speak with the technical-department manager. I told him I was interested in becoming a counselor and asked him when I could come in for an interview. I noticed that on the phone his voice was loud, clear and quick. He arranged to meet with me later that day.

At the agency, he told me to sit down next to his desk. He studied my card with a look of concern. He asked me why I wanted to become a counselor. As he stared at me intensely and looked over my clothes, I had the feeling he was trying to make me feel ill at ease. Then he would stare at my card again and tap his fingers loudly on the desk; soon, his foot was also tapping as fast and as loud as his fingers.

The technical-department manager then asked me about my experience as a salesman. He wanted to know how much I was interested in selling. Then he handed me a manual to read, which explained in detail how the agency operates with regard to commissions, bonuses and promotions. Afterwards, I was given a personality test. It sought to measure my disposition toward selling and making money. He studied my test paper for a few minutes. Apparently satisfied that my intentions were clearly to make money, he told me to come to work the next day.

The three prime criteria for a good counselor, therefore, would seem to be:
1) an ability to sell his own personality;
2) a great concern with money; and
3) a neat appearance.

One type that the agency definitely did *not* want was the "humanitarian," to whom service might be as important as money.

Counselors and managers are young; the median age for both, in my agency, was 31. They are young, in part, because the field itself is relatively young. Then too, managers prefer younger counselors, whom they can train more easily. It also seems to be true that most counselors with some experience eventually leave the field.

Still, some of the counselors had considerable experience in employment work, and managers had usually been highly successful counselors before promotion. But, though all were supposed to be expert at placing other people, few had had any valuable background experience or training other than counseling. Personality and salesmanship were what counted most.

The department manager usually hired his own counselors, and was expected to be a "driver" with them. He constantly asserted his authority, freely bawling out anyone, even the best counselors, he thought might be loafing. He accepted only one explanation when a counselor "lost a placement"—the applicant had not been properly conditioned.

What does this do to the counselor's self-image? Peter M. Blau has described three basic situations that produce feelings of inequality and alienation in employees. Managers inflict all three on counselors. They constantly ride them, and aggressively check their work, and in a personal way; they assert their authority through immediate punishments (in my agency, usually a public bawling-out) and immediate rewards; and their exercise of power seemed arbitrary and sometimes almost whimsical.

Still, I found that counselors did, nevertheless, often strongly identify with their departments and the agency. Perhaps they saw reason, even consideration, behind the method: Managers told them that they constantly scrutinized their work because they wanted the counselors to make more money; and the punishments and rewards might indicate how important the counselors' work was. And counselors *did* get quick recognition: When one made a placement, he immediately walked to the center of the office, banged a large brass gong to inform everyone, and took a prize from a table loaded with $2 gimmicks.

Moreover, the manager was a "model" to his counselors. As a formerly successful counselor, he could give them expert advice and criticism. They turned to him for guidance. More important, he lent them moral support. When they became depressed by abuse from applicants and employers, he encouraged them, and taught them how to accept disappointment. This support can be very important to a counselor, because much of his job is deeply frustrating. When he calls an employer about a possible placement, he is in a position of servitude. Employers occasionally become angry about being bothered, and may chew him out, or hang up on him. The applicants, too, can be very difficult. As Valiere Camell points out:

> The employer is looking for an intelligent, present-able, hard-working, highly trained experienced worker under 35, willing to work long hours at the lowest possible salary; while the applicant is seeking the easiest, most conveniently located job in the company with utopian benefits.

Just as the counselor tries to shape the self-conception of the applicant, so the manager shapes the self-conception of his counselors. But he can afford to be more genuinely sincere and understanding.

As might be expected, the turnover of counselors was very great. My agency's manager said this was because "Many men cannot take it." By "it" he meant the pressures from employers and applicants; apparently he never entertained the idea that the heavy pressures from him and his department heads might have some effect.

Conditioning of counselors also includes regulating their personal attitudes and behavior, at work and even off-duty. The rulebook forbade discussion of agency business in any public places, open fraternization with other counselors in the office neighborhood, and frater-nization with stenographers anywhere. Counselors were often shifted around, at least partly to discourage friendships. However, some friendships did form.

Under the guidance of their managers, counselors develop a moralizing rationale for the conditioning they give applicants. They are doing it for their own good.

Both applicants and employers must be forced to wake up and face reality. "They cannot have what they really want because it does not exist. They have to be like the rest of us." Some counselors believe they are a great help to everyone, including society, because they "put people to work." With such responsibilities, they cannot be very much concerned with what individuals want: "They don't *know* what they want."

Counselors maintain that experience teaches them that applicants and employers pay closer attention to, and are more easily led by, someone who never asks or suggests but tells them exactly what is good for them. Gradually, then, the counselor's orientation and self-image develop along the line of aggressive salesmanship. And those who adjust best and do not drop out were inclined that way to begin with. One of the more vociferous managers told me that he had had a mean temper before he entered the business—and now his temper was making money for him.

Private employment agencies play a large and ever-increasing role in our economy. Apparently this role is valuable to industry—in the agency in which I worked, close to 90 percent of the larger firms (those with over 100 employees) and half of the smaller ones paid most or all of the agency fees. The role is also valuable to job-seekers, who pay the rest.

It was not the purpose of this report, however, to judge how well the agencies perform their function. I am interested instead in the processes and extent of conditioning of counselors and applicants and in the altering of self-conceptions, all of which the agencies seem to find necessary.

The people who own or work in the private employment agencies regard them not as social utilities, but as money-making businesses. They deal with a commodity. They use aggressive salesmanship to process it and to sell it. They face growing and tough competition; they serve a growing market. Their income comes from fees. Fees come from placements. The faster and more certain the placements, the greater and more certain the income. As they see it, proper conditioning of the applicant is the specific means to achieve more and quicker placements.

To perform this conditioning, the counselors themselves are specially selected and conditioned. Hard-driving, manipulative counselors create compliant applicants with altered self-images. And this is the commodity they send to market.

March 1968

IV. EDUCATION

The Wrong Way to
Find Jobs for Negroes

DAVID WELLMAN

In the summer of 1966 I studied a Federal government program designed to help lower-class youths find jobs. The program was known as TIDE. It was run by the California Department of Employment, and classes were held five days a week in the Youth Opportunities Center of West Oakland.

The TIDE program was anything but a success. "I guess these kids just don't want jobs," one of the teacher-counselors told me. "The clothes they wear are loud. They won't talk decent English. They're boisterous. And they constantly fool around. They refuse to take the program seriously."

"But isn't there a job shortage in Oakland?" I asked. "Does it really *matter* how the kids act?"

"There's plenty of jobs. They're just not interested."

The students were 25 young men and 25 young women selected by poverty-program workers in the Bay

Area. Their ages ranged from 16 to 22, and most were Negroes. The government paid them $5 a day to participate. Men and women usually met separately. I sat in on the men's classes.

The young men who took part in TIDE had a distinctive style. They were "cool." Their hair was "processed." All sported sunglasses—very lightly tinted, with small frames. They called them "pimp's glasses." Their clothes, while usually inexpensive, were loud and ingeniously altered to express style and individuality. They spoke in a "hip" vernacular. Their vocabularies were small but very expressive. These young men, as part of the "cool world" of the ghetto, represent a distinctively black working-class culture.

To most liberals these young men are "culturally deprived" or "social dropouts." Most had flunked or been kicked out of school. Few had any intention of getting a high-school degree. They seemed uninterested in "making it." They had long and serious arrest and prison records. They were skeptical and critical of both the TIDE program and white society in general.

The TIDE workers were liberals. They assumed that if the young men would only act a little less "cool" and learn to smooth over some of their encounters with white authorities, they too could become full-fledged, working members of society. The aim of TIDE was not to train them for jobs, but to train them how to *apply* for jobs—how to take tests, how to make a good impression during a job interview, how to speak well, how to fill out an application form properly. They would play games, like dominoes, to ease the pain associated with numbers and arithmetic; they would conduct mock interviews, take mock tests, meet with management representatives, and tour places where jobs might be available. They were told to consider the TIDE program itself as a job—to be at the Youth Opportunities Center office on time, dressed as if they were at work. If they were late or made trouble, they would be docked. But if they took the program seriously and did well, they were told, they stood a pretty good chance of getting a job at the end of four weeks. The unexpressed aim of TIDE, then, was to prepare Negro youngsters for white society. The government would serve as an employment agency for white, private enterprise.

The program aimed to change the youngsters by making them more acceptable to employers. Their grammar and pronunciation were constantly corrected. They were indirectly told that, in order to get a job, their appearance would have to be altered: For example, "Don't you think you could shine your shoes?" Promptness, a virtue few of the youngsters possessed, was lauded. The penalty for tardiness was being put on a clean-up committee, or being docked.

For the TIDE workers, the program was a four-week exercise in futility. They felt they weren't asking very much of the youngsters—just that they learn to make a good impression on white society. And yet the young men were uncooperative. The only conclusion the TIDE workers could arrive at was: "They just don't want jobs."

Yet most of the youngsters took *actual* job possibilities very seriously. Every day they would pump the Youth Opportunities Center staff about job openings. When told there was a job at such-and-such a factory and that a particular test was required, the young men studied hard and applied for the job in earnest. The TIDE program *itself,* however, seemed to be viewed as only distantly related to getting a job. The youngsters wanted jobs, but to them their inability to take tests and fill out forms was *not* the problem. Instead, they talked about the shortage of jobs available to people without skills.

Their desire for work was not the problem. The real problem was what the program demanded of the young men. It asked that they change their manner of speech and dress, that they ignore their lack of skills and society's lack of jobs, and that they act as if their arrest records were of no consequence in obtaining a job. It asked, most important, that they pretend *they*, and not society, bore the responsibility for their being unemployed. TIDE didn't demand much of the men: Only that they become white.

What took place during the four-week program was a daily struggle between white, middle-class ideals of conduct and behavior and the mores and folkways of the black community. The men handled TIDE the way the black community in America has always treated white threats to Negro self-respect. They used subtle forms of subversion and deception. Historians and sociologists have pointed to slave subversion, to the content and ritual of Negro spirituals, and to the blues as forms of covert black resistance to white mores.

Today, "putting someone on," "putting the hype on someone," or "running a game on a cat" seem to be important devices used by Negroes to maintain their integrity. "Putting someone on," which is used as much with black people as with whites, allows a person to maintain his integrity in a hostile or threatening situation. To put someone on is to publicly lead him to believe that you are going along with what he has to offer or say, while privately rejecting the offer and subtly subverting it. The tactic fails if the other person recognizes what is happening. For one aim of putting someone on is to take pride in feeling that you have put something over on him, often at his expense. (Putting someone on differs from "putting someone down," which means active defiance and public confrontation.)

TIDE was evidently interpreted by the men as a threat to their self-respect, and this was the way they responded to it. Sometimes TIDE was put on. Sometimes it was put down. It was taken seriously only when it met the men's own needs.

There was almost no open hostility toward those in charge of TIDE, but two things quickly led me to believe that if the men accepted the program, they did so only on their own terms.

First, all of them appeared to have a "tuning-out" mechanism. They just didn't hear certain things. One young man was a constant joker and talked incessantly, even if someone else was speaking or if the group was supposed to be working. When told to knock it off, he never heard the command. Yet when he was interested in a program, he could hear perfectly.

Tuning out was often a collective phenomenon. For instance, there was a radio in the room where the youngsters worked, and they would play it during lunch and coffee breaks. When the instructor would enter and tell them to begin work, they would continue listening and dancing to the music as if there were no one else in the room. When *they* were finished listening, the radio went off and the session began. The youngsters were going along with the program—in a way. They weren't challenging it. But they were undermining its effectiveness.

A second way in which the young men undermined the program was by playing dumb. Much of the program consisted of teaching the youngsters how to fill out employment applications. They were given lengthy lectures on the importance of neatness and lettering. After having filled out such forms a number of times, however, some students suddenly didn't know their mother's name, the school they last attended, or their telephone number.

This "stupidity" was sometimes duplicated during the mock job interviews. Five or more of the students would interview their fellow trainees for an imaginary job. These interviewers usually took their job seriously. But after it became apparent that the interview was a game, many of the interviewees suddenly became incredibly incompetent. They didn't have social-security numbers, they couldn't remember their last job, they didn't know what school they went to, they didn't know if they really wanted the job—to the absolute frustration of their interviewers and instructors alike. Interestingly enough, when an instructor told them one morning that *this* time those who did well on the interview would actually be sent out on a real job interview with a real firm, the stupid and incompetent were suddenly transformed into model job applicants.

The same thing happened when the youngsters were given job-preference tests, intelligence tests, aptitude tests, and tests for driver's licenses. The first few times the youngsters took these tests, most worked hard to master them. But after they had gotten the knack, and still found themselves without jobs and taking the same tests, their response changed. Some of them no longer knew how to do the test. Others found it necessary to cheat by looking over someone's shoulder. Still others flunked tests they had passed the day before. Yet when they were informed of actual job possibilities at the naval ship yard or with the post office, they insisted on giving and taking the tests themselves. In one instance, some of them read up on which tests were relevant for a particular job, then practiced that test for a couple of hours by themselves.

Tuning out and playing stupid were only two of the many ways the TIDE program was "put-on." Still another way: Insisting on work "breaks." The young men "employed" by TIDE were well acquainted with this ritual and demanded that it be included as part of their job. Since they had been given a voice in deciding the content of the program, they insisted that breaks become part of their daily routine. And no matter what the activity, or who was addressing them, the young men religiously adhered to the breaks.

The program started at 9:30 A.M. The youngsters decided that their first break would be for coffee at 10:30. This break was to last until 11. And while work was never allowed to proceed a minute past 10:30, it was usually 11:15 or so before the young men actually got back to work. Lunch began exactly at 12. Theoretically, work resumed at 1. This usually meant 1:15, since they had to listen to "one more song" on the radio. The next break was to last from 2:30 to 3. However, because they were finished at 3:30 and because it took another 10 minutes to get them back to work, the fellows could often talk their way out of the remaining half hour. Considering they were being paid $5 a day for five hours' work, of which almost half were regularly devoted to breaks, they didn't have a bad hustle.

Games were another part of the TIDE program subverted by the put-on. Early in the program an instructor told the students that it might be helpful if they mastered arithmetic and language by playing games—dominoes, Scrabble, and various card games. The students considered this a fine idea. But what their instructor had intended for a pastime during the breaks, involving at most an hour a day, they rapidly turned into a major part of the instruction. They set aside 45 minutes in the morning and 45 minutes in the afternoon for games. But they participated in these games during their breaks as well, so that the games soon became a stumbling block to getting sessions back in order after breaks. When the instructor would say, "Okay, let's get back to work," the men would sometimes reply, "But we're already working on our math—we're playing dominoes, and you said that would help us with our math."

To familiarize the students with the kinds of jobs potentially available, the TIDE instructors took them on excursions to various work situations. These excursions were another opportunity for a put-on. It hardly seemed to matter what kind of company they visited so long as the visit took all day. On a trip to the Oakland Supply Naval Station, the men spent most of their time putting the make on a cute young WAVE who was their guide. One thing this tour did produce, however, was a great deal of discussion about the war in Vietnam. Almost none of the men wanted to serve in the armed forces. Through the bus windows some of them would yell at passing sailors: "Vietnam, baby!" or "Have a good time in Vietnam, man!"

The men would agree to half-day trips only if there was no alternative, or if the company would give away samples. Although they knew that the Coca-Cola Company was not hiring, they wanted to go anyway, for the free Cokes. They also wanted to go to many candy and cookie factories. Yet they turned down a trip to a local steel mill that they knew was hiring. TIDE, after all, was not designed to get them an interview—its purpose was to show them what sorts of jobs might be available. Given the circumstances, they reasoned, why not see what was enjoyable as well?

When the men were not putting on the TIDE program and staff, they might be putting them down. When someone is put down, he knows it. The tactic's success depends on his knowing it, whereas a put-on is successful only when its victim is unaware of it.

Among the fiercest put-downs I witnessed were those aimed at jobs the students were learning to apply for. These jobs were usually for unskilled labor: post-office, assembly-line, warehouse, and longshore workers, truck drivers, chauffeurs, janitors, bus boys and so on.

The reaction of most of the students was best expressed by a question I heard one young man ask an instructor: "How about some tests for I.B.M.?" The room broke into an uproar of hysterical laughter. The instructor's response was typically bureaucratic, yet disarming: "Say, that's a good suggestion. Why don't you put it in the suggestion box?" The students didn't seem to be able to cope with that retort, so things got back to normal.

Actual employers, usually those representing companies that hired people only for unskilled labor, came to TIDE to demonstrate to the men what a good interview would be like. They did *not* come to interview men for real jobs. It was sort of a helpful-hints-for-successful-interviews session. Usually one of the more socially mobile youths was chosen to play the role of job applicant. The entire interview situation was played through. Some employers even went so far as to have the "applicant" go outside and knock on the door to begin the interview. The students thought this was both odd and funny, and one said to the employer: "Man, you've already *seen* the cat. How come you making him walk out and then walk back in?"

With a look of incredulity, the employer replied: "But that's how you get a job. You have to sell yourself from the moment you walk in that door."

The employer put on a real act, beginning the interview with the usual small talk.

"I see from your application that you played football in high school."

"Yeah."

"Did you like it?"

"Yeah."

"Football really makes men and teaches you team-work."

"Yeah."

At this point, the men got impatient: "Man, the cat's here to get a job, not talk about football!"

A wisecracker chimed in: "Maybe he's interviewing for a job with the Oakland Raiders."

Usually the employer got the point. He would then ask about the "applicant's" job experience, draft status, school record, interests, skills and so on. The young man being interviewed usually took the questions seriously and answered frankly. But after a while, the rest of the group would tire of the game and (unrecognized, from the floor) begin to ask about the specifics of a real job:

"Say man, how much does this job pay?"

"What kind of experience do you need?"

"What if you got a record?"

It didn't take long to completely rattle an inter-viewer. The instructor might intervene and tell the students that the gentleman was there to help them, but this would stifle the revolt for only a short while. During one interview, several of the fellows began loudly playing dominoes. That got the response they were looking for.

"Look!" shouted the employer. "If you're not interested in learning how to sell yourself, why don't you just leave the room so that others who are interested can benefit from this?"

"Oh no!" responded the ringleaders. "We work here. If you don't dig us, then *you* leave!"

Not much later, he did.

Sometimes during these mock interviews, the very nature of the work being considered was put down. During one mock interview for a truck-driving job, some of the men asked the employer about openings for salesmen. Others asked him about executive positions. At one point the employer himself was asked point blank how much he was paid, and what his experience was. They had turned the tables and were enjoying the opportunity to interview the interviewer. Regardless of a potential employer's status, the young men treated him as they would their peers. On one tour of a factory, the students were escorted by the vice-president in charge of hiring. To the TIDE participants, he was just another guide. After he had informed the students of the large number of unskilled positions available, they asked him if he would hire some of them, on the spot. He replied that this was just a tour and that he was in no position to hire anyone immediately. One youth looked at him and said: "Then you're just wasting our time, aren't you?"

Although shaken, the executive persisted. Through-out his talk, however, he innocently referred to his audience as "boys," which obviously bothered the students. Finally one of the more articulate men spoke up firmly: "We are young *men* not boys!"

The vice-president blushed and apologized. He made a brave attempt to avoid repeating the phrase. But habit was victorious, and the word slipped in again and again. Each time he said "you boys," he was corrected, loudly, and with increasing hostility.

The students treated State Assemblyman Byron Rumford, a Negro, the same way. The meeting with Rumford was an opportunity for them to speak with an elected official about the job situation in the state. The meeting was also meant to air differences and to propose solutions. At the time, in fact, the men were quite angry about their rate of pay at TIDE. An instructor had suggested that they take the matter up with Rumford.

The meeting was attended by both the young men and women in the TIDE program. The young women were very well dressed and well groomed. Their clothes were not expensive, but were well cared for and in "good taste." Their hair was done in high-fashion styles. They looked, in short, like aspiring career women. The young men wore their usual dungarees or tight trousers, brightly colored shirts and sweaters, pointed shoes and sunglasses.

The women sat quietly and listened politely. The men spoke loudly whenever they felt like it, and constantly talked among themselves.

Rumford, instead of speaking about the job situation in the Bay Area, chose to talk about his own career. It was a Negro Horatio Alger story. The moral was that if you work hard, you too can put yourself through college, become a successful druggist, then run for public office.

The moment Rumford finished speaking and asked for questions, one of the men jumped up and asked, "Hey man, how do we get a raise?" A male chorus of "Yeah!" followed. Before Rumford could complete a garbled answer (something like, "Well, I don't really know much about the procedures of a federally sponsored program"), the battle of the sexes had been joined. The women scolded the men for their "disrespectful behavior" toward an elected official. One said: "Here he is trying to help us and you-all acting a fool. You talking and laughing and carrying on while he talking, and then when he finishes you want to know about a raise. Damn!"

"Shit," was a male response. "You don't know what you talking about. We got a *right* to ask the cat about a raise. We elected him."

"We supposed to be talking about jobs," said another. "And we're talking about *our* job. If y'all like the pay, that's your business. We want more!"

The debate was heated. Neither group paid any attention to Rumford, who wisely slipped out of the room.

During the exchanges it became clear to me that the differences in clothing and style between the sexes reflected their different orientations toward the dominant society and its values. In the minds of the young women, respect and respectability seemed paramount. At one point, a young woman said to the men, "You acting just like a bunch of *niggers*." She seemed to identify herself as a Negro, not as a "nigger." For the men, on the other hand, becoming a Negro (as opposed to a "nigger") meant giving up much that they considered positive. As one young man said in answer to the above, "You just ain't got no soul, bitch."

The women's identification with the values of white society became even clearer when the debate moved from what constituted respect and respectability to a direct attack on a personal level: "Do you all expect to get a job looking the way you do?" "Shit, I wouldn't wear clothes like that if I was on welfare." The direction of the female attack corresponded closely with the basic assumptions of the TIDE program: People are without jobs because of themselves. This barrage hit the young men pretty hard. Their response was typical of any outraged male whose manhood has been threatened. In fact, when one young woman gibed, "You ain't no kinda man," some of the fellows had to be physically restrained from hitting her.

One of the men explained that "maybe the reason cats dress the way they do is because they can't afford anything else. Did you ever think of that?"

The woman's response was one I had not heard since the third or fourth grade: "Well, it doesn't matter what you wear as long as it's clean, pressed and tucked in. But hell, you guys don't even shine your shoes."

The battle of the sexes in the black community seems to be almost a class conflict. Many observers have noted that the black woman succeeds more readily in school than the black man. Women are also favored by parents, especially mothers. Moreover, the black woman has been for some time the most stable force and the major breadwinner of the Negro family. All these things put Negro women in harmony with the major values attached to work and success in our society. Black men, however, have been estranged from society, and a culture has developed around this estrangement—a male Negro culture often antagonistic to the dominant white society. The black woman stands in much the same relation to black men as white society does.

Even including Rumford, no group of officials was put down quite so hard as the Oakland police. Police brutality was constantly on the youngsters' minds. A day didn't pass without at least one being absent because he was in jail, or one coming in with a story about mistreatment by the police. A meeting was arranged with a sergeant from the Community Relations Bureau of the Oakland police. The students seemed excited about meeting the officer on their own turf and with the protection provided by the program.

In anticipation of his arrival, the fellows rearranged the room, placing all the separate tables together. Then they sat down in a group at one end of the table, waiting for the officer.

Sergeant McCormack was an older man. And while obviously a cop, he could also pass for a middle-aged businessman or a young grandfather.

"Hi boys," he said as he sat down. His first mistake. He began with the five-minute speech he must give to every community group. The talk was factual, uninteresting and noncontroversial: how the department is run, what the qualifications for policemen are, and how difficult it is for police to do their work and still please everyone. His talk was greeted with complete silence.

"I understand you have some questions," McCormack finally said.

"What about police brutality?" asked one man.

"What is your definition of police brutality?" the sergeant countered.

"How long you been a cop?" someone shouted.

"Over 20 years."

"And you got the nerve to come on sounding like you don't know what we talking about. Don't be jiving us. Shit, if you've been a cop *that* long, you *got* to know what we talking about."

"Righteous on that, brother!" someone chimed in.

"Well, I've been around a while, all right, but I've never seen any brutality. But what about it?"

"What *about* it?" There was a tone of disbelief mixed with anger in the young man's voice. "Shit man, we want to know why you cats always kicking other cats' asses."

The officer tried to draw a distinction between necessary and unnecessary police violence. The fellows weren't buying that. They claimed the police systematically beat the hell out of them for no reason. The officer asked for examples, and the fellows obliged with long, involved and detailed personal experiences with the Oakland Police Department. The sergeant listened patiently, periodically interrupting to check details and inconsistencies. He tried to offer a police interpretation of the incident. But the fellows were simply not in a mood to listen. In desperation the sergeant finally said, "Don't you want to hear *our* side of the story?"

"Hell no, motherfucker, we *see* your side of the story every night on 14th Street."

One young man stood up, his back to the officer, and addressed his contemporaries: "We *tired* of talking! We want some action! There's a new generation now. We ain't like the old folks who took all this shit off the cops." He turned to the sergeant and said, "You take that back to your goddamn Chief Preston and tell him."

McCormack had a silly smile on his face.

Another youngster jumped up and hollered, "You all ain't going to be smiling when we put dynamite in your police station!"

The officer said simply, "You guys don't want to talk."

"You see," someone yelled, "the cat's trying to be slick, trying to run a game on us. First he comes in here all nice-talking, all that shit about how they run the police and the police is to protect us. And then when we tell him how they treat us he wants to say we don't want to talk. Shit! We want to talk, he don't want to listen."

From this point on, they ran over him mercilessly. I, with all my biases against the police, could not help feeling compassion for the sergeant. If the police are an authority figure in the black community, then this episode must be viewed as a revolt against authority—*all* authority. There was nothing about the man's life, both private and public, that wasn't attacked.

"How much money you get paid?"

"About $12,000 a year."

"For being a cop? Wow!"

"What do you do?"

"I work in the Community Relations Department."

"Naw, stupid, what *kind* of work?"

"I answer the telephone, speak to groups, and try to see if the police treat the citizens wrong."

"Shit, we could do that, and we don't even have a high-school education. Is that all you do? And get that much money for it?"

"Where do you live?"

"I'll bet he lives up in the hills."

"I live in the east side of Oakland. And I want you to know that my next-door neighbor is a colored man. I've got nothing against colored people."

"You got any kids?"

"Yeah, two boys and a girl."

"Shit, bet they all went to college and got good jobs. Any of your kids been in trouble?"

"No, not really."

"What do they do?"

"My oldest boy is a fighter pilot in Vietnam."

"What the hell is he doing over there? That's pretty stupid."

"Yeah man, what are we fighting in Vietnam for? Is that your way of getting rid of us?"

"Well, the government says we have to be there, and it's the duty of every citizen to do what his country tells him to do."

"We don't want to hear all that old bullshit, man."

"Hey, how come you wear such funny clothes? You even look like a goddam cop."

"Yeah baby, and he smells like one too!"

The barrage continued for almost half an hour. The instructor finally called a halt: "Sergeant McCormack has to get back, fellows. Is there anything specific that you'd like to ask him?"

"Yeah. How come Chief Preston ain't here? He's always talking to other people all over the country about how good the Oakland cops are and how there ain't going to be no riot here. Why don't he come and tell us that? We want to talk with the chief."

The next day, Deputy Chief Gain came—accompanied by the captain of the Youth Division, the lieutenant of that division, and a Negro sergeant. It was a formidable display of police authority. The youngsters were noticeably taken aback.

Chief Gain is a no-nonsense, businesslike cop. He takes no static from anyone, vigorously defends what he thinks is correct, and makes no apologies for what he considers incorrect. He is an honest man in the sense that he makes no attempt to cover up or smooth over unpleasant things. He immediately got down to business: "All right now, I understand you guys have some beefs with the department. What's the story?"

The fellows started right in talking about the ways they had been mistreated by the police. The chief began asking specific questions: where it happened, when it happened, what the officer looked like and so on. He never denied the existence of brutality. That almost seemed to be assumed. He did want details, however. He always asked whether the youth had filed a complaint with the department. The response was always No. He then lectured them about the need to file such complaints if the situation was to be changed.

He explained the situation as he saw it: "Look fellows, we run a police force of 654 men. Most of them are good men, but there's bound to be a few rotten apples in the basket. I know that there's a couple of men who mistreat people, but it's only a few and we're trying our best to change that."

"Shit, I know of a case where a cop killed a cat and now he's back on the beat."

"Now wait a minute—"

"No more waiting a minute!" someone interrupted. "You had two cops got caught taking bribes. One was black and the other Caucasian. The black cat was kicked off the force and the white cat is back on."

"Yeah, and what about that cat who killed somebody off-duty, what about him?"

"Hold on," Gain said firmly. "Let's take these things one at a time." He didn't get very far before he was back to the "few rotten apples" argument.

"If it's only a few cops, how come it happens all the time?"

The deputy chief told them that he thought it was the same few cops who were causing all the problems. "Unless you file complaints each time you feel you've been mistreated, we can't do anything about it. So it's up to you as much as it is up to us."

For the first time in weeks, I intruded into the discussion. I pointed out to Gain that he was asking citizens to police their own police force. He had argued that in most situations the department had a good deal of control over its own men—the same argument the police had used against a civilian-review board. Now he was saying the opposite: that it was up to the citizens. This seemed to break the impasse, and the students howled with delight.

"What happens if a cop beats my ass and I file a complaint?" demanded one. "Whose word does the judge take?"

"The judge takes the evidence and evaluates it objectively and comes to a decision."

"Yeah, but it's usually two cops against one of us, and if both testify against me, what happens? Do you think the judge is going to listen to me?"

"Bring some witnesses."

"That ain't going to do anything."

"That's your problem. If you don't like the legal system in this country, work to change it."

"Okay man," one fellow said to Gain, "You pretty smart. If I smack my buddy here upside the head and he files a complaint, what you gonna do?"

"Arrest you."

"Cool. Now let's say one of your ugly cops smacks *me* upside the head and I file a complaint—what you gonna do?"

"Investigate the complaint, and if there's anything to

it, why we'll take action—probably suspend him."

"Why do *we* get arrested and *you* investigated?"

The Deputy chief's response was that most private companies with internal difficulties don't want to be investigated by outside agencies. The fellows retorted:

"Police are *not* a private business. You're supposed to work for the people!"

"And shit, you cats get to carry guns. No business-man carries guns. It's a different scene, man."

"How come you got all kinds of squad cars in this neighborhood every night? And have two and three cops in each of them?"

"The crime rate is high in this area," replied Gain, "and we get a lot of calls and complaints about it."

"Yeah, and you smart enough to know that when you come around here, you better be wearing helmets and carrying shotguns. If you that clever, you got to be smart enough to handle your own goddam cops."

At this point the fellows all jumped on the deputy chief the same way they had jumped on the sergeant the day before:

"Why don't you just let us run our own damn community?"

"Yeah. There should be people on the force who've been in jail because they the only people who know what it means to be busted. People in West Oakland should be police because they know their community; you don't."

"Why do we get all the speeding tickets?"

"How come we got to fight in Vietnam?"

"Why the judges so hard on us? They don't treat white cats—I mean dudes—the way they do us."

The chief began assembling his papers and stood up. "You guys aren't interested in talking. You want to yell.

When you want to talk, come down to my office, and if I'm free we'll talk."

But the fellows had the last word. While he was leaving they peppered him with gibes about how *they* were tired of talking; promised to dynamite his office; and called the police chief a coward for not coming down to speak with them.

When the deputy chief had gone, the instructor asked the fellows why they insisted on ganging up on people like the police. The answer provides a lot of insight into the young men's actions toward the police, businessmen and public officials:

"These people just trying to run a game on us. If we give them time to think about answers, they gonna put us in a trick. We've *got* to gang up on them because they gang up on us. Did you dig the way that cat brought three other cats with him? Besides, how else could we put them down?"

In effect, the young men had inverted the meaning and aims of the TIDE program. It was supposed to be an opportunity for them to plan careers and prepare themselves for their life's work. The immediate goal was to help them get started by showing them how to get a job. The youngsters had a different view. The program was a way to play some games and take some outings—an interesting diversion from the boredom and frustration of ghetto life in the summer. In some respects it was also a means of confronting, on equal terms, high-status people normally unavailable to them— and of venting on them their anger and hostility. But primarily they saw it as a $5-a-day job.

The program simply did not meet the needs of these young men. In fact, it was not really meant to. The Great Society was trying to "run a game on" black youth. TIDE asked them to stop being what they are. It tried to lead them into white middle-class America by showing that America was interested in getting them jobs. But America does not provide many jobs—let alone attractive jobs—for those with police records, with few skills, with black skins. The youths knew that; TIDE workers knew that too. They did not train youths for work, but tried to make them believe that if they knew *how* to get a job, they could. The young men saw through the sham.

Ironically, the view that Negro youths, rather than society, are responsible for the employment problem is very similar to the familiar line of white racism. Negroes will not work because they are lazy and shiftless, the old Southern bigot would say. The Northern liberal today would put it a little differently: Negroes cannot get jobs because of their psychological and cultural impediments; what they need is cultural improvement, a proper attitude, the ability to sell themselves. Both views suggest that inequities in the job and opportunity structure of America are minor compared to the deficiencies of Negroes themselves. In the end, Northern liberals and Southern racists agree: The problem is mainly with Negroes, not with our society. This fallacy underlies much of the war on poverty's approach and is indicative of the subtle forms racism is taking in America today.

April 1968

FURTHER READING

Autobiography by Malcolm X (New York: Grove Press, 1965).

Manchild in the Promised Land by Claude Brown (New York: Macmillan, *1965).*

Tally's Corner by Elliot Liebow (Boston: Little Brown 1967).

Genetic Psychology Monographs (Provincetown, Mass.: Journal Press, 1967) edited by John E. Horrocks.

"Why Should Negroes Work?" by Jan E. Dizard in *Negroes and Jobs* (Ann Arbor: University of Michigan Press, 1968) edited by Louis A. Ferman *et al.*

"American Slaves and Their History" by Eugene Genovese, *New York Review of Books*, Vol. 15, No. 10 (December 3, 1970).

The Warrior Dropouts

ROSALIE H. WAX

A Note on Methodology

In studying the adolescents on Pine Ridge we concentrated on two areas, the high school and a particular day school community with a country Indian population of about 1,000. We interviewed somewhat less than half the young people then enrolled in the high school plus a random sample of 48 young country Indians. Subsequently, we obtained basic socioeconomic and educational data from all the young people who had graduated from the day school in 1961, 1962 and 1963. We interviewed 153 young people between the ages of 13 and 21, about 50 of whom were high school dropouts. We used many approaches and several types of questionnaires, but our most illuminating and reliable data were obtained from interviews conducted by Indian college students who were able to associate with Sioux adolescents and participate in some of their activities.

While "country Sioux" or "country Indian" might loosely be considered a synonym for "full-blood," I have avoided the latter term as connoting a traditional Indian culture which vanished long ago and whose unchanging qualities were a mythology of white observers rather than a social reality of Indian participants.

289

In any case, I use "country Indian" to refer to the people raised and living "out on the reservation (prairie)" who participate in the social and ceremonial activities of their local rural communities, as opposed to those persons, also known as Indians, who live in Pine Ridge town and make a point of avoiding these backwoods activities.

Scattered over the prairie on the Pine Ridge reservation of South Dakota, loosely grouped into bands along the creeks and roads, live thousands of Sioux Indians. Most live in cabins, some in tents, a few in houses; most lack the conventional utilities—running water, electricity, telephone and gas. None has a street address. They are called "country Indians" and most speak the Lakota language. They are very poor, the most impoverished people on the reservation.

For four years I have been studying the problems of the high school dropouts among these Oglala Sioux. In many ways these Indian youths are very different from slum school dropouts—Negro, Mexican-American, rural white—just as in each group individuals differ widely one from another. Yet no one who has any familiarity with their problems can avoid being struck by certain parallels, both between groups and individuals.

In slum schools and Pine Ridge schools scholastic achievement is low, and the dropout rate is high; the children's primary loyalties go to friends and peers, not schools or educators; and all of them are confronted by teachers who see them as inadequately prepared, uncultured offspring of alien and ignorant folk. They are classified as "culturally deprived." All such schools serve as the custodial, constabulary and reformative arm of one element of society directed against another.

Otherwise well-informed people, including educators themselves, assume on the basis of spurious evidence that dropouts dislike and voluntarily reject school, that they all leave it for much the same reasons, and that they are really much alike. But dropouts leave high school under strikingly different situations and for quite different reasons.

Many explicitly state that they do not wish to leave and are really "pushouts" or "kickouts" rather than "dropouts." As a Sioux youth in our sample put it, "I quit, but I never did *want* to quit!" Perhaps the fact that educators consider all dropouts to be similar tells us more about educators and their schools than about dropouts.

The process that alienates many country Indian boys from the high schools they are obliged to attend begins early in childhood and reflects the basic Sioux social structure. Sioux boys are reared to be physically reckless and impetuous. One that does not perform an occasional brash act may be accepted as "quiet" or "bashful," but he is not considered a desirable son, brother or sweetheart. Sioux boys are reared to be proud and feisty and are expected to resent public censure. They have some obligations to relatives; but the major social controls after infancy are exerted by their fellows—their "peer group."

From about the age of seven or eight, they spend almost the entire day without adult supervision, running or riding about with friends of their age and returning home only for food and sleep. Even we (my husband, Dr. Murray L. Wax, and I), who had lived with Indian families from other tribal groups, were startled when we heard a responsible and respected Sioux matron dismiss a lad of six or seven for the entire day with the statement, "Go play with Larry and John." Similarly, at a ceremonial gathering in a strange community with hundreds of people, boys of nine or ten often take off and stay away until late at night as a matter of course. Elders pay little attention. There is much prairie and many creeks for roaming and playing in ways that bother nobody. The only delinquencies we have heard Sioux elders complain about are chasing stock, teasing bulls, or occasionally some petty theft.

Among Sioux males this kind of peer-group raising leads to a highly efficient yet unverbalized system of intragroup discipline and powerful intragroup loyalties and dependencies. During our seven-month stay in a reservation community, we were impressed by how rarely the children quarreled with one another. This behavior was not imposed by elders but by the children themselves.

For example, our office contained some items very attractive to them, especially a typewriter. We were astonished to see how quietly they handled this prize that only one could enjoy at a time. A well-defined status system existed so that a child using the typewriter at once gave way and left the machine if one higher in the hierarchy appeared. A half-dozen of these shifts might take place within an hour; yet, all this occurred without a blow or often even a word.

Sioux boys have intense loyalties and dependencies. They almost never tattle on each other. But when forced to live with strangers, they tend to become inarticulate, psychologically disorganized or withdrawn.

With most children the peer group reaches the zenith of its power in school. In middle-class neighborhoods, independent children can usually seek and secure support from parents, teachers or adult society as a whole. But when, as in an urban slum or Indian reservation, the teachers stay aloof from parents, and parents feel that teachers are a breed apart, the peer group may become so powerful that the children literally take over the school. Then group activities are carried on in class—jokes, notes, intrigues, teasing, mock combat, comic-book reading, courtship—all without the teacher's knowledge and often without grossly interfering with the learning process.

Competent and experienced teachers can come to terms with the peer group and manage to teach a fair amount of reading, writing and arithmetic. But teachers who are incompetent, overwhelmed by large classes, or sometimes merely inexperienced may be faced with groups of children who refuse even to listen.

We marveled at the variety and efficiency of the devices developed by Indian children to frustrate formal learning—unanimous inattention, refusal to go to the board, writing on the board in letters less than an inch high, inarticulate responses, and whispered or pantomime teasing of victims called on to recite. In some seventh and eighth-grade classes there was a withdrawal so uncompromising that no voice could be heard for hours except the teacher's, plaintively asking questions or giving instructions.

Most Sioux children insist they like school, and most Sioux parents corroborate this. Once the power and depth of their social life within the school is appreciated, it is not difficult to see why they like it. Indeed, the only unpleasant aspects of school for them are the disciplinary regulations (which they soon learn to tolerate or evade), an occasional "mean" teacher, bullies or feuds with members of other groups. Significantly, we found that notorious truants had usually been rejected by classmates and also had no older relatives in school to protect them from bullies. But the child who has a few friends or an older brother or sister to stand by him, or who "really likes to play basketball," almost always finds school agreeable.

By the time he has finished the eighth grade, the country Indian boy has many fine qualities: zest for life, curiosity, pride, physical courage, sensibility to human relationships, experience with the elemental facts of life, and intense group loyalty and integrity. His experiences in day school have done nothing to diminish or tarnish his ideal—the physically reckless and impetuous youth, who is admired by all.

But, on the other hand, the country Indian boy is almost completely lacking in the traits most highly valued by the school authorities: narrow and absolute respect for "regulations," "government property," routine, discipline and diligence. He is also deficient in other skills apparently essential to rapid and easy passage through high school and boarding school—especially the abilities to make short-term superficial social adjustments with strangers. Nor can he easily adjust to a system which demands, on the one hand, that he study competitively as an individual, and, on the other, that he live in barrack-type dormitories where this kind of study is impossible.

Finally, his English is inadequate for high-school work. Despite eight or more years of formal training in reading and writing, many day-school graduates cannot converse fluently in English even among themselves. In contrast, most of the students with whom they will compete in higher schools have spoken English since childhood.

To leave home and the familiar and pleasant day school for boarding life at the distant and formidable high school is a prospect both fascinating and frightening. To many young country Indians the agency town of Pine Ridge is a center of sophistication. It has blocks of Indian Bureau homes with lawns and fences, a barber shop, big grocery stores, churches, gas stations, a drive-in confectionary, and even a restaurant with a juke box. While older siblings or cousins may have reported that at high school "they make you study harder," that "they just make you move every minute," or that the "mixed-bloods" or "children of bureau employees" are "mean" or "snotty," there are the compensatory highlights of movies, basketball games and the social (white man's) dances.

For the young men there is the chance to play high-school basketball, baseball or football; for the young women there is the increased distance from overwatchful, conservative parents. For both, there is the freedom, taken or not, to hitchhike to White Clay, with its beer joints, bowling hall, and archaic aura of Western wickedness. If, then, a young man's close friends or relatives decide to go to high school, he will usually want to go too rather than remain at home, circumscribed, "living off his folks." Also, every year, more elders coax, tease, bribe, or otherwise pressure the young men into "making a try" because "nowadays only high school graduates get the good jobs."

The student body of the Oglala Community High School is very varied. First, there are the children of the town dwellers, who range from well-paid white and Indian government employees who live in neat government housing developments to desperately poor people who live in tar-paper shacks. Second, there is the large number of institutionalized children who have been attending the Oglala Community School as boarders for the greater part of their lives. Some are orphans, others come from isolated sections of the reservation where there are no day schools, others come from different tribal areas.

But these town dwellers and boarders share an advantage—for them entry into high school is little more than a shift from eighth to ninth grade. They possess an intimate knowledge of their classmates and a great deal of local know-how. In marked contrast, the country Indian freshman enters an alien environment. Not only is he ignorant of how to buck the rules, he doesn't even know the rules. Nor does he know anybody to put him wise.

Many country Indians drop out of high school before they have any clear idea what high school is all about. In our sample, 35 percent dropped out before the end of the ninth grade and many of these left during the first semester. Our first interviews with them were tantalizingly contradictory—about half the young men seemed to have found high school so painful they could scarcely talk about it; the other half were also laconic, but insisted that they had liked school. In time, those who had found school unbearable confided that they had left school because they were lonely or because they were abused by more experienced boarders. Only rarely did they mention that they had trouble with their studies.

The following statement, made by a mild and pleasant boy, conveys some idea of the agony of loneliness, embarrassment, and inadequacy that a country Indian newcomer may suffer when he enters high school:

> At day school it was kind of easy for me. But high school was really hard, and I can't figure out even simple questions that they ask me. . . . Besides I'm

so quiet [modest and unaggressive] that the boys really took advantage of me. They borrow money from me every Sunday night and they don't even care to pay it back. . . . I can't talk English very good, and I'm really bashful and shy, and I get scared when I talk to white people. I usually just stay quiet in the [day school] classroom, and the teachers will leave me alone. But at boarding school they wanted me to get up and talk or say something. . . . I quit and I never went back. . . . I can't seem to get along with different people, and I'm so shy I can't even make friends. . . . [Translated from Lakota by interviewer.]

Most of the newcomers seem to have a difficult time getting along with the experienced boarders and claim that the latter not only strip them of essentials like soap, paper and underwear, but also take the treasured gifts of proud and encouraging relatives, wrist watches and transistor radios.

Some of the kids—especially the boarders—are really mean. All they want to do is steal—and they don't want to study. They'll steal your school work off you and they'll copy it. . . . Sometimes they'll break into our suitcase. Or if we have money in our pockets they'll take off our overalls and search our pockets and get our money. . . . So finally I just came home. If I could be a day scholar I think I'll stay in. But if they want me to board I don't want to go back. I think I'll just quit.

Interviews with the dropouts who asserted that school was "all right"—and that they had not wished to quit—suggest that many had been almost as wretched during their first weeks at high school as the bashful young men who quit because they "couldn't make friends." But they managed to find some friends and, with this peer support and protection, they were able to cope with and (probably) strike back at other boarders. In any case, the painful and degrading aspects of school became endurable. As one lad put it: "Once you *learn* to be a boarder, it's not so bad."

But for these young men, an essential part of having friends was "raising Cain"—that is, engaging in daring and defiant deeds forbidden by the school authorities. The spirit of these escapades is difficult to portray to members of a society where most people no longer seem capable of thinking about the modern equivalents of Tom Sawyer, Huckleberry Finn or Kim, except as juvenile delinquents. We ourselves, burdened by sober professional interest in dropouts, at first found it hard to recognize that these able and engaging young men were taking pride and joy in doing exactly what the school authorities thought most reprehensible; and they were not confessing, but boasting, although their stunts had propelled them out of school.

For instance, this story from one bright lad of 15 who had run away from high school. Shortly after entering ninth grade he and his friends had appropriated a government car. (The usual pattern in such adventures is to drive off the reservation until the gas gives out.) For this offense (according to the respondent) they were restricted for the rest of the term—they were forbidden to leave the high school campus or attend any of the school recreational events, games, dances or movies. (In effect, this meant doing nothing but going to class, performing work chores, and sitting in the dormitory.) Even then our respondent seems to have kept up with his class work and did not play hookey except in reading class:

It was after we stole that car Mrs. Bluger [pseudonym for reading teacher] would keep asking who stole the car in class. So I just quit going there. . . . One night we were the only ones up in the older boys' dorm. We said, "Hell with this noise. We're not going to be the only ones here." So we snuck out and went over to the dining hall. I pried this one window open about this far and then it started to crack, so I let it go. . . . We heard someone so we took off. It was show that night I think. [motion picture was being shown in school auditorium.] . . . All the rest of the guys was sneaking in and getting something. So I said I was going to get my share too. We had a case of apples and a case of oranges. Then I think it was the night watchman was coming, so we run around and hid behind those steps. He shined that light on us. So I thought right then I was going to keep on going. That was around Christmas time. We walked back to Oglala [about 15 miles] and we were eating this stuff all the way back.

This young man implied that after this escapade he simply did not have the nerve to try to return to the high school. He insisted, however, that he would like to try another high school:

I'd like to finish [high school] and get a good job some place. If I don't I'll probably just be a bum around here or something.

Roughly half the young Sioux who leave high school very early claim they left because they were unable to conform to school regulations. What happens to the country boys who remain? Do they "shape-up" and obey the regulations? Do they, even, come to "believe" in them? We found that most of these older and more experienced youths were, if anything, even *more* inclined to boast of triumphs over the rules than the younger fellows who had left. Indeed, all but one assured us that they were adept at hookey, and food and car stealing, and that they had frequent surreptitious beer parties and other outlaw enjoyments. We do not know whether they (especially the star athletes) actually disobey the school regulations as frequently and flagrantly as they claim. But there can be no doubt that most Sioux young men above 12 wish to be regarded as hellions in school. For them, it would be unmanly to have any other attitude.

An eleventh grader in good standing explained his private technique for playing hookey and added proudly: "They never caught me yet." A twelfth grader and first-string basketball player told how he and some other students "stole" a jeep from the high school machine shop and drove it all over town. When asked why, he patiently explained: "To see if we can get away with it. It's for the enjoyment . . . to see if we can take the car without getting caught." Another senior told our male staff worker: "You can always get out and booze it up."

The impulse to boast of the virile achievements of youth seems to maintain itself into middle and even into old age. Country Indians with college training zestfully told how they and a group of proctors had stolen large amounts of food from the high-school kitchen and were never apprehended, or how they and their friends drank three fifths of whiskey in one night and did not pass out.

Clearly, the activities school administrators and teachers denounce as immature and delinquent are regarded as part of youthful daring, excitement, manly honor, and contests of skill and wits by the Sioux young men and many of their elders.

They are also, we suspect, an integral part of the world of competitive sports. "I like to play basketball" was one of the most frequent responses of young men to the question: "What do you like most about school?" Indeed, several ninth and tenth graders stated that the opportunity to play basketball was the main reason they kept going to school. One eighth grader who had run away several times stated:

> When I was in the seventh grade I made the B team on the basketabll squad. And I made the A team when I was in the eighth grade. So I stayed and finished school without running away anymore.

The unselfconscious devotion and ardor with which many of these young men participate in sports must be witnessed to be appreciated even mildly. They cannot communicate their joy and pride in words, though one 17-year-old member of the team that won the state championship tried, by telling how a team member wearing a war bonnet "led us onto the playing floor and this really gave them a cheer."

Unfortunately, we have seen little evidence that school administrators and teachers recognize the opportunity to use sports as a bridge to school.

By the eleventh and twelfth grades many country Indians have left the reservation or gone into the armed services, and it is not always easy to tell which are actual dropouts. However, we did reach some. Their reasons for dropping out varied. One pled boredom: "I was just sitting there doing anything to pass the time." Another said he didn't know what made him quit: "I just didn't fit in anymore. . . . I just wasn't like the other guys anymore." Another refused to attend a class in which he felt the teacher had insulted Indians. When the principal told him that he must attend this class or be "restricted," he left. Significantly, his best friend dropped out with him, even though he was on the way to becoming a first-class basketball player.

Different as they appear at first, these statements have a common undertone: They are the expressions not of immature delinquents, but of relatively mature young men who find the atmosphere of the high school stultifying and childish.

Any intense cross-cultural study is likely to reveal as many tragicomic situations as social scientific insights. Thus, on the Pine Ridge reservation, a majority of the young men arrive at adolescence valuing elan, bravery, generosity, passion, and luck, and admiring outstanding talent in athletics, singing and dancing. While capable of wider relations and reciprocities, they function at their social best as members of small groups of peers or relatives. Yet to obtain even modest employment in the greater society, they must graduate from high school. And in order to graduate from high school, they are told that they must develop exactly opposite qualities to those they possess: a respect for humdrum diligence and routine, for "discipline" (in the sense of not smoking in toilets, not cutting classes and not getting drunk), and for government property. In addition, they are expected to compete scholastically on a highly privatized and individualistic level, while living in large dormitories, surrounded by strangers who make privacy of any type impossible.

If we were dealing with the schools of a generation or two ago, then the situation might be bettered by democratization—involving the Sioux parents in control of the schools. This system of local control was not perfect, but it worked pretty well. Today the problem is more complicated and tricky; educators have become professionalized, and educational systems have become complex bureaucracies, inextricably involved with universities, education associations, foundations and federal crash programs. Even suburban middle-class parents, some of whom are highly educated and sophisticated, find it difficult to cope with the bureaucratic barriers and mazes of the schools their children attend. It is difficult to see how Sioux parents could accomplish much unless, in some way, their own school system were kept artificially small and isolated and accessible to their understanding and control.

How does our study of the Sioux relate to the problems of city dropouts? A specific comparison of the Sioux dropouts with dropouts from the urban working class—Negroes, Puerto Ricans or whites—would, no doubt, reveal many salient differences in cultural background and world view. Nevertheless, investigations so far undertaken suggest that the attitudes held by these peoples toward education and the schools are startlingly similar.

Both Sioux and working class parents wish their children to continue in school because they believe that graduating from high school is a guarantee of employment. Though some teachers would not believe it, many working-class dropouts, like the Sioux dropouts, express a generally favorable attitude toward school, stating that teachers are generally fair and that the worst thing about dropping out of school is missing one's friends. Most important, many working-class dropouts assert that they were pushed out of school and frequently add that the push was fairly direct. The Sioux boys put the matter more delicately, implying that the school authorities would not really welcome them back.

These similarities should not be seized on as evidence that all disprivileged children are alike and that they will respond as one to the single, ideal, educational policy. What it does mean is that the schools and their administrators are so monotonously alike that the boy brought up in a minority social or ethnic community can only look at and react to them in the same way. Despite their differences, they are all in much the same boat as they face the great monolith of middle-class society and its one-track education escalator.

An even more important—if often unrecognized—point is that not only does the school pose a dilemma for the working-class or Sioux, Negro, or Puerto Rican boy—he also poses one for the school. In many traditional or ethnic cultures boys are encouraged to be virile adolescents and become "real men." But our schools try to deprive youth of adolescence—and they demand that high school students behave like "mature people"—which, in our culture often seems to mean in a pretty dull, conformist fashion.

Those who submit and succeed in school can often fit into the bureaucratic requirements of employers, but they are also likely to lack independence of thought and creativity. The dropouts are failures—they have failed to become what the school demands. But the school has failed also—failed to offer what the boys from even the most "deprived" and "underdeveloped" peoples take as a matter of course—the opportunity to become whole men.

S. M. Miller and Ira E. Harrison, studying working class youth, assert that individuals who do poorly in school are handicapped or disfavored for the remainder of their lives, because "the schools have become the occupational gatekeepers" and "the level of education affects the kind and level of job that can be attained." On the other hand, the investigations of Edgar Z.

Friedenberg and Jules Henry suggest that the youths who perform creditably in high school according to the views of the authorities are disfavored in that they emerge from this experience as permanently crippled persons or human beings.

In a curious way our researches among the Sioux may be viewed as supporting both of these contentions, for they suggest that some young people leave high school because they are too vital and independent to submit to a dehumanizing situation.

May 1966

FURTHER READING

Formal Education in an American Indian Community by Murray L. Wax, Rosalie H. Wax and Robert V. Dumont (The Society for the Study of Social Problems, Spring 1964).

Blue-Collar World: Studies of the American Worker edited by Arthur B. Shostak and William Gomberg (Englewood Cliffs, N.J.: Prentice-Hall, 1964).

The Dignity of Youth and Other Atavisms by Edgar Z. Friedenberg (Boston: Beacon Press, 1966).

Indian Americans: Unity and Diversity by Murray L. Wax (Englewood Cliffs, N.J.: Prentice-Hall, 1971).

The Face of the Fox by Frederick O. Gearing (Chicago: Aldine-Atherton, Inc., 1971).

Programmed for Social Class: Tracking in High School

WALTER E. SCHAFER
CAROL OLEXA *and* KENNETH POLK

If, as folklore would have it, America is the land of opportunity, offering anyone the chance to raise himself purely on the basis of his or her ability, then education is the key to self-betterment. The spectacular increase in those of us who attend school is often cited as proof of the great scope of opportunity that our society offers: 94 percent of the high school age population was attending school in 1967, as compared to 7 percent in 1890.

Similarly, our educational system is frequently called more democratic than European systems, for instance, which rigidly segregate students by ability early in their lives, often on the basis of nationally administered examinations such as England's "11-plus." The United States, of course, has no official national policy of educational segregation. Our students, too, are tested and retested throughout their lives and put into faster or slower classes or programs on the basis of their presumed ability, but this procedure is carried out in a decentralized fashion that varies between each city or state.

However, many critics of the American practice claim that, no matter how it is carried out, it does not meet the needs of the brighter and duller groups, so much as it solidifies and widens the differences between them. One such critic, the eminent educator Kenneth B. Clark, speculates: "It is conceivable that the detrimental effects of segregation based upon intellect are similar to the known detrimental effects of schools segregated on the basis of class, nationality or race."

Patricia Cayo Sexton notes that school grouping based on presumed ability often reinforces already existing social divisions:

> Children from higher social strata usually enter the "higher quality" groups and those from lower strata the "lower" ones. School decisions about a child's ability will greatly influence the kind and quality of education he receives as well as his future life, including whether he goes to college, the job he will get, and his feelings about himself and others.

And Arthur Pearl puts it bluntly:

> . . . "special ability classes," "basic track," or "slow learner classes" are various names for another means of systematically denying the poor adequate access to education.

In this article we will examine some evidence bearing on this vital question of whether current educational practices tend to reinforce existing social class divisions. We will also offer an alternative aimed at making our public schools more effective institutions for keeping open the opportunities for social mobility.

Since the turn of the century, a number of trends have converged to increase enormously the pressure on American adolescents to graduate from high school: declining opportunity in jobs, the upgrading of educational requirements for job entry, and the diminishing need for teenagers to contribute to family income. While some school systems, especially in the large cities, have adapted to this vast increase in enrollment by creating separate high schools for students with different interests, abilities or occupational goals, most communities have developed comprehensive high schools serving all the youngsters within a neighborhood or community.

In about half the high schools in the United States today, the method for handling these large and varied student populations is through some form of tracking system. Under this arrangement, the entire student body is divided into two or more relatively distinct career lines, or tracks, with such titles as college preparatory, vocational, technical, industrial, business, general, basic and remedial. While students on different tracks may take some courses together in the same classroom, they are usually separated into entirely different courses or different sections of the same course.

School men offer several different justifications for tracking systems. Common to most, however, is the notion that college-bound students are academically more able, learn more rapidly, should not be deterred in their progress by slower, non-college-bound students, and need courses for college preparation which non-college-bound students do not need. By the same token, it is thought that non-college-bound students are less bright, learn more slowly, should not be expected to progress as fast or learn as much as college-bound students, and need only a general education or work-oriented training to prepare themselves for immediate entry into the world of work or a business or vocational school.

In reply, the numerous critics of tracking usually contend that while the college-bound are often encouraged by the tracking system to improve their performance, non-college-bound students, largely as a result of being placed in a lower-rated track, are discouraged from living up to their potential or from showing an interest in academic values. What makes the system especially pernicious, these critics say, is that non-college-bound students more often come from low-income and minority group families. As a result, high schools, through the tracking system, inadvertently close off opportunities for large numbers of students from lower social strata, and thereby contribute to the low achievement, lack of interest, delinquency and rebellion which school men frequently deplore in their noncollege track students.

If these critics are correct, the American comprehensive high school, which is popularly assumed to be the very model of an open and democratic institution, may not really be open and democratic at all. In fact, rather than facilitating equality of educational opportunity, our schools may be subtly denying it, and in the process widening and hardening existing social divisions.

During the summer of 1964, we collected data from official school transcripts of the recently graduated senior classes of two midwestern three-year high schools. The larger school, located in a predominantly middle-class, academic community of about 70,000, had a graduating class that year of 753 students. The smaller school, with a graduating class of 404, was located nearby in a predominantly working-class, industrial community of about 20,000.

Both schools placed their students into either a college prep or general track. We determined the positions of every student in our sample by whether he took tenth grade English in the college prep or the general section. If he was enrolled in the college prep section, he almost always took other college prep sections or courses, such as advanced mathematics or foreign languages, in which almost all enrollees were also college prep.

Just how students in the two schools were assigned to—or chose—tracks is somewhat of a mystery. When we interviewed people both in the high schools and in their feeder junior highs, we were told that whether a student went into one track or another depended on various factors, such as his own desires and aspirations, teacher advice, achievement test scores, grades, pressure from parents, and counselor assessment of academic promise. One is hard put to say which of these weighs most heavily, but we must note that one team of researchers, Cicourel and Kitsuse showed in their study of *The Educational Decision-Makers* that assumptions made by counselors about the character, adjustment and potential of incoming students are vitally important in track assignment.

Whatever the precise dynamics of this decision, the outcome was clear in the schools we studied: socioeconomic and racial background had an effect on which track a student took, quite apart from either his achievement in junior high or his ability as measured by IQ scores. In the smaller working-class school, 58 percent of the incoming students were assigned to the college prep track; in the larger, middle-class school, 71 percent were placed in the college prep track. And, taking the two schools together, whereas 83 percent of students from white-collar homes were assigned to the college prep track, this was the case with only 48 percent of students from blue-collar homes. The relationship of race to track assignment was even stronger: 71 percent of the whites and only 30 percent of the blacks were assigned to the college prep track. In the two schools studied, the evidence is plain: Children from low income and minority-group families more often found themselves in low ability groups and non-college-bound tracks than in high ability groups or college-bound tracks.

Furthermore, this decision-point early in the students' high school careers was of great significance for their futures, since it was virtually irreversible. Only 7 percent of those who began on the college prep track moved down to the noncollege prep track, while only 7 percent of those assigned to the lower, noncollege track, moved up. Clearly, these small figures indicate a high degree of rigid segregation within each of the two schools. In fact, greater mobility between levels has been reported in English secondary modern schools, where streaming—the British term for tracking—is usually thought to be more rigid and fixed than tracking in this country. (It must be remembered, of course, that in England the more rigid break is between secondary modern and grammar schools.)

As might be expected from the schoolmen's justification for placing students in separate tracks in the first place, track position is noticeably related to academic performance. Thirty-seven percent of the college prep students graduated in the top quarter of their class (measured by grade-point average throughout high school), while a mere 2 percent of the noncollege group achieved the top quarter. By contrast, half the noncollege prep students fell in the lowest quarter, as opposed to only 12 percent of the college prep.

Track position is also strikingly related to whether a student's academic performance improves or deteriorates during high school. The grade-point average of all sample students in their ninth year—that is, prior to their being assigned to tracks—was compared with their grade point averages over the next three years. While there was a slight difference in the ninth year between those who would subsequently enter the college and noncollege tracks, this difference had increased by the senior year. This widening gap in academic performance resulted from the fact that a higher percentage of students subsequently placed in the college prep track improved their grade point average by the senior year, while a higher percentage of noncollege prep experienced a decline in grade point average by the time they reached the senior year.

Track position is also related strongly to dropout rate. Four percent of the college prep students dropped out of high school prior to graduation, as opposed to 36 percent of the noncollege group.

Track position is also a good indication of how deeply involved a student will be in school, as measured by participation in extracurricular activities. Out of the 753 seniors in the larger school, a comparatively small number of college prep students—21 percent—did not participate in any activities, while 44 percent took part in three or more such activities. By contrast, 58 percent, or more than half of the noncollege group took part in no extracurricular activities at all, and only 11 percent of this group took part in three or more activities.

Finally, track position is strikingly related to delinquency, both in and out of school. Out of the entire school body of the larger school during the 1963-1964 school year—that is, out of 2,565 boys and girls—just over one-third of the college-bound, as opposed to more than half of the non-college-bound committed one or more violations of school rules. Nineteen percent of the college-bound, compared with 70 percent of the non-college-bound, committed three or more such violations. During this year, just over one-third of all the college-bound students were suspended for infractions of school rules, while more than half of all the non-college-bound group were suspended.

Furthermore, using juvenile court records, we find that out of the 1964 graduating class in the larger school, 6 percent of the college prep, and 16 percent of the non-college-bound groups, were delinquent while in high school. Even though 5 percent of those on the noncollege track had already entered high school with court records, opposed to only 1 percent of the college prep track, still more non-college-bound students became delinquent during high school than did college prep students (11 percent compared with 5 percent). So the relation between track position and delinquency is further supported.

We have seen, then, that when compared with college prep students, noncollege prep students show lower achievement, great deterioration of achievement, less participation in extracurricular activities, a greater tendency to drop out, more misbehavior in school, and more delinquency outside of school. Since students are assigned to different tracks largely on the basis of presumed differences in intellectual ability and inclination for further study, the crucial question is whether assignment to different tracks helped to meet the needs of groups of students who were already different, as many educators would claim, or actually contributed to and reinforced such differences, as critics like Sexton and Pearl contend.

The simplest way to explain the differences we have just seen is to attribute them to characteristics already inherent in the individual students, or—at a more sophisticated level—to students' cultural and educational backgrounds.

It can be argued, for example, that the difference in academic achievement between the college and noncollege groups can be explained by the fact that college prep students are simply brighter; after all, this is one of the reasons they were taken into college prep courses. Others would argue that non-college-bound students do less well in school work because of family background: they more often come from blue-collar homes where less value is placed on grades and college, where books and help in schoolwork are less readily available, and verbal expression limited. Still others would contend that lower track students get lower grades because they performed less well in elementary and junior high, have fallen behind, and probably try less hard.

Fortunately, it was possible with our data to separate out the influence of track position from the other suggested factors of social class background (measured by father's occupation), intelligence (measured by IQ—admittedly not a perfectly acceptable measure), and previous academic performance (measured by grade point average for the last semester of the ninth year). Through use of a weighted percentage technique known as test factor standardization, we found that even when the effects of IQ, social class and previous performance are ruled out, there is still a sizable difference in grade point average between the two tracks. With the influence of the first three factors eliminated we nevertheless find that 30 percent of the college prep, as opposed to a mere 4 percent of the noncollege group attained the top quarter of their class; and that only 12 percent of the college prep, as opposed to 35 percent of the noncollege group, fell into the bottom quarter. These figures, which are similar for boys and girls, further show that track position has an independent effect on academic achievement which is greater than the effect of each of the other three factors—social class, IQ and past performance. In particular, assignment to the noncollege track has a strong negative influence on a student's grades.

Looking at dropout rate, and again controlling for social class background, IQ and past performance, we find that track position in itself has an independent influence which is higher than the effect of any of the other three factors. In other words, even when we rule out the effect of these three factors, non-college-bound students still dropped out in considerably greater proportion than college-bound students (19 percent vs. 4 percent).

So our evidence points to the conclusion that the superior academic performance of the college-bound students, and the inferior performance of the noncollege students is partly caused by the tracking system. Our data do not explain how this happens, but several studies of similar educational arrangements, as well as basic principles of social psychology do provide a number of probable explanations. The first point has to do with the pupil's self-image.

Stigma. Assignment to the lower track in the schools we studied carried with it a strong stigma. As David Mallory was told by an American boy, "Around here you are *nothing* if you're not college prep." A noncollege prep girl in one of the schools we studied told me that she always carried her "general" track books upside down because of the humiliation she felt at being seen with them as she walked through the halls.

The corroding effect of such stigmatizing is well known. As Patricia Sexton has put it, "He [the low track student] is bright enough to catch on very quickly to the fact that he is not considered very bright. He comes to accept this unflattering appraisal because, after all, the school should know."

One ex-delinquent in Washington, D.C. told one of us how the stigma from this low track affected him.

It really don't have to be the tests, but after the tests, there shouldn't be no separation in the classes. Because, as I say again, I felt good when I was with my class, but when they went and separated us—that changed us. That changed our ideas, our thinking, the way we thought about each other and turned us to enemies toward each other—because they said I was dumb and they were smart.

When you first go to junior high school you do feel something inside—it's like ego. You have been from elementary to junior high, you feel great inside. You say, well daggone, I'm going to deal with the *people* here now, I am in junior high school. You get this shirt that says Brown Junior High or whatever the name is and you are proud of that shirt. But then you go up there and the teacher says—"Well, so and so, you're in the basic section, you can't go with the other kids." The devil with the whole thing—you lose—something in you—like it just goes out of you.

Did you think the other guys were smarter than you?

Not at first—I used to think I was just as smart as anybody in the school—I knew I was smart. I knew some people were smarter, and I *wanted* to go to school, I wanted to get a diploma and go to college and help people and everything. I stepped into there in junior high—I felt like a fool going to school—I really felt like a fool.

Why?

Because I felt like I wasn't a part of the school. I couldn't get on special patrols, because I wasn't qualified.

What happened between the seventh and ninth grades?

I started losing faith in myself—after the teachers kept downing me. You hear "a guy's in basic section, he's dumb" and all this. Each year—"you're ignorant—you're stupid."

Considerable research shows that such erosion of self-esteem greatly increases the chances of academic failure, as well as dropping out and causing "trouble" both inside and outside of school.

Moreover, this lowered self-image is reinforced by the expectations that others have toward a person in the non-college group.

The Self-fulfilling Prophecy. A related explanation rich in implications comes from David Hargreaves' *Social Relations in a Secondary School*, a study of the psychological, behavioral and educational consequences of the student's position in the streaming system of an

English secondary modern school. In "Lumley School," the students (all boys) were assigned to one of five streams on the basis of ability and achievement, with the score on the "11-plus" examination playing the major role.

Like the schools we studied, students in the different streams were publicly recognized as high or low in status and were fairly rigidly segregated, both formally in different classes and informally in friendship groups. It is quite probable, then, that Hargreaves' explanations for the greater antischool attitudes, animosity toward teachers, academic failure, disruptive behavior and delinquency among the low stream boys apply to the noncollege prep students we studied as well. In fact, the negative effects of the tracking system on non-college-bound students may be even stronger in our two high schools, since the Lumley streaming system was much more open and flexible, with students moving from one stream to another several times during their four-year careers.

As we noted, a popular explanation for the greater failure and misbehavior among low stream or non-college-bound students is that they come from homes that fail to provide the same skills, ambition or conforming attitude as higher stream or college-bound students. Hargreaves demonstrates that there is some validity to this position: in his study, low stream boys more often came from homes that provided less encouragement for academic achievement and higher level occupations, and that were less oriented to the other values of the school and teachers. Similar differences may have existed among the students we studied, although their effects have been markedly reduced by our control for father's occupation, IQ and previous achievement.

But Hargreaves provides a convincing case for the position that whatever the differences in skills, ambition, self-esteem or educational commitment that the students brought to school, they were magnified by what happened to them in school, largely because low stream boys were the victims of a self-fulfilling prophecy in their relations with teachers, with respect to both academic performance and classroom behavior. Teachers of higher stream boys expected higher performance and got it. Similarly, boys who wore the label of streams "C" or "D" were more likely to be seen by teachers as limited in ability and troublemakers, and were treated accordingly.

In a streamed school the teacher categorizes the pupils not only in terms of the inferences he makes of the child's class room behavior but also from the child's stream level. It is for this reason that the teacher can rebuke an "A" stream boy for being like a "D" stream boy. The teacher has learned to *expect* certain kinds of behavior from members of different streams. . . . It would be hardly surprising if "good" pupils thus became "better" and the "bad" pupils become "worse." It is, in short, an example of a self-fulfilling prophecy. The negative expectations of the teacher reinforce the negative behavioral tendencies.

A recent study by Rosenthal and Jacobson in an American elementary school lends further evidence to the position that teacher expectations influence student's performance. In this study, the influence is a positive one. Teachers of children randomly assigned to experimental groups were told at the beginning of the year to expect "unusual intellectual" gains, while teachers of the control group children were told nothing. After eight months, and again after two years, the experimental group children, the "intellectual spurters," showed significantly greater gains in IQ and grades. Further, they were rated by the teachers as being significantly more curious, interesting, happy and more likely to succeed in the future. Such findings are consistent with theories of interpersonal influence and with the interactional or labelling view of deviant behavior.

If, as often claimed, American teachers underestimate the learning potential of low track students and expect more negative attitudes and greater trouble from them, it may well be that they partially cause the very failure, alienation, lack of involvement, dropping out and rebellion they are seeking to prevent. As Hargreaves says of Lumley, "It is important to stress that if this effect of categorization is real, it is entirely unintended by the teachers. They do not wish to make low streams more difficult than they are!" Yet the negative self-fulfilling prophecy was probably real, if unintended and unrecognized, in our two schools as well as in Lumley.

Two further consequences of the expectation that students in the noncollege group will learn less well are differences in grading policies and in teacher effectiveness.

Grading Policies. In the two schools we studied, our interviews strongly hint at the existence of grade ceilings for noncollege prep students and grade floors for college-bound students. That is, by virtue of being located in a college preparatory section or course, college prep students could seldom receive any grade lower than "B" or "C," while students in non-college-bound sections or courses found it difficult to gain any grade higher than "C," even though their objective performance may have been equivalent to a college prep

"B." Several teachers explicitly called our attention to this practice, the rationale being that noncollege prep students do not deserve the same objective grade rewards as college prep students, since they "clearly" are less bright and perform less well. To the extent that grade ceilings do operate for non-college-bound students, the lower grades that result from this policy, almost by definition, can hardly have a beneficial effect on motivation and commitment.

Teaching Effectiveness. Finally, numerous investigations of ability grouping, as well as the English study by Hargreaves, have reported that teachers of higher ability groups are likely to teach in a more interesting and effective manner than teachers of lower ability groups. Such a difference is predictable from what we know about the effects of reciprocal interaction between teacher and class. Even when the same individual teaches both types of classes in the course of the day, as was the case for most teachers in the two schools in this study, he is likely to be "up" for college prep classes and "down" for noncollege prep classes—and to bring out the same reaction from his students.

A final, and crucial factor that contributes to the poorer performance and lower interest in school of non-college-bound students is the relation between school work and the adult career after school.

Future Payoff. Non-college-bound students often develop progressively more negative attitudes toward school, especially formal academic work, because they see grades—and indeed school itself—as having little future relevance or payoff. This is not the case for college prep students. For them, grades are a means toward the identifiable and meaningful end of qualifying for college, while among the non-college-bound, grades are seen as far less important for entry into an occupation or a vocation school. This difference in the practical importance of grades is magnified by the perception among non-college-bound students that it is pointless to put much effort into school work, since it will be unrelated to the later world of work anyway. In a study of *Rebellion in a High School* in this country, Arthur Stinchcombe describes the alienation of non-college-bound high school students:

> The major practical conclusion of the analysis above is that rebellious behavior is largely a reaction to the school itself and to its promises, not a failure of the family or community. High school students can be motivated to conform by paying them in the realistic coin of future advantage. Except perhaps for pathological cases, any student can be motivated to conform if the school can realistically promise something valuable to him as a reward for working hard. But for a large part of the population, especially the adolescent who will enter the male working class or the female candidates for early marriage, the school has nothing to offer. . . . In order to secure conformity from students, a high school must articulate academic work with careers of students.

Being on the lower track has other negative consequences for the student which go beyond the depressing influence on his academic performance and motivation. We can use the principles just discussed to explain our findings with regard to different rates of participation in school activities and acts of misbehavior.

For example, the explanations having to do with self-image and the expectations of others suggest that assignment to the non-college-bound track has a dampening effect on commitment to school in general, since it is the school which originally categorized these students as inferior. Thus, assignment to the lower track may be seen as independently contributing to resentment, frustration and hostility in school, leading to lack of involvement in all school activities, and finally ending in active withdrawal. The self-exclusion of the noncollege group from the mainstream of college student life is probably enhanced by intentional or unintentional exclusion by other students and teachers.

Using the same type of reasons, while we cannot prove a definite causal linkage between track position and misbehavior, it seems highly likely that assignment to the non-college prep track often leads to resentment, declining commitment to school, and rebellion against it, expressed in lack of respect for the school's authority or acts of disobedience against it. As Albert Cohen argued over a decade ago in *Delinquent Boys*, delinquency may well be largely a rebellion against the school and its standards by teenagers who feel they cannot get anywhere by attempting to adhere to such standards. Our analysis suggests that a key factor in such rebellion is noncollege prep status in the school's tracking system, with the vicious cycle of low achievement and inferior self-image that go along with it.

This conclusion is further supported by Hargreaves' findings on the effect of streaming at Lumley:

> There is a real sense in which the school can be regarded as a generator of delinquency. Although the aims and efforts of the teachers are directed towards deleting such tendencies, the organization of the school and its influence on subcultural development unintentionally fosters delinquent values. . . . For low stream boys . . . , school

simultaneously exposes them to these values and deprives them of status in these terms. It is at this point they may begin to reject the values because they cannot succeed in them. The school provides a mechanism through the streaming system whereby their failure is effected and institutionalized, and also provides a situation in which they can congregate together in low streams.

Hargreaves' last point suggests a very important explanation for the greater degree of deviant behavior among the non-college-bound.

The Student Subculture. Assignment to a lower stream at Lumley meant a boy was immediately immersed in a student subculture that stressed and rewarded antagonistic attitudes and behavior toward teachers and all they stood for. If a boy was assigned to the "A" stream, he was drawn toward the values of teachers, not only by the higher expectations and more positive rewards from the teachers themselves, but from other students as well. The converse was true of lower stream boys, who accorded each other high status for doing the opposite of what teachers wanted. Because of class scheduling, little opportunity developed for interaction and friendship across streams. The result was a progressive polarization and hardening of the high and low stream subcultures between first and fourth years and a progressively greater negative attitude across stream lines, with quite predictable consequences.

The informal pressures within the low streams tend to work directly against the assumption of the teachers that boys will regard promotion into a higher stream as a desirable goal. The boys from the low streams were very reluctant to ascend to higher streams because their stereotypes of "A" and "B" stream boys were defined in terms of values alien to their own and because promotion would involve rejection by their low stream friends. The teachers were not fully aware that this unwillingness to be promoted to a higher stream led the high informal status boys to depress their performance in examinations. This fear of promotion adds to our list of factors leading to the formation of anti-academic attitudes among low stream boys.

Observations and interviews in the two American schools we studied confirmed a similar polarization and reluctance by noncollege prep students to pursue the academic goals rewarded by teachers and college prep students. Teachers, however, seldom saw the antischool attitudes of noncollege prep students as arising out of the tracking system—or anything else about the school—but out of adverse home influences, limited intelligence or psychological problems.

Implications. These, then, are some of the ways the schools we studied contributed to the greater rates of failure, academic decline, uninvolvement in school activities, misbehavior and delinquency among non-college-bound students. We can only speculate, of course, about the generalization of these findings to other schools. However, there is little reason to think the two schools we studied were unusual or unrepresentative and, despite differences in size and social class composition, the findings are virtually identical in both. To the extent the findings are valid and general, they strongly suggest that, through their tracking system, the schools are partly causing many of the very problems they are trying to solve and are posing an important barrier to equal educational opportunity to lower income and black students, who are disproportionately assigned to the noncollege prep track.

The notion that schools help cause low achievement, deterioration of educational commitment and involvement, the dropout problem, misbehavior and delinquency is foreign and repulsive to many teachers, administrators and parents. Yet our evidence is entirely consistent with Kai Erikson's observation that " . . . deviant forms of conduct often seem to derive nourishment from the very agencies devised to inhibit them."

What, then, are the implications of this study? Some might argue that, despite the negative side effects we have shown, tracking systems are essential for effective teaching, especially for students with high ability, as well as for adjusting students early in their careers to the status levels they will occupy in the adult occupational system. We contend that however reasonable this may sound, the negative effects demonstrated here offset and call into serious question any presumed gains from tracking.

Others might contend that the negative outcomes we have documented can be eliminated by raising teachers' expectations of noncollege track students, making concerted efforts to reduce the stigma attached to noncollege classes, assigning good teachers to noncollege track classes, rewarding them for doing an effective job at turning on their students, and developing fair and equitable grading practices in both college prep and noncollege prep classes.

Attractive as they may appear, efforts like these will be fruitless so long as tracking systems, and indeed schools as we now know them, remain unchanged. What is needed are wholly new, experimental environments of teaching-learning-living, even outside today's public schools, if necessary. Such schools of the future must address themselves to two sets of problems highlighted by our findings: ensuring equality of opportunity for students now "locked out" by tracking, and offering—to all students—a far more fulfilling and satisfying learning process.

One approach to building greater equality of opportunity, as well as fulfillment, into existing or new secondary schools is the New Careers model. This model, which provides for fundamentally different ways of linking up educational and occupational careers, is based on the recognition that present options for entering the world of work are narrowly limited: one acquires a high school diploma and goes to work, or he first goes to college and perhaps then to a graduate or professional school. (Along the way, of course, young men must cope with the draft.)

The New Careers model provides for new options. Here the youth who does not want to attend college or would not qualify according to usual criteria, is given the opportunity to attend high school part time while working in a lower level position in an expanded professional career hierarchy (including such new positions as teacher aide and teacher associate in education). Such a person would then have the options of moving up through progressively more demanding educational and work stages; and moving back and forth between the work place, the high school and then the college. As ideally conceived, this model would allow able and aspiring persons ultimately to progress to the level of the fully certified teacher, nurse, librarian, social worker or public administrator. While the New Careers model has been developed and tried primarily in the human service sector of the economy, we have pointed out elsewhere that it is applicable to the industrial and business sector as well.

This alternative means of linking education with work has a number of advantages: students can try different occupations while still in school; they can earn while studying; they can spend more time outside the four walls of the school, learning what can best be learned in the work place; less stigma will accrue to those not immediately college bound, since they too will have a future; studying and learning will be inherently more relevant because it will relate to a career in which they are actively involved; teachers of such students will be less likely to develop lower expectations because these youth too will have an unlimited, open-ended future; and antischool subcultures will be less likely to develop, since education will not be as negative, frustrating or stigmatizing.

To ensure equality of opportunity is not enough. Merely to open the channels for lower income youth to flow into educational careers that are now turning off millions of middle class, college-bound youth is hardly doing anyone a favor. Though not reflected in our data, many middle class students now find school even less tolerable than do low income youth. The empty grade-scrambling, teacher-pleasing and stultifying passivity such youth must endure stands in greater and greater contrast to their home and other non-school environments which usually yield much greater excitement, challenge and reward. More and more are dropping out psychologically, turning instead to drugs, apathy or political activism, often of an unthinking and self-defeating kind.

What is needed, then are entirely new and different models that will assure not only equality of opportunity but also much more in the way of an enriching and rewarding growth process. Educational environments of the future, incorporating New Careers as well as other new forms, must follow several simple guidelines.

First, successful new learning environments must be based on the recognition and acceptance of each individual's uniqueness. Each person must be allowed and stimulated to develop, learn and grow as an individual, not as a standardized occupant of any gross human category. As Kenneth Keniston stated in *The Uncommitted*, "Human diversity and variety must not only be tolerated, but rejoiced in, applauded, and encouraged."

At the beginning, we pointed out that tracking was an educational response to the increased pupil diversity created by pressure on adolescents from employers, parents and educators themselves to stay in school longer. While it may be an efficient way to screen large numbers of youth out of the educational and economic systems, and while it may be bureaucratically convenient, tracking is crude at best and destructive at worst in psychological and educational terms. Predictably, the occupants of the categories created by tracking come to be perceived, treated and taught according to what they are thought to have in common: college material or not college material, bright or not bright, motivated or not motivated, fast or not fast. Yet psychologists of individual differences and learning have told us for years what every parent already knows from common sense and experience: each child is unique in aptitudes, style of interaction, learning style and rate, energy level, interests, self-attitudes, reactions to challenge and stress, and in countless other ways. New educational environments must be adaptable to these differences.

The second guideline must be that the potential for

individual growth and development is virtually unlimited and must be freed and stimulated to develop as
fully as possible during each student's lifetime. We must
stop assuming human potential is somehow fixed or
circumscribed. Tragically, tracking—and indeed the
whole structure of schooling—is founded on this premise. George Leonard puts it well in his *Education and
Ecstasy*: " . . . the task of *preventing* the new generation
from changing in any deep or significant way is precisely
what most societies require of their educators." Not
surprisingly, then, "The most obvious barrier between
our children and the kind of education that can free
their enormous potential seems to be the educational
system itself: a vast, suffocating web of people, practices, and presumptions, kindly in intent, ponderous in
response." In building new environments for becoming—
with rich and limitless opportunities for exploration
into self and others, other places, times and ideas, and
the unknown—educators can play a part in seeing to it
that more than today's mere fraction of potential
learning and growing is unleashed.

The third guideline must be that "learning is sheer
delight," to quote Leonard. For the non-college bound—
indeed for the vast majority, including neat and tidy
"high achievers"—"schooling" (we can hardly call it
learning) is the very opposite. Tragically, Leonard may
be all too right: "A visitor from another planet might
conclude that our schools are hell bent on creating—in a
society that offers leisure and demands creativity—a
generation of joyless drudges . . . when joy is absent, the
effectiveness of the learning process falls and falls until
the human being is operating hesitantly, grudgingly,
fearfully at only a tiny fraction of his potential." For
joy to enter learning, "cognitive learning" must be
reunited with affective, physical and behavioral growth.

The payoff must be now. Will learning then stop with the diploma?

If new learning-teaching-living environments follow these simple guidelines, not only will the negative effects of tracking be eliminated, but several features of the student role that alienate all types of students can also be avoided: passivity, subordination, forced separation from self, fragmented sequencing of learning, age segregation, isolation from community life with the unrealities of school that follow, an almost exclusive instrumental emphasis on future gains from schooling.

In summary, then, education must afford a chance for every student to experience an individualized, mind-expanding, joy-producing educational process, based on equity of opportunity. But it must do even more. Education must, in the final analysis, address itself to the vital issues of man and his survival. Educators then can take a long step toward preserving life itself.

"Right answers," specialization, standardization, narrow competition, eager acquisition, aggression, detachment from the self. Without them, it has seemed, the social machinery would break down. Do not call the schools cruel or unnatural for furthering what society had demanded. The reason we now need radical reform in education is that society's demands are changing radically. It is quite safe to say that the human characteristics now being inculcated will not work much longer. Already they are not only inappropriate, but destructive. If education continues along the old tack, humanity sooner or later will simply destroy itself (Leonard).

We must start now.

October 1970

FURTHER READING

New Careers for the Poor, by Arthur Pearl and Frank Riessman (New York: Free Press, 1965).

Social Relations in a Secondary School, by David H. Hargreaves (New York: Humanities Press, 1967).

"Delinquency and the Schools," by Walter E. Schafer and Kenneth Polk, in *Task Force Report: Juvenile Delinquency and Youth Crime* (President's Commission of Law Enforcement and Administration of Justice, 1967).

Schools and Delinquency, by Kenneth Polk and Walter E. Schafer (Englewood Cliffs, N.J.: Prentice-Hall, 1972).

V. HEALTH

Medical Ghettos

ANSELM L. STRAUSS

In President Johnson's budget message to Congress in 1967 he proposed a quadrupling of federal spending on health care and medical assistance for the poor to $4.2 billion in fiscal 1968:

> The 1968 budget maintains the forward thrust of federal programs designed to improve health care in the nation, to combat poverty, and assist the needy.... The rise reflects the federal government's role in bringing quality medical care, particularly to aged and indigent persons.

Three years earlier in a special message to Congress the President had prefaced reintroduction of the medicare bill by saying:

> We can—and we must—strive now to assure the availability of and accessibility to the best health care for all Americans, regardless of age or geography or economic status.... Nowhere are the needs

greater than for the 15 million children of families who live in poverty.

Then, after decades of debate and massive professional and political opposition, the medicare program was passed. It promised to lift the poorest of our aged out of the medical ghetto of charity and into private and voluntary hospital care. In addition, legislation for heart disease and cancer centers was quickly enacted. It was said that such facilities would increase life expectancy by five years and bring a 20 percent reduction in heart disease and cancer by 1975.

Is the medical millenium, then, on its way? The President, on the day before sending the 1968 budget to Congress, said: "Medicare is an unqualified success."

"Nevertheless," he added, "there are improvements which can be made and shortcomings which need prompt attention." The message also noted that there might be some obstacles on the highroad to health. The rising cost of medical care, President Johnson stated, "requires an expanded and better organized effort by the federal government in research and studies of the organization and delivery of health care." If the President's proposals are adopted, the states will spend $1.9 billion and the federal government $1 billion in a "Partnership for Health" under the Medicaid program.

Considering the costs to the poor—and to the taxpayers—why don't the disadvantaged get better care? In all the lively debate on that matter, it is striking how little attention is paid to the mismatch between the current organization of American medicine and the life styles of the lower class. The major emphasis is always on how the *present* systems can be a little better supported or a trifle altered to produce better results.

I contend that the poor will never have anything

approaching equal care until our present medical organization undergoes profound reform. Nothing in current legislation or planning will accomplish this. My arguments, in brief, are these:

1) The emphasis in all current legislation is on extending and improving a basically sound system of medical organization.

2) This assumes that all those without adequate medical services—especially the poor—can be reached with minor reforms without radical transformation of the systems of care.

3) This assumption is false. The reason the medical systems have not reached the poor is because they were never designed to do so. The way the poor think and respond, the way they live and operate, has hardly ever (if ever) been considered in the scheduling, paperwork, organization and mores of clinics, hospitals and doctors' offices. The life styles of the poor are different; they must be specifically taken into account. Professionals have not been trained and are not now being trained in the special skills and procedures necessary to do this.

4) These faults result in a vicious cycle which drives the poor away from the medical care they need.

5) Major reforms in medical organizations must come, or the current great inequities will continue, and perhaps grow.

I have some recommendations designed specifically to break up that vicious cycle at various points. These recommendations are built directly upon aspects of the life styles of the poor. They do not necessarily require new money or resources, but they do require rearrangement, reorganization, reallocation—the kind of change and reform which are often much harder to attain than new funds or facilities.

In elaborating these arguments, one point must be nailed down first: The poor definitely get second-rate medical care. This is self-evident to anyone who has worked either with them or in public medical facilities; but there is a good deal of folklore to the effect that the very poor share with the very rich the best doctors and services—the poor getting free in the clinics what only the rich can afford to buy.

The documented statistics of the Department of Health, Education, and Welfare tell a very different story. As of 1964, those families with annual incomes under $2,000 average 2.8 visits per person to a physician each year, compared to 3.8 for those above $7,000. (For children during the crucial years under 15, the ratio is 1.6 to 5.7. The poor tend to have larger families; needless to add, their child mortality rate is also higher.) People with higher incomes (and $7,000 per year can hardly be considered wealthy) have a tremendous advantage in the use of medical specialists—27.5 percent see at least one of them annually, compared to about 13 percent of the poor.

Health insurance is supposed to equalize the burden; but here, too, money purchases better care. Hospital or surgical insurance coverage is closely related to family income, ranging from 34 percent among those with family income of less than $2,000 to almost 90 percent for persons in families of $7,000 or more annual income. At the same time, the poor, when hospitalized, are much more apt to have more than one disorder—and more apt to exhaust their coverage before discharge.

Among persons who were hospitalized, insurance paid for some part of the bill for about 40 percent of patients with less than $2,000 family income, for 60 percent of patients with $2,000-$3,999 family income, and for 80 percent of patients with higher incomes. Insurance paid three-fourths or more of the bill for approximately 27 percent, 44 percent and 61 percent of these respective income groups. Preliminary data from the 1964 survey year showed, for surgery or delivery bills paid by insurance, an even more marked association of insurance with income.

Similar figures can be marshaled for chronic illness, dental care and days of work lost.

Strangely enough, however, *cash* difference (money actually spent for care) is not nearly so great. The under $2,000 per year group spent $112 per person per year, those families earning about three times as much ($4,000-$7,000) paid $119 per person, and those above $7,000, $153. Clearly, the poor not only get poorer health services but less for their money.

As a result, the poor suffer much more chronic illness and many more working days lost—troubles they are peculiarly ill-equipped to endure. Almost 60 percent of the poor have more than one disabling condition compared to about 24 percent of other Americans. Poor men lose 10.2 days of work annually compared to 4.9 for the others. Even medical research seems to favor the affluent—its major triumphs have been over acute, not chronic, disorders.

Medical care, as we know it now, is closely linked with the advancing organization, complexity and maturity of our society and the increasing education, urbanization and need for care of our people. Among the results: Medicine is increasingly practiced in hospitals in metropolitan areas.

The relatively few dispensaries for the poor of yesteryear have been supplanted by great numbers of outpatient hospital clinics. These clinics and services are still not adequate—which is why the continuing cry for reform is "more and better." But even when medical services *are* readily available to the poor, they are not used as much as they could and should be. The reasons fall into two categories:

—factors in the present organization of medical care that act as a brake on giving quality care to everyone;

—the life styles of the poor that present obstacles even when the brakes are released.

The very massiveness of modern medical organization is itself a hindrance to health care for the poor. Large buildings and departments, specialization, division of labor, complexity and bureaucracy lead to an impersonality and an overpowering and often grim atmosphere of hugeness. The poor, with their meager experience in organizational life, their insecurity in the middle-class world, and their dependence on personal contacts, are especially vulnerable to this impersonalization.

Hospitals and clinics are organized for "getting work done" from the staff point of view; only infrequently are they set up to minimize the patient's confusion. He fends for himself and sometimes may even get lost when sent "just down the corridor." Patients are often sent for diagnostic tests from one service to another with no explanations, with inadequate directions, with brusque tones. This may make them exceedingly anxious and affect their symptoms and diagnosis. After sitting for hours in waiting rooms, they become angry to find themselves passed over for latecomers—but nobody explains about emergencies or priorities. They complain they cannot find doctors they really like or trust.

When middle-class patients find themselves in similar situations, they can usually work out some methods of "beating the system" or gaining understanding that may raise staff tempers but will lower their own anxieties. The poor do not know how to beat the system. And only very seldom do they have that special agent, the private doctor, to smooth their paths.

Another organizational barrier is the increasing professionalism of health workers. The more training and experience it takes to make the various kinds of doctors, nurses, technicians and social workers, the more they become oriented around professional standards and approaches, and the more the patient must take their knowledge and abilities on trust. The gaps of communications, understanding and status grow. To the poor, professional procedures may seem senseless or even dangerous—especially when not explained—and professional manners impersonal or brutal, even when professionals are genuinely anxious to help.

Many patients complain about not getting enough information; but the poor are especially helpless. They don't know the ropes. Fred Davis quotes from a typical poor parent, the mother of a polio-stricken child:

> Well they don't tell you anything hardly. They don't seem to want to. I mean you start asking questions and they say, "Well, I only have about three minutes to talk to you." And then the things that you ask, they don't seem to want to answer you. So I don't ask them anything any more. . . .

For contrast, we witnessed an instance of a highly educated woman who found her physician evasive. Suddenly she shot a question: "Come now, Doctor, don't I have the same cancerous condition that killed my sister?" His astonished reaction confirmed her suspicion.

Discrimination also expresses itself in subtle ways. As Frank Riessman and Sylvia Scribner note (for psychiatric care), "Middle class patients are preferred by most treatment agents, and are seen as more treatable. . . . Diagnoses are more hopeful. . . ." Those who understand, follow, respond to, and are grateful for treatment are good patients; and that describes the middle class.

Professional health workers are themselves middle class, represent and defend its values and show its biases. They assume that the poor (like themselves) have regular meals, lead regular lives, try to support families, keep healthy, plan for the future. They prescribe the same treatment for the same diseases to all, not realizing that their words do not mean the same things to all. (What does "take with each meal" mean to a family that eats irregularly, seldom together, and usually less than three times a day?)

And there is, of course, some open bias. A welfare case worker in a large Midwestern city, trying to discover why her clients did not use a large, nearby municipal clinic more, described what she found:

> People are shouted at, ridiculed, abused, pushed around, called "Niggers," told to stand "with the rest of the herd," and in many instances made to feel terribly inferior if not inadequate. . . . This . . . was indulged in by personnel other than doctors and nurses. . . .

Even when no bias is intended, the hustle, impersonality and abstraction of the mostly white staff tend to create this feeling among sensitive and insecure people: "And I do think the treatment would have been different if Albert had been white."

The poor especially suffer in that vague area we call "care," which includes nursing, instructions about regimens, and post-hospital treatment generally. What happens to the lower-class patient once released? Middle-class patients report regularly to their doctors who check on progress and exert some control. But the poor are far more likely to go to the great, busy clinics where they seldom see the same doctor twice. Once out they are usually on their own.

Will the poor get better care if "more and better" facilities are made available? I doubt it. The fact is that they underutilize those available now.

Distances are also important. Hospitals and clinics are usually far away. The poor tend to organize their lives around their immediate neighborhoods, to shut out the rest of the city. Some can hardly afford bus fare (much less cab fare for emergencies). Other obstacles include unrealistic eligibility rules and the requirement by some hospitals that clinic patients arrange a blood donation to the blood bank as a prerequisite for prenatal care.

Medical organization tends to assume a patient who is educated and well motivated, who is interested in ensuring a reasonable level of bodily functioning and generally in preserving his own health. But health professionals themselves complain that the poor come to the clinic or hospital with advanced symptoms, that parents don't pay attention to children's symptoms early enough, that they don't follow up treatments or regimens, and delay too long in returning. But is it really the fault of whole sections of the American population if they don't follow what professionals expect of them?

What are the poor really like? In our country they are distinctive. They live strictly, and wholeheartedly, in the present; their lives are uncertain, dominated by re-curring crises (as S.M. Miller puts it, theirs "is a crisis-life constantly trying to make do with string where rope is needed"). To them a careful concern about health is unreal—they face more pressing troubles daily, just getting by. Bad health is just one more condition they must try to cope—or live—with.

Their households are understaffed. There are no servants, few reliable adults. There is little time or energy to care for the sick. If the mother is ill, who will care for her or take her to the clinic—or care for the children if she goes? It is easier to live with illness than use up your few resources doing something about it.

> As Daniel Rosenblatt and Edward Suchman have noted: The body can be seen as simply another class of objects to be worn out but not repaired. Thus, teeth are left without dental care. . . . Corrective eye examinations, even for those who wear glasses, are often neglected. . . . It is as though . . . blue-collar groups think of the body as having a limited span of utility; to be enjoyed in youth and then to suffer with and to endure stoically with age and decrepitude.

They are characterized by low self-esteem. Lee Rainwater remarks that low-income people develop "a sense of being unworthy; they do not uphold the sacredness of their persons in the same way that middle-class people do. Their tendency to think of themselves as of little account is . . . readily generalized to their bodies." And this attitude is transferred to their children.

They seek medical treatment only when practically forced to it. As Rosenblatt and Suchman put it: "Symptoms that do not incapacitate are often ignored." In clinics and hospitals they are shy, frustrated, passively submissive, prey to brooding, depressed anxiety. They reply with guarded hostility, evasiveness and withdrawal. They believe, of their treatment, that "what is free is not much good." As a result, the professionals tend to turn away. Julius Roth describes how the staff in a rehabilitation ward gets discouraged with its apparently unrehabilitatable patients and gives up and concentrates on the few who seem hopeful. The staffs who must deal with the poor in such wards either have rapid turnover or retreat into "enclaves of research, administration, and teaching."

The situation must get worse. More of the poor will come to the hospitals and clinics. Also, with the increasing use of health insurance and programs by unions and employers, more will come as paying patients into the private hospitals, mixing with middle-class patients and staff, upsetting routines, perhaps lowering quality—a frightening prospect as many administrators see it. As things are going now, relations between lower-income patients and hospital staff must become more frequent, intense and exacerbated.

It is evident that the vicious cycle that characterizes medical care for the poor must be broken before anything can be accomplished.

In the first part of this cycle, the poor come into the hospitals later than they should, often delaying until their disorders are difficult to relieve, until they are actual emergency cases. The experiences they have there encourage them to try to stay out even longer the next time—and to cut the visits necessary for treatment to a minimum.

Second, they require, if anything, even more effective communication and understanding with the professionals than the middle-class patient. They don't get it; and the treatment is often undone once they leave.

What to do? The conventional remedies do help some. More money and insurance will tend to bring the poor to medical help sooner, increased staff and facilities can cut down the waits, the rush, the tenseness, and allow for more individual and efficient treatment and diagnosis.

But much more is required. If the cycle is to be *broken*, the following set of recommendations must be adopted:

1) Speed up the initial visit. Get them there sooner.
2) Improve patient experiences.
3) Improve communication given and received about regimens and treatment to be followed.
4) Work to make it more likely that the patient or his family will follow through at home.
5) Make it more likely that the patient will return when necessary.
6) Decrease the time between necessary visits.

This general list is not meant to be the whole formula. Any experienced doctor or nurse, once he recognizes the need, can add to or modify it. An experience of mine illustrates this well. A physician in charge of an adolescent clinic for lower-income patients, finding that my ideas fitted into his own daily experience, invited me to address his staff. In discussion afterward good ideas quickly emerged.

7) Since teen-age acne and late teen-age menstrual pain were frequent complaints and the diagnoses and medications not very complicated, why not let nurses make them? Menstruating girls would be more willing to talk to a woman than a man.
8) Patients spend many hours sitting around waiting. Why not have nursing assistants, trained by the social worker and doctor and drawn from the patients' social class, interview and visit with them during this period, collecting relevant information?

Note two things about these suggestions: Though they do involve some new duties and some shifting around, they do not call for any appreciable increase of money, personnel, or resources; and such recommendations, once the need is pointed out, can arise from the initiative and experience of the staff themselves.

Here in greater detail are my recommendations:

Increased efforts are needed for early detection of disease among the poor. Existing methods should be increased and improved, and others should be added— for instance, mobile detection units of all kinds, public drives with large-scale educational campaigns against common specific disorders and so on. The poor themselves should help in planning, and their ideas should be welcomed.

The schools could and should become major detection units with large-scale programs of health inspection. The school nurse, left to her own initiative, is not enough. The poor have more children and are less efficient at noting illness; those children do go to school, where they could be examined. Teachers should also be given elementary training and used more effectively in detection.

Train more sub-professionals, drawn from the poor themselves. They can easily learn to recognize the symptoms of the more common disorders and be especially useful in large concentrations, such as housing projects. They can teach the poor to look for health problems in their own families.

The large central facilities make for greater administrative and medical efficiency. But fewer people will come to them than to smaller neighborhood dispensaries. Imperfect treatment may be better than little or no treatment; and the total effectiveness for the poor may actually be better with many small facilities than the big ones.

Neighborhood centers can not only treat routine

cases and act to follow up hospital outpatients, but they can also discover those needing the more difficult procedures and refer them to the large centers—for example, prenatal diagnosis and treatment in the neighborhoods, with high-risk pregnancies sent to the central facilities. (The Children's Bureau has experimented with this type of organization.)

There must be better methods to get the sick to the clinics. As noted, the poor tend to stick to their own neighborhoods and be fearful outside them, to lack bus fare and domestic help. Even when dental or eye defects *are* discovered in schools, often children still do not get treatment. Sub-professionals and volunteers could follow up, provide transportation, bus fare, information, or babysitting and housecare. Block or church organizations could help. The special drives for particular illnesses could also include transportation. (Recent studies show that different ethnic groups respond differently to different pressures and appeals; sub-professionals from the same groups could, therefore, be especially effective.)

Hours should be made more flexible; there should be more evening and night clinics. Working people work, when they have jobs, and cannot afford to lose jobs in order to sit around waiting to be called at a clinic. In short, clinics should adapt to people, not expect the opposite. (A related benefit: Evening clinics should lift the load on emergency services in municipal hospitals, since the poor often use them just that way.)

Neighborhood pharmacists should be explicitly recognized as part of the medical team, and every effort be made to bring them in. The poor are much more apt to consult their neighborhood pharmacist first—and he could play a real role in minor treatment and in referral.

He should be rewarded, and given such training as necessary—perhaps by schools of pharmacy. Other "health healers" might also be encouraged to help get the seriously ill to the clinics and hospitals, instead of being considered rivals or quacks.

Lower-income patients who enter treatment early can be rewarded for it. This may sound strange, rewarding people for benefiting themselves—but it might bring patients in earlier as well as bring them back, and actually save money for insurance companies and government and public agencies.

Hospital emergency services must be radically reorganized. Such services are now being used by the poor as clinics and as substitutes for general practitioners. Such use upsets routine and arouses mutual frustrations and resentments. There are good reasons why the poor use emergency services this way, and the services should be reorganized to face the realities of the situation.

Clinics and hospitals could assign *agents* to their lower-income patients, who can orient them, allay anxiety, listen to complaints, help them cooperate, and help them negotiate with the staff.

Better accountability and communication should be built into the organization of care. Much important information gets to doctors and nurses only fortuitously, if at all. For instance, nurses' aides often have information about cardiac or terminal patients that doctors and nurses could use; but they do not always volunteer the information nor are they often asked, since they are not considered medically qualified. This is another place where the *agent* might be useful.

It is absolutely necessary that medical personnel lessen their class and professional biases. Anti-bias training is virtually nonexistent in medical schools or associations. It must be started, especially in the professional schools.

Medical facilities must carefully consider how to allow and improve the lodging of complaints by the poor against medical services. They have few means and little chance now to make their complaints known, and this adds to their resentment, depression, and helplessness. Perhaps the agent can act as a kind of medical ombudsman; perhaps unions, or the other health insurance groups, can lodge the complaints; perhaps neighborhood groups can do it. But it must be done.

Treatment and regimens are supposed to continue in the home. Poor patients seldom do them adequately. Hospitals and clinics usually concentrate on diagnosis and treatment and tend to neglect what occurs after. Sometimes there is even confusion about who is supposed to tell the patient about such things as his diet at home, and there is little attempt to see that he does it. Here again, follow-up by sub-professionals might be useful.

Special training given to professionals will enable them to give better instructions to the poor on regimens. They are seldom trained in interviewing or listening—and the poor are usually deficient in pressing their opinions.

Clinics and hospitals could organize their services to include checking on ex-patients who have no private physicians. We recommend that hospitals and clinics try to bring physicians in poor neighborhoods into some sort of association. Many of these physicians do not have hospital connections, practice old-fashioned or substandard medicine—yet they are in most immediate contact with the poor, especially before hospitalization.

Medical establishments should make special efforts to

discover and understand the prevalent life styles of their patients. Since this affects efficiency of treatment, it is an important medical concern.

I strongly recommend greater emphasis on research in medical devices or techniques that are simple to operate and depend as little as possible on patients' judgment and motivation. Present good examples include long-term tranquilizers and the intrauterine birth-control device which requires little of the woman other than her consent. Such developments fit lower-class life style much better than those requiring repeated actions, timing and persistence.

As noted, these recommendations are not basically different from many others—except that they all relate to the idea of the vicious cycle. A major point of this essay is that equal health care will not come unless all portions of that cycle are attacked simultaneously.

To assure action sufficiently broad and strong to demolish this cycle, *responsibility must also be broad and strong.*

1) Medical and professional schools must take vigorous steps to counteract the class bias of their students, to teach them to relate, communicate, and adapt techniques and regimens to the poor, and to learn how to train and instruct sub-professionals.

2) Specific medical institutions must, in addition to the recommendations above, consider how best to attack *all* segments of the cycle. Partial attacks will not do—medicine has responsibility for the total patient and the total treatment.

3) Lower class people must themselves be enlisted in the campaign to give them better care. Not to do this would be absolutely foolhardy. The sub-professionals we mention are themselves valuable in large part because

they come from the poor, and understand them. Where indigenous organizations exist, they should be used. Where they do not exist, organizations that somehow meet their needs should be aided and encouraged to form.

4) Finally, governments, at all levels, have an immense responsibility for persuading, inducing, or pressuring medical institutions and personnel toward reforming our system of medical care. If they understand the vicious cycle, their influence will be much greater. This governmental role need not at all interfere with the patient's freedom. Medical influence is shifting rapidly to the elite medical centers; federal and local governments have a responsibility to see that medical influence and care, so much of it financed by public money, accomplishes what it is supposed to.

What of the frequently heard argument that increasing affluence will soon eliminate the need for special programs for the poor?

5) Most sociologists agree that general affluence may never "trickle down" to the hard-core poverty groups; that only sustained and specialized effort over a long period of time may relieve their poverty.

6) Increased income does not necessarily change life styles. Some groups deliberately stand outside our mainstream. And there is usually a lag at least of one generation, often more, before life styles respond to changed incomes.

In the long run, no doubt, prosperity for all will minimize the inferiority of medical care for the poor. But in the long run, as the saying goes, we will all be dead. And the disadvantaged sick will probably go first, with much unnecessary suffering.

May 1967

FURTHER READING

"Delivery of Personal Health Services and Medical Services for the Poor: Concessions or Prerogatives" by Howard Brown, in *Milbank Memorial Fund Quarterly* (Vol. XLVI, 1968, Part 2).

The Lower Class, Health Illness and Mental Institutions" by I. Deutscher and E.L. Thompson from *Among the People* (New York: Basic Books, 19——).

"Metropolitan Medical Economics" by Nora Piore in *Scientific American* (Vol. 212, 1965).

"The Underutilization of Medical-Care Services by Blue Collarities" by Daniel Rosenblatt and Edward Suchman in *Blue Collar World* edited by Arthur Shostak and William Gomberg (New York: Prentice-Hall, 1964).

"Professionalism and the Poor—Structural Effects and Professional Behavior" by James Walsh and Ray Elling in *Journal of Health and Social Behavior* (Vol. 9, 1968).

"Illness Behavior of the Working Classes" by Irving Zola in *Blue Collar World* edited by Arthur Shostak and William Gomberg (New York: Prentice-Hall, 1964).

The Gift of Blood

RICHARD TITMUSS

There is a bond that links all men and women in the world so closely and intimately that every difference of color, religious belief and cultural heritage is insignificant beside it. Never varying in temperature more than five or six degrees, composed of 55 percent water, the life stream of blood that runs in the veins of every member of the human race proves that the family of man is a reality.

The "blood is the life," says Deuteronomy (12:23). "For this is my blood of the New Testament which is shed for you" (Matthew 26:28). Ancient Egyptians were said to bathe in blood to refresh their powers, and to anoint heads with oil and blood to treat graying and baldness. Ovid describes how Aeson recovered his youthfulness after drinking the blood of his son Jason. The Romans were said to have drunk the blood of dying gladiators to imbue them with courage. Blood brother ceremonies in various countries of the world still fulfill functions of reconciliation and other social purposes, while blood feuds—blood being repaid with blood—represented a powerful institution in medieval Europe and form part of the conventions of some societies today.

Symbolically and functionally, blood is deeply embedded in religious doctrine, in the psychology of human relationships, and in theories and concepts of race, kinship, ancestor worship and the family. From time immemorial it has symbolized qualities of fortitude, vigor, nobility, purity and fertility. Men have been terrified by the sight of blood; they have killed each other for it, believed it could work miracles and have preferred death rather than receive it from a member of a different ethnic group.

In more recent times, the growth of scientific knowledge about blood has provided us with a more rational framework. But it is only in the last 30 years or so that scientific advances have made the transfer of blood from one human being to another an increasingly indispensable part of modern medicine.

Blood transfusion represents one of the greatest therapeutic instruments in the hands of contemporary physicians. It has made possible the saving of life on a scale undreamt of several decades ago, and for conditions that were long considered hopeless. Moreover, the demand for blood increases yearly in every Western country as physicians adopt more radical surgical techniques entailing the loss of massive amounts of blood, and as new uses are found for blood, both in the saving of life and in the prevention of disease and disability.

All these scientific and technical developments in the field of blood transfusion have not only produced new and as yet unsolved problems for the biological and medical sciences, they have also set in train social, economic and ethical consequences that present society with issues of profound importance. It is part of the purpose of this essay to explore these consequences.

It is difficult to assemble information about the total activities of all blood-banking systems in the United States. It has been estimated that there were in 1966-68 some 9,000 central, regional and local blood banks in the United States concerned with the collection of blood from donors. Some (for example, hospital blood banks) will also be concerned with processing, cross-matching and transfusion; some have the function of producing and preparing blood components; some operate solely as collectors, distributors and suppliers of whole blood; and some provide a comprehensive community service.

This diversity of single and multipurpose agencies may be classified in terms of five distinct types of blood banks:

☐ Fifty-five independent but cooperating American Red Cross Regional Blood Centers based on 1,700 participating local chapters and accounting, according to rough estimates in 1967, for about 40 percent of total blood supplies in the United States.

☐ Some 6,000 individual hospital blood banks, which perform a great variety of services and are estimated to be responsible for about 20 to 30 percent of total blood supplies.

☐ About 100 nonprofit organizations known as community blood banks, which generally aim to ensure an adequate blood supply for the communities in which they are situated. These agencies also perform various services, some simply acting as collectors and distributors to hospitals, others having a wide range of functions. The community banks were thought in 1966 to account for about 15 to 20 percent of total blood supplies.

☐ An unknown number of independent profit-making commercial blood banks, which generally obtain their blood supplies from paid donors, process it and sell it to hospitals at a profit. These banks were believed in the early 1960s to account for some 10 to 15 percent of total blood supplies. As we shall see, however, more recent estimates arrive at substantially higher figures. Indeed there seems to be no doubt that in recent years the percentage of blood supplied by these commercial agencies has been increasing, partly at the expense of voluntary programs.

☐ An unknown number of commercial blood banks directly operated by pharmaceutical firms which rely heavily on a newly developed method of drawing blood, plasmapheresis. In nontechnical terms, this means that after the donor has given a pint of blood, the red cells are separated from the plasma (the liquid part of blood as distinguished from the suspended elements) and injected back into the donor. For the donor, the process takes less than an hour. Provided that the strictest medical standards are observed, and that the donor is in excellent health and eats a nutritious high-protein diet, it is claimed by some authorities that one individual can make several donations a week. Other authorities believe, however, that it is too soon to be certain that plasmapheresis may not involve serious long-term hazards for the donors.

Plasmapheresis of donors is used by these blood banks to obtain plasma, plasma protein components and platelets, for all of which there has been an immensely increasing demand. Various estimates in 1968 suggested that pharmaceutical firms were paying for 1 to 1.5 million donations a year yielding, with "double bleed" sessions, approximately 2 million units. A number of firms operate their own plasmapheresis centers; others obtain their supplies from "independent blood contractors." Some regular donors are, in effect, "semisalaried" and paid $150 to $200 a month for a specified number of donations; some are long-term prisoners.

National estimates of the quantities of blood collected by these different types of blood banks generally exclude the commercial plasmapheresis centers because no comprehensive figures exist as to the scale of their operations. Excluding such supplies, however, national estimates of collections in the early 1960s range from 5 to 6 million units a year. Of this total, it has been suggested that anywhere from 17 to 20 percent, and more, is provided by donors who are paid in cash for their blood. One might assume, therefore, that the remainder of the total annual collection was provided by voluntary donors. Much depends, however, on the definition of "voluntary donor."

To "donate" is to give implying an altruistic motive. Strictly and perhaps more neutrally speaking, "suppliers" should replace "donors" in the vocabulary of this study, as we shall see presently. We will, however, conform to the common usage, even though it is somewhat misleading.

To obtain sufficient quantities of blood in the required blood-group proportions, at the required times and in the required places are not processes that can be determined and controlled by the medical profession alone, despite its power to decide who may and who may not give and the destination of the gifts. To give or not to give, to lend, repay or even to buy and sell blood—these are the questions that lead us beyond any one profession into the fundamentals of social and economic life.

The forms and functions of giving embody moral, social, psychological, religious, legal and esthetic ideas. They may reflect, sustain, strengthen or lessen the cultural bonds of the group, large or small. They may inspire the worst excesses of war and tribal nationalism or the tolerances of the community. They may contribute to integrative processes in a society (binding together different ethnic, religious and generational groups), or they may spread, through separatist and segregationist acts, the sense and reality of alienation—as in South Africa and the southern states of the United States.

Customs and practices of noneconomic giving—unilateral and multilateral social transfers—thus may tell us much (as Marcel Mauss so sensitively demonstrated in his book *The Gift*) about the texture of personal and group relationships in different cultures, past and present. But the gift of blood has about it certain unique attributes that distinguish it from other forms of giving. We enumerate some of these now; all derive from the assumption that the gift is a voluntary, altruistic act:

☐ The gift of blood takes place in impersonal situations, sometimes with physically hurtful consequences to the donor.

☐ The recipient is in almost all cases not personally

known to the donor; there can, therefore, be no personal expressions of gratitude or of other sentiments.
□ Only certain groups in the populations are allowed to give; the selection of those who can is determined on rational and not cultural rules by external arbiters.
□ There are no personal, predictable penalties for not giving, no socially enforced sanctions of remorse, shame or guilt.
□ For the giver there is no certainty of a corresponding gift in return, present or future.
□ No givers require or wish for corresponding gifts in return; they do not expect and would not wish to have a blood transfusion.
□ In most systems, there is no obligation imposed on the recipient himself to make a corresponding gift in return.
□ Whether the gift itself is beneficial or harmful to an unknown recipient will depend to some extent on the truthfulness and honesty of the giver. Moreover, the intermediaries—those who collect and process the gift— may determine in certain systems whether it is potentially beneficial or harmful.
□ Both givers and recipients might, if they were known to each other, refuse to participate in the process on religious, ethnic, political or other grounds.
□ Blood as a gift is highly perishable (its value rapidly diminishes), but neither the giver nor the recipient wields any power in determining whether it is used or wasted.
□ To the giver, the gift is quickly replaced by the body. There is no permanent loss. To the recipient, the gift may be everything: life itself.

There are many myths in all societies, and America is no exception. One of the most deeply held myths in this country today is that the voluntary donor is the norm, that most blood donations are contributed by volunteers.

In weighing the truth of this myth, one should bear in mind the many inadequacies, gaps and errors in the statistical data. At various points in the breakdown of types of donors that follows, we have been forced to employ what one can only call "informed guesswork" based on months of work tabulating, checking and comparing the statistics in all the survey reports since 1956. In general, we believe we have erred on the conservative side in our estimates of the proportions of paid blood supplies. However, with these cautions in mind, we now sum up these approximate figures:

Table 1—ESTIMATES OF SOURCE OF BLOOD COLLECTED
BY TYPE, UNITED STATES, EACH YEAR, 1965-67

Type	Number of Units	
A The Paid Donor B The Professional Donor	1,737,800	29%
C The Paid-Induced Voluntary Donor	211,600	4
D The Responsibility Fee Donor E The Family Credit Donor	3,188,000	52
F The Captive Voluntary Donor	324,800	5
G The Fringe Benefit Voluntary Donor	26,500	1
H The Voluntary Community Donor	561,300	9
Total	6,000,000	100

This table shows that about one-third of all donations were bought and sold (types A,B and C). Approximately 52 percent (types D and E) were "tied" by contracts of various kinds; that is, these donations represented the contracted repayment in blood of blood debts, encouraged or enforced by monetary penalties. Some of these donors will have themselves benefited financially, and some will have paid other donors to provide the blood. About 5 percent were captive voluntary donors—members of the armed forces and prisoners. About 9 percent approximated the concept of the voluntary community donor who sees his donation as a free gift to strangers in society.

But this picture is incomplete. We have already noted the recent growth of plasmapheresis programs operated by commercial banks and pharmaceutical firms. Their annual harvest of 2 million units has had the effect of making the contribution of the voluntary donor an even less significant one in the United States, for almost all of these units were bought: some from registered, quasi-salaried donors, some from "walk-in," irregular and occasional donors. In all, perhaps 400,000 or so different individuals are paid for this yield of 2 million units a year.

We now have to add these estimates to the totals in Table 1. The effect is to raise the annual national collection total to 8 million units and the combined figure for types A and B ("paid" and "professional" donors) to 3,737,800 units. The adjusted percentages are:

Table 2—ESTIMATES OF SOURCE OF BLOOD (INCLUDING PLASMAPHERESIS PROGRAMS) COLLECTED BY TYPE, UNITED STATES, 1965-67

A The Paid Donor ⎤ B The Professional Donor ⎦	47%
C The Paid-Induced Voluntary Donor	3
D The Responsibility Fee Donor ⎤ E The Family Credit Donor ⎦	39
F The Captive Voluntary Donor	4
G The Fringe Benefit Voluntary Donor	0
H The Voluntary Community Donor	7
Total	100

On the basis of 8 million units a year, then, approximately one-half are bought and sold. The contribution of the voluntary community donor is only 7 percent.

Apart from the great increase in paid plasma donations, all the evidence we have brought together suggests that the proportion of paid donations in the country as a whole has increased in recent years. Thirteen years ago the Joint Blood Council survey estimated the proportion of paid donations for the country as a whole at about 14 to 17 percent. It would seem, therefore, from Table 1 that the proportion has doubled and, if the 2 million plasma donations are included, trebled.

The only other trend figures that have been published relate to New York City. The proportions of paid donations were: 1952, 14 percent; 1956, 42 percent; 1966, 55 percent. The proportion of voluntary community donations fell from 20 percent in 1956 to about 1 percent in 1966.

As the blood transfusion services of the United States become increasingly dependent on the paid or professional donor, it is important that we have some sense of the social characteristics of those who sell their blood. A survey we conducted in 1968 was in part designed to produce some evidence on this matter. In all, I received statistics from a large number of commercial banks (some operated by pharmaceutical firms) accounting for some 366,000 units of blood. While very few appear to maintain detailed records on their sources of supply with respect to age, sex, marital status and other characteristics, many provided summary accounts. It would seem that most paid donors (apart from those in prisons, in the armed forces or university students) fall into three categories:

☐ "Professional donors"—registered donors who contribute regularly and who are paid on a fee basis or are semisalaried (this category figures largely in the plasmapheresis programs).

☐ "Call-in" donors—individuals (perhaps with less common blood groups) who are on a register of some kind and who respond to a call for blood on payment of a fee of $5 to $15 or more.

☐ "Walk-in" donors, who may be attracted by advertisements, who are paid $5 or more a pint depending on local circumstances, such as the extent of the shortage of blood and other market considerations.

Many commercial blood banks, often open (at least in New York) from 7:30 in the morning to midnight, are better placed to attract walk-in donors because their "store fronts" are located in Negro and ghetto areas. In 1966, according to one journalistic report, voluntary and private hospitals bought 100,000 pints of "Skid Row blood from New York City's 31 pay-for-blood stores." The hospitals paid $35 a pint or more for the blood. A typical journalistic account which appeared in 1963 described the scene at one of these blood banks:

A bleary-eyed, vacant-faced man shuffles up to a building in an industrial part of town, checks the address with a scrap of paper in his shaking hand, and walks inside. In a bleak third-floor office, he joins a number of other men, many derelicts like himself. One by one they are summoned to a desk where an attendant asks a few quick questions and directs them to an inner room.

This is not a flophouse. It is not an employment agency or a social service bureau for weary, homeless men. This is a blood donor center. Similar accounts have appeared since 1963 of conditions in commercial blood banks in Chicago, Seattle, Georgia, Cleveland, Boston, Miami, Detroit, Cincinnati, Los Angeles, San Francisco, Washington, Baltimore, Philadelphia, New Jersey, Kansas City and many other places in addition to New York.

Most of these accounts, however, are not the products of keen-eyed journalists but of physicians concerned about the problem of serum hepatitis. We will discuss this problem in a moment. Meanwhile, we conclude that, despite all the statistical inadequacies in the data on blood transfusion services in America, the trend appears to be markedly in the direction of the increasing commercialization of blood and donor relationships. Concomitantly, we find that proportionately more blood is being supplied by the poor, the unskilled, the unemployed, Negroes and other low-income groups and, with the rise of plasmapheresis, a new class is emerging of an exploited human population of high blood yielders. Redistribution in terms of "the gift of blood and blood products" from the poor to the rich appears to be one of the dominant effects of the American blood-banking systems.

To the recipient the use of human blood for medical purposes can be more lethal than many drugs. The transfusion and use of whole blood and certain blood products carries with it the risk of transmitting disease, particularly serum hepatitis, malaria, syphilis and brucellosis. Not only are there risks in infected blood and plasma but there are also risks in the use of contaminated needles and apparatus in the collection and transfusion processes.

In the United States and other modern societies the most dangerous of these hazards is serum hepatitis. It is becoming a major public health problem throughout the world. No scientific means have yet been found to detect in the laboratory the causative agents of hepatitis in the blood before it is used for a transfusion or for conversion into various blood products. The quantity of infected blood that can transmit hepatitis may be as little as one-millionth of a milliliter. The absence of a scientific check on quality and safety means that the subsequent biological condition of those who receive blood constitutes the ultimate test of whether the virus was present in the donation; in effect, therefore, the patient is the laboratory for testing the quality of the gift of blood.

But few—if any—patients know that their bodies perform this role. They do not ask and in most cases are in no condition to ask: Will this blood cause hepatitis? Who supplied it? In what circumstances? What safeguards were employed to ensure as far as humanly possible that this blood is not going to harm or kill me? Even if such questions were asked, it has to be recognized that they could not be satisfactorily answered by those administering transfusions or blood products.

In these situations of consumer ignorance and uncertainty, as in many others in the field of medical care, the patient has to trust the medical profession and the organized system of medical care. He has no alternative but to trust. If, subsequently, he develops hepatitis and it is clinically diagnosed as such (which in many instances it is difficult to do), it is still virtually impossible in most cases to establish a causal relationship and to connect the infection or the ill health to the blood transfusion or the blood product. Many complex factors are involved in these difficulties of diagnosing, identifying and naming the causal agent(s), one being the long incubation period in serum hepatitis—possibly up to six months.

Not only, therefore, has the patient no alternative to trust when receiving blood but, subsequently, and apart from a very small proportion of obvious cases of infection where causal attribution can be established, he can have no redress. He is not only unknowingly the laboratory test of "goodness," he and his family must bear the biological, social and economic costs of infected blood and misplaced trust in terms of physical incapacity, loss of earnings and career prospects, the effects on family life and other unquantifiable factors. These costs may be mitigated, but they may never be entirely eliminated. In many cases, the costs are irreversible.

For these and many other reasons those responsible for blood transfusion services have stressed the great importance of maintaining the most rigorous standards in the selection of donors. The state of health, the health history and the social habits of the donor become crucial because the laboratory cannot identify the virus. Again, however, there are definite limits to the clinical assessment of "health"; no single test or battery of liver function tests has yet been devised which will reliably distinguish carriers of the virus from "normal" subjects.

A great deal depends, therefore, on the truthfulness of the donor in the processes of medical examination, history taking and selection. Just as the recipient of blood has to trust the doctor, so the doctor has, within limits, to trust the giver. Those responsible for making medical decisions and administering blood have to act in certain circumstances on the assumption that donors have been truthful. In situations of total ignorance and total helplessness this is one social right the patient has—the right to truthfulness. Essentially, this is because he can exercise no preferences, and because one man's untruthfulness can reduce another man's welfare.

In different blood donation systems, therefore, we are led to ask: What particular set of conditions and arrangements permits and encourages maximum truthfulness on the part of donors? To what extent can honesty be maximized? Can this objective be pursued regardless of the donor's motives for giving blood? What principles should the medical profession, in the interests of patients and of the profession, consider as fundamental in the organization and operation of blood donor programs?

Martin L. Gross has summarized the evidence on the risks of hepatitis:

> Hepatitis is the most widespread transfusion danger for the hospital patient, the result of contaminated blood. Its exact toll is elusive, but the *Journal of the American Medical Association* has editorially indicated that the hepatitis transfusion problem is significant and considerably more prevalent than previously thought. "It has been reliably shown," (ran the editorial), "that an essential therapeutic measure, blood transfusion, causes death in approximately one of every 150 transfusions in persons over 40 years of age as a result of serum hepatitis. Since this is the age group to which most blood transfusions are given, and since many hundreds are given daily, such a high fatality rate becomes a problem."

Key area studies—in Chicago, New Jersey, Philadelphia, Los Angeles and Baltimore—which have carefully followed up transfused patients are discouraging. The hepatitis scourge, they show, strikes about one in 25 to

50 patients, with sizable death rates of up to 20 percent of those stricken. "It appears that the incidence of hepatitis after blood transfusion is greater than prior estimates have indicated," states Dr. John R. Senior, a Philadelphia researcher. Dr. Garrott Allen of Chicago has reported hepatitis danger so extensive that it surprised the most inured of the profession: 3.6 percent of all transfused hospital patients later contracted the disease (the risk rises with the number of units transfused). Judging from these samples, there may be 75,000 cases of hepatitis yearly, with almost 10,000 deaths.

More optimistic statistics have been garnered in Boston by Tufts University School of Medicine researchers with a hopeful transfusion rationale for the future. A 12-year study of the nine Boston teaching hospitals has produced only 171 patients rehospitalized for posttransfusion hepatitis, 12 percent of whom died. Since their total study represents about 5 percent of the nation's one-year blood use, we might thus expect 3,500 cases nationally. The actual toll of blood transfusion hepatitis is possibly between the extremes of the Boston and Chicago studies.

One of the main keys to preventing hepatitis after transfusion, the Boston physicians found, was in the careful checking of the source of the blood. The epidemic-like hepatitis in other cities, they believe, is a direct result of prebottled blood supplied by commercial sources: 40 percent of the blood in the Chicago sample was bought, and more than 75 percent of the blood in the Baltimore group was commercial. In the teaching hospitals of Boston, conversely, none of the blood was purchased from commercial blood firms.

"No matter what method of case finding was used,

the lowest incidence of posttransfusion hepatitis was seen when commercially supplied blood was avoided," state the Tufts University researchers.

Dr. Allen, one of the foremost authorities in the United States, has shown in a series of studies that the risk of serum hepatitis from transfusions derived from prison and Skid Row populations is at least ten times that from the use of voluntary donors.

> This greater risk rate is attributed to the fact that the paid donor is often a cloistered resident of Skid Row where he and his colleagues are alleged to enjoy frequently the practice of the communal use of unsterile needles and syringes for the self-administration of drugs. These rates increase with the numbers of transfusions, but they do not continue as a linear relationship after the first 5 or 6 units are given. There are also other unsanitary practices that prevail among this kind of population which favor repeated exposures to infectious hepatitis as well. Still another contributing factor, allegedly higher in this group than in the general population, is that of alcoholism, which appears to make such individuals more susceptible to an initial attack of either infectious or serum hepatitis.

A later study (in New Jersey) showed that the risk of hepatitis "developing in recipients of blood known to have been donated by convicted or suspected narcotics addicts was 70 times that in the controls."

Over the past decade many studies in different parts of the United States have incriminated the paid donor (and blood obtained from commercial blood banks) as the major source of infection. The most recently reported of these studies was conducted by Dr. Paul Schmidt and his colleagues at the National Institutes of Health, Bethesda.

This was a controlled prospective study (unlike many previous retrospective ones) of two groups of patients 21 years and older who were undergoing cardiac surgery at the National Institutes of Health hospital. There were no significant differences between the groups with respect to age, sex, type of heart disease, type of operation and severity of preoperative symptoms. One group received 94 percent of their blood from one or both of two commercial blood sources employing paid donors (in the Mississippi Valley area and an East Coast port city). The second group received 97 percent of their blood from voluntary donors in the Washington area. The average number of units of blood transfused per patient was 18.5 in the commercial group and slightly more (19.6) in the voluntary group.

In the commercial group, the total hepatitis attack rate was 53 percent; in the voluntary group, nil. This study suggests not only that there is an extremely high attack rate among cardiac surgery cases (average age 47) transfused with paid blood in the United States but also that an immense number of cases of infection are at present undetected. Because the number of patients involved was small (a total of 68), surveillance of the hepatitis risk is being continued and expanded on a nationwide basis. Further studies are also under way to eliminate the possibility of a geographic factor (because some of the paid blood was obtained from the Mississippi Valley area).

Nor is the problem of serum hepatitis confined to the use of whole blood. There is a serious risk in the use of whole pooled plasma and certain blood products, the production of which has been, as we saw, greatly aided by the use of plasmapheresis programs. It has been argued, however, that, compared with the hepatitis risks involved in the use of walk-in, irregular, Skid Row donor types, more regular, selected, longer-term plasmapheresis donors have a lower carrier rate. But a great deal depends here—as it does with all donors—on two factors: the precise nature of external quality and safety controls exercised by some scientific supervisory agency (even though there are limits to effective screening) and, second, the degree of *continued* truthfulness among paid donors.

As to the controls, it has been repeatedly shown in the United States that the official public health standards designed to insure the continued safety, purity and potency of biological products are only minimal standards and in many cases are either inapplicable, inadequate or ineffective (partly because of the inherent difficulties of continually inspecting and checking all procedures at blood banks). "Under the standards set by the National Institutes of Health, an ancient physician, a nurse and a former bartender can theoretically combine their resources to form a blood bank. They can draw most of their blood from Skid Row donors at the minimum fee and sell their blood to hospitals that seek the lowest bidder and are not concerned with the scientific aspects of blood banking." Moreover, the great expansion during 1968-69 in chains of profit-making hospitals (newly built hospitals as well as voluntary hospitals bought by some 33 nationwide investor-owned companies) is likely to increase the risks as more blood is purchased from commercial banks. Altruistic donors can hardly be expected to give their blood to profit-making hospitals.

With regard to the issue of truthfulness, again it has been repeatedly shown that paid donors—and especially poor donors badly in need of money—are, on an average and compared with voluntary donors, relatives and friends, more reluctant and less likely to reveal a full medical history and to provide information about recent contacts with infectious disease, recent inoculations and about their diets, drinking and drug habits that would disqualify them as donors.

The hazards involved in the commercial blood transfusion system, both to the American people and internationally, were made more explicit in 1969 by reports on the activities of Southern Food and Drug Research and its associated corporations. These corporations, operating in three states, acted as "intermediate contractors" to some 37 major American pharmaceutical firms, a number of which have large international markets. Their main role, as commercial enterprises, was to supply plasma, hyperimmune immunoglobulin and other products and to carry out clinical trials on human beings of proposed new pharmaceutical products. The supply of hyperimmune immunoglobulin (used for therapeutic purposes in connection with mumps, whooping cough, tetanus and smallpox) involved vaccinating donors to build up the antibodies in the plasma. The technique mainly used was plasmapheresis.

With the assistance of prison physicians (some of whom were remunerated by these corporations) extensive use was made of prisoners (who were paid for taking pills, vaccinations and supplying plasma) from 1962 to 1969. In all, these corporations are said to have conducted between 25 and 50 percent of the initial drug tests (or first-phase tests usually carried out on healthy subjects) annually undertaken in the United States.

A series of investigations and inquiries into the activities of these corporations reported:
□ Potentially fatal new compounds have been tested on prisoners with little or no direct medical observation of the results.
□ Prisoners failed to swallow pills, failed to report

serious reactions to those they did swallow and failed to receive careful laboratory tests.

☐ Control records for validation purposes were totally inadequate, plasmapheresis rooms were "sloppy" and gross contamination of the rooms containing donors' plasma was evident.

☐ One prisoner on plasmapheresis received back another man's red cells and was seriously damaged for life.

☐ Another prisoner, injected with a whooping cough vaccine, died.

☐ Large outbreaks of hepatitis occurred at various prisons, involving over 1,000 prisoners of whom at least six died.

☐ It is alleged that several agencies of the Department of Health, Education and Welfare knew for years about the activities and standards of these corporations and did not curtail or stop them.

☐ Many internationally known pharmaceutical firms knew of the standards of medical supervision, laboratory and quality control being exercised by these corporations. No concerted or collective action was taken to stop using these intermediaries. Some firms remained the biggest consumers of Southern Food and Drug Research and its associated corporations. Those who were still using these facilities in 1969 are reported to have defended the validity of the data provided.

This is only a brief summary of an immense amount of documentation available in the United States. We have not included here much material raising ethical and political issues similar to those made explicit in the Nuremberg Code.

This case—or series of cases—is relevant in a number of ways to the problems raised here: the issues of donor "truthfulness," theories of social costs in relation to blood and blood products and questions of safety, purity and potency.

In private market terms, we see that "untruthfulness" was maximized at many points in the system, from the prisoners themselves to officials employed by the pharmaceutical firms. The social costs involved extend far beyond the areas of cost-benefit analysis conventionally studied by economists and statisticians. They embrace the prisoners and their families (many of whom were Negroes), the prison system itself, the medical profession, the pharmaceutical industry in the United States and the consumers of these products not only in the United States but in many countries of the world.

At least one conclusion can be drawn at this point. Governmental systems of licensing, inspection and quality validation appear to be helpless to control private markets in blood and blood products. Their ineffectiveness has contributed in recent years to the phenomenon in the United States of numerous legal suits based on negligence, implied warranty and various food and drug acts. What is involved, of course, is the question whether blood transfusion is a commercial transaction or a professional service.

All these issues were crystallized and debated in the now famous Kansas City case of 1962. Before we pursue them it is instructive to review the causes and implications of this particular event. Briefly, the facts are these.

In 1953 a meeting of doctors, pathologists, hospital administrators and local citizens decided to form a nonprofit community blood bank in Kansas City. There was a need for more blood which the local hospital blood banks were not fully supplying, and the local branch of the American Red Cross was at the time channeling the blood it collected to the armed forces in

Korea. For the next two years there were endless disputes among the various interests involved (which need not concern us here) about power, institutional control and finance. Then, in May 1955, a commercial blood bank (calling itself the Midwest Blood Bank and Plasma Center) started operations.

The bank was owned and operated by a husband-and-wife team. The husband had completed grade school, had no medical training and had previously worked as a banjo teacher, secondhand car salesman and photographer. The blood-bank procedures seem to have been actually directed by the wife. She called herself an RN but was not licensed as a nurse in either Kansas or Missouri and did not show any evidence of experience or training in blood banking. Originally there had been a third partner, but he had been chased out of the bank by the husband with a gun. A medical director was appointed to comply with public health regulations. He was 78, a general practitioner with no training in blood banking. The bank was inspected and licensed by the relevant federal authority, the National Institutes of Health.

Situated in a slum area, the blood bank displayed a sign reading "Cash Paid for Blood" and drew blood from donors described as "Skid Row derelicts." It was said by one witness to have "worms all over the floor." In 1958 another commercial bank, the World Blood Bank, was established in Kansas City and also began operations.

From 1955 onwards pressures of various kinds were brought to bear on relatives of hospital patients, members of associations and trade unions to provide blood on a replacement basis to these commercial banks. But local hospitals refused to accept blood from these sources to discharge patients' blood fees. These and other developments seem to have forced a solution to the disputes over the control of the nonprofit community blood bank, and in April 1958 it commenced operations. Subsequently, it appears from the evidence that practically all the large local hospitals entered into blood-supply contracts with the Community Blood Bank and ceased operating their own banks. The Community Blood .Bank thus had a virtual monopoly.

The two commercial banks then complained to the Federal Trade Commission alleging restraint of trade. In July 1962, after an investigation lasting several years, the commission issued a complaint against the Community Blood Bank and its officers, directors, administrative director and business manager; the Kansas City Area Hospital Association and its officers, directors and executive director; three hospitals, individually and as representatives of the 40 members of the hospital association; 16 pathologists; and two hospital administrators.

The complaint charged the respondents with having entered into an agreement or planned course of action to hamper and restrain the sale and distribution of human blood in interstate commerce. They were charged with conspiring to boycott a commercial blood bank in the sale and distribution of blood in commerce, and that the conspiracy was to the injury of the public and unreasonably restricted and restrained interstate commerce in violation of Section 5 of the Federal Trade Commission Act of 1952. This section of the act declares that "uniform methods of competition in commerce, and unfair or deceptive acts or practices in commerce, are declared unlawful." Violation of a commission "cease and desist order," after it becomes final, subjects the violator to civil penalties up to $5,000 for each day the violation continues.

The respondents appealed. After lengthy hearings before an examiner for the commission in 1963, a further appeal and more hearings before the full Trade Commission of five members, a ruling was issued in October 1966. By a majority of three to two the commission decided that the Community Blood Bank and the hospitals, doctors and pathologists associated with it were illegally joined together in a conspiracy to restrain commerce in whole human blood.

Part of the Federal Trade Commission's case that blood was an article of commerce was based on arguments for extending the doctrine of implied warranty (fitness for use) in the financial interests of consumers—in short, to make it easier for them to sue doctors, hospitals, blood banks, laboratories and so forth. A doctor should, for example, be found guilty of negligence if he obtained human blood from a bank that failed to meet adequate standards; he "should have known" that the hepatitis virus was present in the blood. This doctrine could be extended to all other areas of medical practice as well as to other service relationships. Nonprofit hospitals would be regarded as engaged in trade or commerce for profit. Until 1964 hospitals, like churches, schools, colleges, universities, public libraries and charitable institutions not operated for profit, were exempt from the price discrimination provisions of the United States Code.

The American Medical Association, in protesting the Federal Trade Commission ruling in the Kansas City case, warned hospitals and doctors to change their "billing" practices and not to state the charge for blood as a separate charge. This proposal put the American Medical Association in a dilemma, however, for it struck at the basis of competition in private medical care and the association's own announced support of commercial blood banks in 1964. Other interests found themselves confronted with similar dilemmas. Pathologists and physicians working in privately owned clinical laboratories, for example, found themselves arguing against the profit motive. This was not a small group for, in 1967, 95 percent of all clinical laboratories in the United States certified for participation in the Medicare program were under commercial proprietary control. Most of them were approved for hematology tests. Commercial blood insurance companies, however, strongly supported the Federal Trade Commission's ruling in the interests of competition and "sound business practices." They were joined by sections of the pharmaceutical industry who did not wish to see commercial blood banking discouraged by "restrictive practices."

In January 1969 the Federal Trade Commission's ruling of 1966 in the Kansas City case was set aside by the Eighth United States Circuit Court of Appeals in Saint Louis. Up to the end of 1969 no appeal had been made to the Supreme Court.

Though this may be the end of this particular case, the fact that it happened is one illustration among many of the increasing commercialization of the blood-banking system and of hospital and medical services in general. This trend must logically lead to more and more recourse to the laws and practices of the marketplace. There is no inconsistency in this development. If blood as a living human tissue is increasingly bought and sold as an article of commerce and profit accrues from such transactions, then it follows that the laws of commerce must, in the end, prevail. What this trend holds in store for the future of medicine in the United States as legally it is increasingly treated as a trade and as the doctrine of charitable immunity disappears into the mists of history is not a matter for this particular study. To consider all such legal ramifications would eventually lead us away from law and into the broader issues of medical ethics, the purpose of medicine and, ultimately, the value of human life.

Nevertheless, the choice of blood as an illustration and case study was no idle academic thought; it was deliberate. Short of examining humankind itself and the institution of slavery—of men and women as market commodities—blood as a living tissue may now constitute in Western societies one of the ultimate tests of where the "social" begins and the "economic" ends. If blood is considered in theory, in law and is treated in practice as a trading commodity, then ultimately human hearts, kidneys, eyes and other organs of the body may also come to be treated as commodities to be bought and sold in the marketplace.

Profitable competition for blood "is a healthy thing," it is argued by some in the United States. It improves services, increases supplies of blood and is the answer to a "shiftless, socialistic approach." If competition for blood were eliminated, it is warned, it would "be the entering wedge for the destruction of our entire antimonopoly structure" and would threaten the interests of "great pharmaceutical companies."

In London, two authors, writing in a 1968 publication of the Institute of Economic Affairs, urged that payment of donors and competition for blood be introduced in Britain, where all blood is now given voluntarily, and where the incidence of tainted blood is virtually nil. Productivity would rise, the writers argue; supplies of blood would increase; "a movement towards more efficiency in the blood market is a movement towards more efficiency in the economy as a whole." The editor, Arthur Seldon, in a preface said that the authors "have made an unanswerable case for a trial period in which the voluntary donor is supplemented by the fee-paid donor so that the results can be judged in practice, and not prejudged by doctrinaire obfuscation."

In essence, these writers, American and British, are making an economic case against a monopoly of altruism in blood and other human tissues. They wish to set people free from the conscience of obligation. Although their arguments are couched in the language of price elasticity and profit maximization, they have far-reaching implications for human values and all "social service" institutions. They legitimate, for instance, the great increase since 1967 in the number of commercial hospitals in the United States.

The moral issues that are raised extend far beyond theories of pricing and operations of the marketplace. Moreover, they involve the foundations of professional freedom in medical care and other service relationships with people, the concept of the hospital and the university as non-profit-making institutions and the legal doctrine in the United States of charitable immunity. Charitable enterprises in that country would be subject under competitive conditions to the same laws of restraint and warranty and have the same freedoms as businessmen in the private market.

Is medical care—analyzed in its many component parts, such as blood transfusion services—a consumption good indistinguishable from other goods and services in the private economic market? What are the consequences, national and international, of treating human blood as a commercial commodity? If blood is morally sanctioned as something to be bought and sold, what ultimately is the justification for not promoting individualistic private markets in all other component areas of medical care, social work skills, the use of patients and clients for professional training and other "social service" institutions and processes?

Where are the lines to be drawn—can indeed any lines at all be pragmatically drawn—if human blood be legitimated as a consumption good? To search for an identity and sphere of concern for social policy would thus be to search for the nonexistent. All policy would become in the end economic policy, and the only values that would count are those that can be measured in terms of money and pursued in the dialectic of hedonism. To abolish the moral choice of giving to strangers could lead to an ideology to end all ideologies. This study, in one small sector of human affairs, disputes both the death of ideology and the philistine resurrection of economic man in social policy. It is thus concerned with the values we accord to people for what they give to strangers, not what they get out of society.

January 1971

FURTHER READING

Beyond Economics, paperback by Kenneth E. Boulding (Ann Arbor: University of Michigan Press, 1968).

Relative Deprivation and Social Justice by Walter G. Runciman (Berkeley: University of California Press, 1966).

Commitment to Welfare by Richard M. Titmuss (London:

Allen & Unwin, 1968).

The Future of Inequality by Seymour M. Miller and Pamela Roby (New York: Basic Books, 1970).

Economic Philosophy by Joan Robinson (Chicago: Aldine, 1962).

About the Authors

Harold M. Baron is a staff member of the urban studies program of the Associated Colleges of the Midwest. He is completing a book on racism in metropolitan America under a grant from the Russell Sage Foundation.

Barbara Brandt is a community organizer in Somerville, Massachusetts and has worked with Gordon Fellman on the forthcoming *The Deceived Majority: Politics and Protest in Middle America*.

Robert Coles has written extensively on the people of Appalachia. He has recently finished two more volumes of *Children of Crisis*, entitled *Migrants, Sharecroppers, Mountaineers* and *The South Goes North*.

Alan J. Davis, a former editor of the *Harvard Law Review*, is a Philadelphia lawyer who specializes in civil and criminal trial work. This essay is based on a study conducted by the Philadelphia District Attorney's office and the Police Department.

James W. Davis, Jr. is associate professor of political science at Washington University, St. Louis. His most recent book is *The National Executive Branch: An Introduction*.

Kenneth Dolbeare is chairman of the department of political science at the University of Washington in Seattle. He is co-author with Murray J. Edelman of *American Politics: Policies, Power and Change* and has written four other books on American politics.

Gordon Fellman is author, with Barbara Brandt, of *The Deceived Majority: Politics and Protest in Middle America* and is associate professor of sociology at Brandeis University.

James M. Graham is supervising instructor of the legal writing program at the University of Wisconsin Law School.

Theodore J. Lowi is professor of political science at the University of Chicago. He is author of *The End of Liberalism*.

Thomas M. Martinez is professor of sociology at Stanford University and has written on public-employee strikes in the United States.

Gary T. Marx is a lecturer in sociology at Harvard. (For more information see the cover.)

Stuart Nagel is professor of political science at the University of Illinois and practices law in Illinois. He has written many articles on inequality in the American legal system.

Dorothy Nelkin is a senior research associate in the Cornell University program on science, technology and society. She is author of *On the Season* and co-author with William H. Friedland of *Migrant: Agricultural Workers in America's Northeast*.

Carol Olexa is a faculty member at Evergreen State College, Olympia, Washington. She is co-author with Walter Schafer of *Tracking and Opportunity*.

Kenneth Polk is associate professor of sociology at the University of Oregon. He is co-author with Walter Schafer of *Schools and Delinquency*.

Roger Rosenblatt is pursuing a joint M.D.-Master of Public Health degree at the Harvard School of Public Health.

Walter E. Schafer is visiting associate professor of social work at the University of Michigan and is co-author of the afore-mentioned volumes.

Anselm L. Strauss is professor of sociology at the University of California at San Francisco. He has written 18 books on social psychology, the most recent of which are *Work, Careers and Professions* and *The Contexts of Social Mobility*.

Richard Titmuss is professor of social administration at the University of London and a department chairman at the London School of Economics. He also served as a member of the Royal Commission on Medical Education.

Rosalie H. Wax is professor of anthropology at the University of Kansas at Lawrence. She is author of *Magic, Fate and History: The Changing Ethos of the Vikings* and co-author with Murray L. Wax and Robert V. Dumont, Jr. of *Formal Education in an American Indian Community*.

Lenore J. Weitzman is assistant professor of sociology at the University of California at Davis and a faculty member of the law school. This article was written while she and her co-author were Russell Sage fellows at the Yale Law School.

David Wellman is assistant professor of sociology at the University of Oregon. As a graduate student at Berkeley he was affiliated with SNCC and SDS.